The Making of
U.S. China Policy

THE MAKING OF
U.S. CHINA POLICY

From Normalization to
the Post–Cold War Era

Tan Qingshan

Lynne Rienner Publishers □ Boulder & London

Published in the United States of America in 1992 by
Lynne Rienner Publishers, Inc.
1800 30th Street, Boulder, Colorado 80301

and in the United Kingdom by
Lynne Rienner Publishers, Inc.
3 Henrietta Street, Covent Garden, London WC2E 8LU

Library of Congress Cataloging-in-Publication Data
Tan Qingshan, 1957–
    The making of U.S. China policy : from normalization to the post-
    cold war era / by Tan Qingshan.
        p.   cm.
    Includes bibliographical references and index.
    ISBN 1-55587-336-7 — ISBN 1-55587-314-6 (pbk.)
    1. United States—Foreign relations—China. 2. China—Foreign
relations—United States. I. Title.
E183.8.C5T296 1992
327.73051—dc20

                                    92-41402
                                        CIP

British Cataloguing in Publication Data
A Cataloguing in Publication record for this book
is available from the British Library

Printed and bound in the United States of America

The paper used in this publication meets the requirements
of the American National Standard for Permanence of
Paper for Printed Library Materials Z39.48-1984.

For Garland and Nick

Contents

Figures

Preface

As a student at the Beijing Institute of International Relations in the early 1980s, I took a course in U.S. politics. I was frustrated to find that the course offered little insight into U.S. politics and political processes because the course depicted the U.S. government as the captive of U.S. capitalists and financiers. I questioned whether it is intellectually satisfactory and politically wise to overlook the division of power in U.S. politics. Despite China's reluctance to distinguish the U.S. Congress from the administration in terms of policymaking, Congress began to play a more assertive role in the making of U.S. China policy after normalization.

To find an answer to my question, I decided to come to the United States to study. I chose Emory University, because of its Carter Center, to study U.S. China policy since normalization. I cannot claim that I have found a complete answer, for any political system is dynamic. But I have gained a much better understanding of the importance of U.S. political institutions in China policymaking.

The U.S.-China relationship expanded rapidly in the early post-normalization period. The bilateral relations extended from diplomatic arenas to exchanges involving security, trade, tourism, business, culture, education, health, environment, science, and technology. These new developments in U.S.-China relations have had a profound impact on the governmental process regarding China policymaking. First, U.S. China policy objectives became diversified with the expansion of Sino-U.S. relations after normalization. As a result, U.S. China policymaking was pluralized and decentralized. Second, U.S.-China relations were institutionalized as the relationship expanded to other areas of interest. The institutionalization had an effect on China policymaking in that it involved different interests of governmental agencies with various policy goals. Bureaucratic players exerted greater influence in China policymaking. Third, the rapid expansion of U.S.-China ties led to an increasing role for Congress in providing a legal framework for China policy and sharing China policymaking power with the executive. Institutional differences in goals, priorities, and approaches highlighted a China policymaking process with conflict and compromise. In this regard, interbranch politics is the key to understanding and predicting U.S. China policy.

The Tiananmen Square event in June 1989 has had a long-term impact on U.S. politics in China policymaking. It altered the past policy norm of encouraging Chinese domestic political and socioeconomic reforms, but not making U.S. policy contingent upon Chinese domestic practices. While the change is less explicit in the Bush administration's China policy, there is a much more explicit change in the congressional orientation toward China policy. A new pattern of decisionmaking has emerged from the interbranch policymaking process. Congress has shown an assertive posture in China policymaking, and the president has been equally determined to take control of Chinese policymaking. As a result, the China policy process has been characterized by a reverse role of Congress taking policy initiatives and the executive proposing amendments and trying to take control of the process. The old car-driving metaphor that the president drives the car of state and Congress applies the brakes may not capture the change of interbranch politics in China policymaking, as Congress is more eager to drive the car and the president has to apply the brakes occasionally. Future U.S. China policy will be less likely to be conducted on the premise of strategic interests and more likely to be directed toward addressing bilateral political, economic, cultural, human rights, and arms sales issues. U.S. China policy will inevitably embrace broader U.S. interests and objectives, which will have domestic implications in both countries. Congress will persistently promote its interests as regards Chinese human rights and push the executive to link China policy to Chinese domestic affairs. Differences between the executive and Congress on China policy goals, priorities, and approaches will continue to affect China policy outcomes. The interbranch policy process will become more important in reconciling and compromising policy differences and in shaping future China policy.

In the course of preparing this research, I benefited greatly from many U.S. government officials and people working in the field of Sino-U.S. relations. Their time and insightful comments have been invaluable. I would like to thank Congressman Chester Atkins for providing me with his office facilities for my research. I am especially indebted to Robert A. Pastor, who helped me in my intellectual growth as he encouraged and guided my research from its inception. I would also like to express my great indebtedness to Randall Strahan, Richard Doner, and Thomas Remington, who spent many hours reviewing drafts and providing constructive and critical comments. I would like to thank Garland Davies, Sung Hui Kim, Dale Nordenberg, Deng Jing, and many anonymous readers, all of whom made it possible for this study to come to fruition. With so much advice and assistance, I alone am responsible for the shortcomings that remain.

Tan Qingshan

Introduction: China Policy Issues Since Normalization

Whether U.S. foreign policy toward China is a function of U.S. strategic interests or U.S. government processes poses a theoretical as well as an empirical question to students of international relations. Studies of U.S. foreign policy toward China have tended to give predominant weight to strategic interests as both a motive and an explanation of U.S. policy. Important as it is, this approach cannot explain sufficiently those policies that mainly reflected political compromises resulting from U.S. governmental processes—for two reasons. First, the transformation of international politics in the 1980s has reduced the importance of balance of power to a new low level. U.S. strategic considerations have been altered to accommodate other foreign policy goals. Second, the rise of bilateral issues that reflected domestic political interests in both countries has had a great effect on the policy process and policymaking. Thus, the emphasis on strategic importance often left unexplained the variance in U.S. China policies that did not necessarily comply with U.S. strategic interests.

Along with the rapid expansion in Sino-U.S. relations as the result of normalization, many new issues arose in the areas of diplomacy, security dialogue, economic exchange, and scientific and technological cooperation. The complex nature of those issues called for bureaucratic expertise and required new laws, thus creating opportunities for more policymakers to participate in China policymaking. Unlike the decision of normalization, for which the president was solely responsible, the solution of those issues would inevitably involve different governmental processes and invite various policymakers from different branches of government and the bureaucracy to compete for their political interests and policy objectives. Therefore, it is important to examine governmental processes and institutional and bureaucratic factors in explaining U.S. China policy since normalization.

In contrast to the strategic explanation, this study takes a different approach to the question by employing three decisionmaking models: the rational actor model, the bureaucratic politics model, and the interbranch politics model. These three models provide a theoretical framework for the analysis of China policy. This book does not intend to study all the U.S. decisions concerning China; rather, it examines some major U.S. China

1

policies since normalization with the purpose of evaluating the importance of institutions (the presidency or Congress), the policy process by which these institutions and their subunits relate to one another, and the role of individual officials in the process. The objective of this study is to look into U.S. governmental processes, or the "black box," to see what the factors are that led U.S. decisionmakers to choose particular policies toward China.

U.S. China policy refers to governmental decisions that affect the way the United States relates to the People's Republic of China (PRC). To serve the purpose of this study, four cases will be analyzed: the Taiwan Relations Act (TRA) in 1979; U.S. arms sales to Taiwan, 1980–1982; the U.S.-China trade agreement in 1979; and U.S. technology transfer to China, 1980–1985. These four cases were selected for several reasons. First, they defined the context and the substance of U.S. policy because they encompassed the major aspects of Sino-U.S. political, economic, and technological relations. Second, these cases revealed the importance of Congress in U.S. China policymaking after normalization. The TRA case signified the congressional role in pulling the executive toward stressing the U.S.-Taiwan security objective. It displayed congressional assertiveness in sharing foreign policymaking power with the executive. Third, arms sales to Taiwan represent another important area in U.S.-China relations. On this issue, the executive and Congress found themselves more often at odds with each other in their approaches to achieving Taiwan policy goals. The policy outcome very often turned out to be controversial. Congress complained that the executive had not done enough to fulfill its commitment to Taiwan, and the Beijing government blamed the administration for not observing the normalization principles. The question is: Is the arms sales policy a compromise in executive-congressional interaction? What factors can explain the outcome? Fourth, as political relations were normalized, the importance of economic relations became more apparent. The two economic cases here represent important, yet controversial, aspects of U.S.-China economic relations. Should the United States have entered into most-favored-nation (MFN) status with China but not with the former USSR? To what extent can economic relations affect U.S. security interests? What are the institutional biases and bureaucratic preferences concerning U.S.-PRC economic relations? What impact can these biases and preferences make on U.S. China policy?

* * *

In order to study the making of U.S. China policy since normalization, it is important to understand and grasp the context of U.S. policymakers' concerns over some basic issue areas in Sino-U.S. relations: U.S.-China strategic cooperation; U.S. policy toward Taiwan; Sino-U.S. economic relations; and technology transfer.

Sino-U.S. relations had remained hostile since 1949, partly due to the Cold War between the West and the East, and partly due to the Korean War. The United States supported the Taiwan regime as an ally against communism. It also regarded Taiwan as an unsinkable aircraft carrier and an important strategic ally in Asia during the Cold War. It was not until the end of the 1960s, when profound changes took place in international affairs, that the United States began to reassess its strategic posture in Asia. First, U.S. power declined relative to the Soviet Union in military terms and to Japan and West Germany in economic terms. The United States had to readjust its global commitments. Second, the rift between China and the Soviet Union came to the surface, and China saw the Soviets as its number one enemy. Consequently, China was seen as a de facto ally in countering Soviet power in Asia. Third, the Vietnam War had a serious impact on U.S. Asian policy: U.S. public opinion and many decisionmakers wanted to reduce U.S. commitments in Asia. Thus, a new Asia strategy was needed so that the United States could reduce some of its military presence and at the same time maintain its Asian interests. In this context, China was viewed as a viable factor to maintain the balance of power in Asia after the United States withdrew from Vietnam. Given China's own security concerns, U.S.-China strategic cooperation in dealing with the Soviet threat for the first time became an attractive idea among U.S. policymakers and finally led to normalization of U.S.-China diplomatic relations in 1978.

U.S.-PRC Strategic Cooperation

In the face of Soviet expansionist activities in the 1970s, the choice of whether or not the United States should develop strategic cooperation with China became an issue among U.S. policymakers. The domestic dispute on U.S.-China strategic cooperation had been profound and consequential. Some policymakers believed that an improved Sino-U.S. relationship could enhance broader U.S. foreign policy interests, especially regarding the Soviet Union. Others advocated an "evenhanded policy" toward both China and the Soviet Union.[1] The debate on the implications of improving U.S.-PRC relations raised a policy issue of whether the United States should build up a security tie with China and, particularly, whether the United States should sell military equipment to China. When the Soviets invaded Afghanistan in 1979, U.S.-Soviet relations underwent a steady decline, which prompted a strong perception in the United States of the growing menace posed by the Soviet military power. At the same time, Chinese leaders repeatedly stressed their opposition to Soviet global expansion. Under these circumstances, those in the Carter administration who favored closer ties with China, including security ties, gained an upper hand in China policymaking. Defense Secretary Harold Brown's China trip in January 1980 resulted in an important policy shift: For the first time since 1949 the U.S. government was willing to consider selling selected military equipment and technology with military support applications to China.

The prospect of further expanding security ties with China was complicated by the Reagan administration's reassessment of China's strategic importance and U.S. policy toward Taiwan. On the one hand, the administration continued the previous policy of maintaining security ties with China.[2] On the other hand, the administration tried to downplay China's strategic importance and promote new relations with Taiwan at the same time.

U.S. Taiwan Policy

The key issue regarding U.S. Taiwan policy is the security of Taiwan; this was reflected in the disagreement over arms sales to Taiwan during the normalization negotiations. Because of the primacy of normalization, both sides compromised on arms sales. The Beijing government decided not to push for a complete ban on arms sales; Carter, on the other hand, announced a one-year moratorium on selling arms to Taiwan. However, some U.S. policymakers in Congress expressed their strong opposition to Carter's policies toward Taiwan. During congressional consideration of the Taiwan legislation in February and March 1979, Congress sought to amend the bill proposed by the administration.[3]

The legislation was needed to govern unofficial relations such as commercial and cultural exchanges with Taiwan after normalization. Congress used the opportunity to register its own concern over Taiwan security, despite the administration's initial opposition to any congressional amendments. The new legislation contained two controversial provisions concerning Taiwan security and arms sales. The arms sales provision already caused problems in Sino-U.S. relations when the Reagan administration sold F-15 E/F aircraft to Taiwan in 1982. It also posed a problem for future administrations in deciding whether or not they should abide by the TRA, which was then considered by China as "the fundamental obstacle to the development of Sino-American relations."[4]

U.S. China Economic Policy

U.S. economic policy toward China has carried strong political and bureaucratic overtones, partly because of U.S. security concerns,[5] and partly because it has involved different governmental institutions and agencies with different political interests and policy preferences. The diversification of political opinion about China and institutional interests has complicated the whole process of U.S. China economic policymaking.

Since normalization, Congress has become more assertive in U.S.-PRC economic relations. Many economic exchanges require legislative approval, especially in the area of trade. Congress, as a lawmaker, used the opportunity of legislative power to address its concerns over issues in U.S.-China relations. Congress has increasingly strengthened its role in maintaining and enhancing its share of power in making U.S. China policy.[6] Congress, in many areas, retains its own priorities and seeks to balance executive preferences in making China policy. Therefore, variations in China policy can emerge from institutional predispositions and from different policy priorities.

There were different views among U.S. policymakers on the goals of U.S. China economic policy. Proponents said that U.S.-China economic cooperation would consolidate the newly established relationship and enhance U.S. foreign policy interests.[7] Opponents of closer U.S.-PRC cooperation, mainly members of Congress, stood against the administration's goals of promoting U.S. strategic and economic interests on the grounds that U.S. economic initiatives toward China would result in an imbalance of the administration's previously avowed policy of evenhandedness and would thus cause more problems in U.S.-USSR relations. They argued that the goal of U.S. China economic policy is not to develop economic leverage to promote political ties between the United States and China. In fact, some of them were not even sure that economic exchange would benefit the United States at all. They took an active role in opposing those who wanted to push for closer economic ties such as granting most-favored-nation status or technical assistance to China. The Carter administration was pressured to put aside proposals that would have changed U.S. laws to allow the United States to grant assistance to China. The Reagan administration was also reluctant to take a stance on granting U.S. aid to China.[8]

U.S. Technology Transfer to China

Technology transfer was a relatively new issue and it was related to security concerns. Prior to normalization, the United States had a very restrictive policy regarding technology transfer to China. The issue first arose when China sought technology from the West to improve its military capability in the mid-1970s. The United States did not involve itself in military sales, but it did not object to a British sale of military equipment to China. After normalization, especially after Secretary of Defense Brown's visit to China, the United States began to sell military equipment to China on the basis of security cooperation. However, this military-oriented technology transfer has its limits. First, the policy of arms sales to China was a controversial one. Some policymakers questioned that such sales would serve U.S. security interests. Second, Chinese decisionmakers also questioned the wisdom of purchasing U.S. military equipment. It was an expensive venture for one thing, and one that could jeopardize China's security in the long run by creating military dependence on the United States. Furthermore, China was badly in need of general technology that could help its modernization drive. And yet, the United States retained restrictive technology transfer policy and exerted significant control over the Coordinating Committee (COCOM) procedures governing technology transfer by its members to communist countries.

These issues are important in that they defined the general direction in which Sino-U.S. relations developed; some, like the TRA, also contain a controversial element that can adversely affect future relations. These issues are also conducive to further study concerning U.S. China policymaking: What are U.S. China policy goals? Who defines U.S. China interests? And who makes China policy? There are two important variations in U.S. China policy that call for an explanation. One type of decision reflected the convergence of strategic interests and cooperation; decisions concerning MFN status, sales of military equipment to China, and technology transfer belong to this category. The other type of decision, including the TRA and arms sales to Taiwan, involved U.S. policy objectives that are incompatible with the construction of a close strategic relationship.

Chapter 1 outlines a theoretical framework for explaining congression-al-executive politics, bureaucratic interests, and roles in U.S. China policymaking and develops a series of propositions about the effects of foreign policy interests and objectives and domestic policy processes on China policies since normalization. Congressional-executive politics may be understood as institutional interactions in four aspects of decision-making: China policy objectives, the prioritization of the policy agenda, the policy approach, and the proper role in policymaking. Propositions about the effects of governmental policymaking processes on China policy outcomes are drawn from two decisionmaking models: the bureau-cratic politics model and interbranch politics model. Propositions on foreign policy interests and objectives are derived from the rational actor model.

Then, in Chapters 2 through 5, the three models are applied to the four case studies to analyze the decisionmaking involved in forging U.S. China policies. Chapter 2 focuses on legislative-executive politics in U.S. Taiwan policy. Chapter 3 deals with the management of the arms sales crisis in U.S.-China relations. Chapter 4 concentrates on the politics of U.S. China economic policy, particularly the politics of granting China most-favored-nation status. Chapter 5 studies the decisionmaking process that led to the U.S. policy of technology transfer to China. The concluding chapter summarizes the analysis of U.S. China policymaking since normalization and returns to the question of the usefulness of existing theoretical perspectives for explaining U.S. China policies.

Notes

1. According to Oksenberg, Brzezinski advocated a pro-China policy while Secretary Vance maintained an evenhanded foreign policy. See Michel Oksenberg, "A Decade of Sino-American Relations," *Foreign Affairs* 61, no. 1 (Fall 1982), pp. 175–195.

2. Alexander Haig, a key figure in the administration in favor of closer China ties, announced in Beijing in 1981 that the United States was willing to consider weapons sales to China on a case-by-case basis. But the Beijing government made it clear that it would not purchase U.S. military equipment until the administration clarified its policy toward Taiwan. See Alexander Haig, *Caveat: Realism, Reagan, and Foreign Policy* (New York: Macmillan, 1984), pp. 204–208.

3. See Congress, Senate, Committee on Foreign Relations, *The Taiwan Enabling Act: Report of the Committee on Foreign Relations, United States Senate, Together with Additional Views on S. 245*, 96th Cong., 1st sess., 1979.

4. For example, Deng Xiaoping stated his position on several occasions during his visit to the United States in January 1979.

5. The Carter administration made a concerted effort to enhance U.S. strategic cooperation with China. Soon after normalization, the administration moved quickly to restore economic relations. Vice President Mondale visited China in 1979, pledging to provide China with U.S. Export-Import Bank (Ex-Im Bank) financing of up to $2 billion over the next five years; promising to submit to Congress before the end of the year the previously negotiated Sino-U.S. trade agreement, which offered most-favored-nation status for Chinese goods entering the United States; and assuring Chinese leaders that the administration would seek congressional action to provide investment guarantees of the Overseas Private Investment Corporation (OPIC) for U.S. investors in China.

6. The Constitution empowers Congress to regulate commerce—a power shared with the executive to oversee U.S. economic relations with foreign countries. Congress has the constitutional power to appropriate money, which Congress often uses as a means to influence foreign policy. On congressional assertiveness in foreign policy since the Vietnam War, see Thomas Franck and Edward Weisband, *Foreign Policy by Congress* (New York: Oxford University Press, 1979).

7. For their arguments, see Robert G. Sutter, *The China Quandary: Domestic Determinants of U.S. China Policy, 1972–82* (Boulder: Westview Press, 1983), pp. 13–14.

8. Ibid., footnote 13, Chapter 1.

1

Politics and Process:
A Theoretical Framework

Despite the richness of theoretical literature in foreign policy and decision-making, there is a lack of theoretical studies specifically on Sino-U.S. relations and U.S. China policy. The literature tends to be either descriptive or policy oriented. Perhaps one reason is that U.S. China relations embrace a wider array of complicated subfields and issues, and many major universities incorporate the study of those relations into multidisciplined China study or area study programs. Accounts of Sino-U.S. relations, such as John Fairbank's well-known book *The United States and China*, aim at providing cultural and historical understandings. Another reason, which is often taken for granted, is that studies of U.S.-China relations and China policy have strong political, economic, or diplomatic implications and usually bear characteristics of policy studies—that is, they study policy feasibilities, develop potential policies, recommend options, or argue for policy change.

Certainly those works, which constitute a major part of the literature in the field, are important and essential to understanding Sino-U.S. relations and U.S. policy toward China. However, it is also important to place some emphasis on theory. Therefore, this book seeks to shed some light on the theoretical issues concerning China policymaking—a field that still has much room for improvement. Theories should help people understand the essence of complicated issues, ask fundamental questions, and explain the logic of how things develop. In the complexity of Sino-U.S. relations, theories should help "find the central tendency among a confusion of tendencies, to single out the propelling principle even though other principles operate, to seek the essential factors where innumerable factors are present."[1] In sum, a theory should be able to describe how things happened, explain why they happened the way they did, and predict the reoccurrence of similar things in a given situation.[2]

To explain U.S. foreign policy, various theories have been developed from different perspectives. According to Ikenberry, three broad approaches have major significance in the field.[3] They are "system-centered, society-centered, and state-centered" approaches, which concentrate on three levels of analysis: international, state, and societal. Each approach embraces a body of theoretical literature. The international approach emphasizes the power or capabilities of the United States relative to other nation-states in the international system.[4] Foreign policies are more a function of the structural constraints of international systems or balance of power. After the Second World War, despite intentions in both China and the United States to seek improvement in bilateral relations, Sino-U.S. relations were predetermined by the ever bipolarized world. The founding of the People's Republic meant the loss of China to the United States, since China would inevitably and "logically" choose to join the Soviet camp. As far as China was concerned, the Korean War (in which China was initially reluctant to participate) was not fought between the United States and China and its comrade-in-arms, but between the two camps: the socialist camp headed by the Soviet Union, and the capitalist camp headed by the United States.[5] During this period, both U.S. China policy and China U.S. policy reflected the two countries' orientation toward the international system. In the late 1960s, when the tensely bipolar world gave way to a multipolar, regionally power-centered world, the foreign policies of both countries, out of security concerns, became subject to a delicately shifting balance of power in the newly structured international system. Developing new Sino-U.S. relations was once again put in the perspective of the strategic interests of both countries. In the case of opening the China door, U.S. policy was responding to the particular set of constraints and opportunities created by its position in the U.S.-USSR-China triangular relationship at the time.[6]

The state approach sees U.S. foreign policy as a function of institutional rules and norms and the role of decisionmakers as that of transforming domestic and international constraints into policy goals. This approach takes into account the institutional arrangements within the state and the role of political and bureaucratic officials in the policymaking process.[7] The societal approach stresses domestic politics as an important source of foreign policy. This pluralist approach views U.S. foreign policy as a function of domestic interest groups and political parties competing for influence. According to this view, U.S. China policy was the result of public opinion influences, the competitiveness of partisan politics, or the preferences of interest groups.[8]

Both international and domestic politics, in explaining U.S. foreign policy, regard state institutions as reflecting or responding to constraints imposed either by the international system or by domestic interest group pressures. In studying the era between Ambassador John Leighton Stuart's departure from China in 1949 and President Nixon's visit to China in 1972, it is perhaps more important to look into the international environment and the domestic pressures and public opinion that affected state actors in U.S. China policy.[9] International and domestic forces more directly and positively constrained U.S. China policy, even though some decisionmakers wanted to make a move toward China.[10]

However, neither approach recognizes that state officials and institutions can be independent decisionmaking actors in the policy process—the autonomous state.[11] These state actors can either abide by their own rules and norms and thus remain free of external pressures, or they can translate external constraints or opportunities into their own preferences. In this respect, the state-centered approach deals with the policymaking process, or the "black box" of government, through which international and domestic forces and constraints are transmitted.[12]

While not dismissing international and domestic approaches as unimportant, since they may be more useful in the comparative analysis of foreign policy, the state-centered approach focuses more explicitly or positively on the role of state officials, governmental institutions, and the bureaucracy in the policymaking process. Therefore, it becomes more helpful when research concentrates on a few foreign policy cases in one country over time.[13]

Methodological Approach

This study uses a deductive case study method, discussing the strengths and weaknesses of each model, then subjecting each model to all cases for analysis. This approach discusses each case in detail as a means of testing, qualifying, and elaborating the theories. Three strategies of inquiry have been adopted to carry out the research.

The Structured, Focused Comparison strategy focuses on certain aspects of the cases and develops a set of general questions to guide the analysis.[14] This method is used to address the question: What theories best explain the content and terms of U.S. China policy? The intention is to find a general pattern of U.S. China decisionmaking based on the focused comparison analysis of each case.

The Within-Case Analysis strategy utilizes "within-case" observations to evaluate causal relations between independent variables and the dependent variable. It requires a theory (or theories) from which propositions and hypotheses are derived to predict outcomes on the basis of specified initial conditions.[15] A comparison is made between the actual policy outcomes and those predicted by the models. If the outcome is consistent with the prediction, then the possibility of a causal relationship is established. The weakness of the within-case approach is that it only assesses the correlation between observed and predicted outcomes as the basis for causal explanations. It can hardly exhaust causal factors for within-case analysis.

As a supplement, I will use what Alexander George called a "process-tracing" procedure. This strategy seeks to examine and explain the decisionmaking process by which various initial conditions are translated into outcomes. In other words, this approach places the decisionmaking process at the center of the investigation, seeking to identify stimuli to which decisionmakers respond: the decisionmaking process that makes use of these stimuli to arrive at decisions; the effect of institutional factors on actors, processes, and outcomes; and the influence of other variables of interest on actors and outcomes.[16] This approach enables the research to focus on the policymaking process that the "within-case" analysis neglects and to account in more detail for the complicated process of decisionmaking. The utilization of this approach may lead to identification of extra factors in the process, thus enriching and refining some existing theories. The weakness of this approach is the insufficiency of information about actors' behavior in the process. To lessen the problem, this research tries to make good use of public documents, published accounts, and interviews with people who have participated in China policymaking.

Explaining China Policymaking: A Framework

This study utilizes three decisionmaking models—the rational actor model, the interbranch politics model, and the bureaucratic politics model—to analyze and explain U.S. China policy. The rational actor model enables us to seek explanations by examining U.S. foreign policy values and objectives. The other two models lead us to opening the "black box," or looking into U.S. policymaking processes by which institutions are related to each other, to explain U.S. China policy outcomes. Those two models differ from the rational actor model in two major respects. First, they break down the concept of the state as a unitary actor in foreign policymaking by probing into government institutions within the state. The interbranch politics model views the executive and Congress as two government institutions with distinct predispositions and objectives in pursuit of foreign policy.[17] The bureaucratic politics model sees foreign policy as the political result of the interaction of agencies pursuing their bureaucratic interests and preferences.[18] Second, both models deal with governmental processes through which different political interests and policy objectives are reconciled and transformed into foreign policies. In this regard, the rational actor model, the bureaucratic politics model, and the interbranch politics model will provide the theoretical framework for our analysis.

Understanding U.S. China policymaking is of empirical and theoretical interest. Empirically, few studies have applied the interbranch politics model and the bureaucratic politics model to explain U.S. China policy, especially U.S.-PRC trade and technology transfer policy after normalization. Theoretically, the three models have been constructed to explain and predict foreign policy behavior. Which model is useful in explaining U.S. China policy? How and when is each useful? Are there any factors that existing models do not take into account? Are there other intervening variables that may affect U.S. China policy?

The Rational Actor Model

The rational actor analysis, in a way similar to systemic theories, has formal deductive logic and parsimonious power for explaining and predicting a nation's foreign policy. The early application of the model was demonstrated in the study of arms race and strategic deterrence,[19] and was elegantly elaborated and tested in the study of the Cuban missile crisis.[20] This model essentially assumes that a nation is a rational, goal-seeking, and unitary decisionmaker. It assumes there is some shared goal or national interest for the decisionmaker to obtain. The rational actor will develop alternatives from which the most effective means will be selected to maximize the goal.[21]

Critics of the rational actor model have made three arguments: (1) since foreign relations are complicated matters and foreign policy problems are messy, decisionmakers do not always define and share foreign policy goals; (2) it is difficult to assess the consequence of each option and choose the most effective one given the "imperfection of information";[22] and (3) given the interdependent characteristics of the present world, governments are not unitary actors.[23]

The first criticism is a valid one given the complexity of foreign policy problems. Although policy approach and options may differ, some national consensus exists in terms of fundamental national interests and values. The key is to identify those shared interests and values. There are two other questions in the rational actor model that need to be clarified. One is that the model assumes that the state is a unitary actor, but it does not specify the actual decisionmaker. What does "state" mean? Does it refer to the State Department? Or Congress? Who is the sole actor that represents the "state" to act and be acted upon? Thus, the rational actor needs to be specified. The other question is that the model takes for granted that the decisionmaking process is one in which a rational actor defines goals, develops options, assesses consequences that each option may produce, and makes the final selection.[24] The problem with this approach is that it does not specify the kind of decisionmaking process: Is it the executive decisionmaking process? The congressional process? Or the decisionmaking process that requires both executive and congressional participation?

The rational actor can be defined here as those key politicians and bureaucrats in the executive branch, including the president, who, on the whole, are more likely to take a national view as they respond to the parochial concerns of either social groups or particular governmental institutions.[25] To operationalize the rational actor model, it is necessary first to identify U.S. China policy objectives. There were three broadly shared policy objectives. The first objective was to develop strategic cooperation. A better relationship with China would enable the United States to win a de facto ally against Soviet global expansion, especially in the face of the Afghanistan invasion. The second was to stabilize Asian affairs. Better Sino-U.S. relations could serve as a balance of forces in Asia favorable to the

United States and its allies and friends in the region and help stabilize the situation on the Korean peninsula. The last was to gain political and economic benefits. A good bilateral relationship would benefit the United States from economic, cultural, and other exchanges; it would also enable the United States to work closely with China on such issues as environmental protection, population control, and arms sales. Apart from these objectives, U.S. decisionmakers also viewed maintaining Taiwan's political stability and economic prosperity as part of U.S. Asian policy objectives. These objectives in many ways were not incompatible with China's objectives, which can be summarized as follows: first, to counter Soviet expansion in Asia and the world; second, to obtain U.S. investment and technology and to benefit from educational, touristic, and other exchanges; and third, to help resolve the Taiwan issue and achieve its national reunification goal.

With the objectives identified above, the following propositions can be derived from the model.

Proposition 1: That the United States would define U.S. China policies primarily according to shifting strategic balance of power while maximizing other foreign policy interests.

Proposition 2: That China's positions can influence U.S. decisionmakers' perception and calculation of U.S. interests and policy objectives concerning Taiwan, hence U.S. China policy outcomes.

The question of whether the United States pursues its foreign policy in a rational way is an old but key one. The answer depends largely on the criteria for judging rationality. Here rationality is defined as orderly responses to issues concerning Sino-U.S. relations according to foreign policy priorities. Now questions arise: Who defines China policy priorities? This is a tough issue because trying to rank foreign policy priorities runs the risk of being self-fulfilling and cyclical. In fact, no president can come up with a clearly defined China policy agenda. And yet, some national consensus on China policy objectives and priorities does exist among U.S. citizens and decision-makers. Public opinion on China policy can be implicit, or intuitive and explicit; decisionmakers are much less intuitive and more calculative in determining policy priorities. Policymakers have certain parameters in defining policy objectives. In the conduct of national foreign policy, national survival and strategic interests, either military or economic (such as geopolitics or security and oil), preempt other policy objectives. In this respect, questions at hand are: Does the United States always pursue its China policy in a rational way? How did the United States maximize other China policy goals that were in conflict with its strategic interests? And how was the policy made: from the top down, by the bureaucracy, or a combination of both?

The Bureaucratic Politics Model

Although bureaucratic phenomena that affect people's lives existed as early as centuries ago when the Chinese emperor invented the first bureaucratic system in the world, the scientific study and modeling of bureaucratic influence on decisionmaking came much later. The pluralist conception of modern society depicts complex and highly differentiated organizations that seek and maintain their own interests. Power is diffused and dispersed in response to various interests. According to Amos Perlmutter, this pluralist orientation "combined with social scientific (and the game theory) analyses, formed the intellectual and methodological foundations of the bureaucratic politics theory."[26] To seek explanations of foreign policy and its making in this pluralist context, political scientists began to concentrate their study on the role and importance of the executive branch, in which several highly differentiated organizations were created and expanded to deal with foreign policy issues. Accompanied by the overall expansion of the executive branch in terms of power, authority, and staff, the three bureaucratic organizations are the most noticeable: the National Security Council (NSC), the Central Intelligence Agency (CIA), and the Department of State.[27] The State Department, for example, had only nine employees besides the secretary at its creation, and it was limited both in power and status; its jurisdiction was often challenged by the more powerful Department of the Treasury.[28]

The major sources of the bureaucratic politics models, or what Robert Art called the "second wave of bureaucratic politics theories," are Graham Allison's "Conceptual Models and the Cuban Missile Crisis" and *Essence of Decision*, and Morton Halperin's *Bureaucratic Politics and Foreign Policy*.[29] The bureaucratic politics model makes some major assumptions. First, different governmental institutions constrain bureaucratic players with different institutional interests and preferences. That is, the behavior of the bureaucratic players is restrained and therefore can be predicted by their organizational roles. Second, players see the stakes involved in a situation according their own interests. In Allison's words, "Where you stand depends on where you sit."[30] Consensus building, compromising, bargaining, and negotiating are the mechanisms of decisionmaking.[31] In sum, foreign policy is the outcome of a bargaining process structured by bureaucratic power resources and interests.

The bureaucratic politics perspective contributes to the understanding of one of our modern societal dilemmas: the need and demand for efficient and effective decisionmaking on the one hand, and a dysfunctional, pulling, and hauling bureaucratic decisionmaking process on the other. The power of the model lies in its penetrating and enduring insight that "foreign policy is often more the product of dysfunctional decision making process than of a rational assessment of instruments and objectives."[32] Foreign policy is said to be national policy, and foreign policy objectives should be national objectives. Yet, very often in pursuit of foreign policy objectives, the rationality is deflected or refracted by bureaucratic fissures resulting from organizational interests and biases as well as by the bureaucratic decisionmaking process. In this regard, politics and process help explain foreign policy.

Critics of the bureaucratic politics model have focused on three points. First, the bureaucratic politics model gives inadequate treatment to presidential influence in the policymaking process. Jerel Rosati, for example, finds that the president's level of involvement was the critical factor in controlling the SALT negotiations during the Nixon administration.[33] Second, Perlmutter deplores the fact that the bureaucratic politics model failed to take into account the importance of the relationship between the president and his chief political and bureaucratic officials, and was thus unable to explain the degree of bureaucratic influence on the outcome of a specific policy.[34] Third, organizational position does not always determine a bureaucratic politics player's stance on an issue.[35] As Stephen Krasner points out, decisionmakers often do not "stand where they sit. Sometimes they are not sitting anywhere."[36] Other scholars point out that a player's policy stance is more a function of personal values and perceptions of external situations than bureaucratic positions.[37]

In addition, the bureaucratic model neglects the fact that quite often, especially since the Vietnam War, Congress has asserted its power in foreign policymaking. The passage of the War Powers Resolution in 1973 over the executive veto, the arms embargo on Turkey in 1974, and the TRA in 1979 demonstrated the importance of congressional residual in explaining foreign policy. The bureaucratic model, as Robert Pastor pointed out, is "at a loss to explain a foreign policy made by the Congress over the objections of a united bureaucracy."[38]

Nevertheless, the bureaucratic politics model provides some insight into bureaucratic politics and process in which players' preferences and players' resources may affect policy formulation and outcomes.

Proposition 1: That U.S. China policy can be explained and predicted by bureaucratic players' positions and preferences within the bureaucracy and their interactions.

Proposition 2: Incoherent, uncoordinated China policy outcomes can be the result of the pulling and hauling of bureaucratic politics, especially when presidential attention and involvement are low.

In applying the bureaucratic policy model to U.S. China policymaking, several questions need to be addressed concerning U.S. China policymaking. Who created the policy: the State Department, the Defense Department, or the NSC? How was the policy made: by bargaining, compromising, or conforming to the president's directive? What are the interests and resources of the bureaucratic players in the area of China policy? Under what circumstances does the president affect the bureaucratic policy process? Of course, all these questions can be addressed only after the fundamental question: Do bureaucratic politics and process affect U.S. China policy?

The Interbranch Politics Model

The idea of studying interbranch politics in foreign policymaking was prompted by the fact that previous literature focused on separate roles that Congress and the executive played in foreign policymaking. Robert Dahl's study, which concluded that "the President proposes and the Congress disposes," represented one of the pioneer efforts to study Congress's role in foreign policy.[39] James Robinson elaborated on Dahl's theme and found that the role of Congress in foreign policymaking became increasingly one of "legitimating, amending, or vetoing executive proposals."[40]

John Lehman's study of congressional-presidential relations in the Nixon administration presented two interesting points. First, he looked into the policy process for an explanation of foreign policy outcomes.[41] Second, he saw policymaking as a zero-sum game in which both branches have their own processes. In each of the processes the two branches claimed to be in control of policymaking, and the outcome of each process either increased the power of one branch and decreased the power of the other or vice versa. In this exercise, Lehman was able to focus on interbranch behavior in the policy-shaping process. Scholars of interbranch politics and foreign policy believe that this kind of approach touches upon the more relevant question: "Who is pushing whom, for what purpose and to what effect?"[42]

Frans Bax also focused on the interactive process between the two branches. In his proposed competitive acceptance model, he emphasized that foreign policy decisions should be the outcome of a political process in which institutional differences can be expressed, accommodated, and compromised.[43] Arthur Maass examined congressional-executive relations in two separate political processes. He developed a model stressing two different roles, executive and congressional, in two distinct processes: administrative and legislative. The executive role is leadership—"to initiate and impel"; the Congress's role is control—"to oversee and to approve, reject, or amend."[44]

Building upon previous literature, Pastor constructed what he called "the interbranch politics lens," which utilizes the congressional-executive interactive process as the explanatory device for understanding U.S. foreign policy. This model assumes that U.S. foreign policy is the "resultant of a sometimes subtle or tacit, sometimes forceful or conflictual, always interactive process between two branches of institutions, the Executive and Congress."[45] The interactive process can best be understood from the perspective of "two institutions with distinct sets of institutional biases or predispositions."[46] These biases are responsible for each branch ranking its foreign policy objectives differently.

In U.S. China policy, for instance, the executive is likely to put greater weight on policy goals stressing strategic, regional, and other international interests, whereas the Congress is likely to seek policy objectives that carry more domestic implications—policies that are more compatible with political interests (partisan or electoral), ideology (liberal or conservative beliefs), and values (social or cultural). Whether the two branches will reconcile these policy goals into a relatively consistent policy will "depend on the extent of responsiveness and trust between the two branches."[47]

Theoretical components of the interbranch politics model can be identified as follows:

1. Legislative-executive process is important in accounting for foreign policy.
2. There are only two institutional players interacting in the process. Here the model presumes that institutional unity is more important. Congress and the executive overcome their intrabranch division and present themselves with their own internal wills in reaction to each other in the process.
3. Each branch as an institution has its own bias or interest, which determines its own objectives, foreign policy priorities, and policymaking behavior.
4. The reconciliation of these objectives into a relatively coherent policy depends on the extent of responsiveness and trust between the two branches.
5. The degree of institutional will, executive leadership, congressional cohesion, and bargaining skill determines the contours and content of the policy.[48]

Proposition 1: That U.S. China policy can be explained by the pulling and hauling of politics between two government institutions: Congress pulling toward an issue-specific, short-term China policy, and the executive stressing long-term strategic cooperation with China.

Proposition 2: That the more the executive consults with Congress on China policy, the more likely it is for the executive to obtain congressional approval of its China policy initiatives.

Proposition 3: That the success of China policy depends on the combination of presidential influence, leadership skills, and the strength of the president's party in Congress.

The focus in applying the interbranch politics model to analyzing China policy is on the following questions: What were the China policy priorities of each branch? To what degree and in what way can Congress assert its influence on China policymaking? To what degree and in what way can the executive influence congressional debate? Who made the policy: the executive, Congress, or both? How was the policy made: by persuasion, consultation, or exclusion?

* * *

Some literature suggests that Congress as an institution is decentralized and fragmented because of its electoral politics. David Mayhew explored the linkage between congressional representatives' motivation and public policy. He found that the principal motivation of a member of Congress is reelection. This "electoral connection" profoundly affects not only behavior and accountability but the structure of Congress and the way it makes public policy.[49] Thus, policies often reflect "individual responsiveness" without "collective responsibility."[50]

Other congressional theories emphasize that Congress imposes institutional constraints on members' behavior as well, such as institutional arrangements, policy process, rules, etc. Moreover, members of Congress act on other members' expertise in policymaking. They usually follow the lead of those who have developed enough expertise to offer an informed judgment.[51] The "cue-taking" theory also suggests members' willingness to rely on the specialties of and be guided by the cues—e.g., colleagues whose ideologies can be identified with their own philosophies.[52]

Review of the congressional literature shows that while electoral politics produces pork barrel–oriented members of Congress, it is possible to speak of Congress as an institution vis-à-vis the executive for several reasons. First, Congress has an institutional interest in enhancing its image and status in making foreign policy. How Congress is perceived by the general public can either enhance or reduce its legitimacy and effectiveness, especially in light of ambiguous constitutional sharing of power with the executive in the area of foreign policy. Second, unity can be achieved, to an extent, by the cue-taking members following other members with recognized expertise on specific issues. In other cases, as Bax noted, "Congress supports or ratifies the desires of those members interested in an issue."[53] By the same token, members try to keep in line with prevailing sentiment in Congress, which is again defined by public mood and opinion.

The executive branch is not referred to as a branch divided by the president's top advisers and the bureaucracy, or a branch fragmented with divisions in the bureaucracy. It means the president retains a hierarchical control over the bureaucracy and has the final say in policy alternatives advocated by subordinates. Therefore, the executive branch is here defined as the coherent, presidentially directed institution.[54]

Theories of interbranch politics distinguish themselves from other bodies of theoretical work in three aspects. First, they focus on two important institutions of decisionmaking rather than on one single institution or subsets of each institution.[55] Second, they utilize the interactive political process as an independent variable to account for the content of policy and policy outcomes. Other models, such as the rational actor model, focus on a single actor or institution as an explanatory vehicle. Third, these theories assume that the pattern of interaction between Congress and the executive is the key to the understanding of foreign policy, whereas other approaches overlook the congressional-executive interaction in the political process.

* * *

In sum, each model raises a different set of questions and suggests a different set of hypotheses to test. These questions and hypotheses are by no means exclusive and exhaustive in terms of testing the models and explaining U.S. China policy. Nonetheless, for the purpose of this study, we can utilize some basic questions from each model and suggest a few policy outcomes predicted by applying the models.

Other factors, such as international events, presidential ideology, electoral mandate, and actions by China, may also affect different institutional predispositions and decisionmakers' perceptions. These contextual factors may not influence U.S. China policymaking directly, but they may pose some initial conditions that actors have to take into consideration. They may also affect the actors' original stance and their relations with each other in the decisionmaking process. For example, decisionmakers tend to anticipate the attitude and response of countries concerned before they make policies.[56] Very often, international events may also disrupt the decisionmaking process and add additional elements for decisionmakers to consider. Contingent international events usually require information and prompt response, and thus render the executive the prominent position in formulating responsive policy.

Issues may also have independent effects on U.S. China policymaking. Different issues may affect congressional responses to presidential initiatives. As Theodore Lowi points out, policy determines politics.[57] The nature of the issues can have two determinant effects: It can decide the arena in which policies will be fought over and it can enhance institutional predisposition and help rerank institutional priorities. Because the Constitution is ambiguous concerning the division of power in many areas and the government has expanded over the years, the overlapping of responsibilities among branches of government has evolved into such a state that each branch grasps issues that it believes may enhance its own institutional standing. This is particularly true in light of the struggle over foreign policy between Congress and the executive since the Vietnam War.

Therefore, the analysis in this study based on the outlined theoretical framework needs to be sensitive to the possible influence of these factors as well. In the concluding chapter, I will relate these factors to the analysis of U.S. China policy.

Notes

1. Kenneth N. Waltz, *Theory of International Politics* (Reading, Mass.: Addison-Wesley, 1979), p. 10.

2. David J. Singer, "The Level-of-Analysis Problem in International Relations," in Klaus Knorr and Sidney Verba, eds., *The International System: Theoretical Essays* (Princeton: Princeton University Press, 1961), pp. 77–92.

3. John Ikenberry, David A. Lake, and Michel Mastanduno, "Introduction: Approaches to Explaining American Foreign Economic Policy," *International Organization* 42 (Winter 1988), pp. 1–14.

4. Waltz, *Theory of International Politics*; Robert Koehane, "The Theory of Hegemonic Stability and Change in International Economic Regimes," in Ole Holsti, R. Siverson, and A. George, eds., *Change in the International System* (Boulder: Westview Press, 1980).

5. Because the Chinese thought that the United States would attack China sooner or later, it was in the interest of China to fight the Korean War. For a detailed account on why China participated in the war, see Hao Yufan and Zhai Zhihai, "China's Decision to Enter the Korean War: History Revisited," *China Quarterly*, no. 121 (March 1990), pp. 94–115.

6 See Banning Garrett, "China Policy and the Constraints of Triangular Logic," in Kenneth A. Oye, Robert J. Lieber, and Ronald Rothchild, eds., *Eagle Defiant: United States Foreign Policy in the 1980s* (Boston: Little, Brown, 1983); Michael Pillsbury, "U.S.-China Military Ties?" *Foreign Policy*, no. 20 (Fall 1975), pp. 50–64.

7. See Peter J. Katzenstein, "Conclusion: Domestic Structure and Strategies of Foreign Economic Policy," in Katzenstein, ed., *Between Power and Plenty: Foreign Economic Policies of Advanced Industrial States* (Madison: University of Wisconsin Press, 1978); Stephen Krasner, *Defending the National Interest: Raw Materials, Investment, and United States Foreign Policy* (Princeton: Princeton University Press, 1978).

8. Leonard A. Kusnitz, *Public Opinion and Foreign Policy: America's China Policy, 1949–1979* (Westport, Conn.: Greenwood Press, 1984), p. 177.

9. Ibid.; see also Richard H. Solomon, ed., *The China Factor: Sino-American Relations and the Global Scene* (Englewood Cliffs, N.J.: Prentice-Hall, 1981), pp. 9–14.

10. Oksenberg, "The Dynamics of the Sino-American Relationship," in Solomon, *China Factor*, p. 62; William J. Barnds, *China and America: The Search for a New Relationship* (New York: New York University Press, 1977), p. 210; Bradford H. Westerfield, *Foreign Policy and Party Politics: Pearl Harbor to Korea* (New Haven: Yale University Press, 1955).

11. See Ralph Miliband, *The State in Capitalist Society* (New York: Basic Books, 1969).

12. Ikenberry, Lake, and Mastanduno, "Introduction: Approaches to Explaining American Foreign Economic Policy," pp. 2–3.

13. Ibid.

14. Alexander L. George, "Case Studies and Theory Development: The Method of Structured, Focused Comparison," in Paul Gordon Lauren, ed., *Diplomacy: New Approaches in History, Theory, and Policy* (New York: The Free Press, 1979), pp. 61–62.

15. Alexander L. George and Timothy J. McKeown, "Case Studies and Theories of Organizational Decision-Making," *Advances in Information Processing in Organizations,* 2 (1985) pp. 29–30.

16. Ibid., pp. 34–41.

17. The interbranch politics model was developed and utilized by Robert A. Pastor to analyze U.S. foreign economic policies. See his *Congress and the Politics of U.S. Foreign Economic Policy 1929–1976* (Berkeley: University of California Press, 1980).

18. The bureaucratic politics model was developed and used by Graham T. Allison to explain the Cuban missile crisis. See his "Conceptual Models and the Cuban Missile Crisis," *American Political Science Review* 63 (September 1969), pp. 689–718. This model was further elaborated in his *Essence of Decision: Explaining the Cuban Missile Crisis* (Boston: Little, Brown, 1971) and in Morton H. Halperin, *Bureaucratic Politics and Foreign Policy* (Washington, D.C.: Brookings Institution, 1974).

19. Thomas Schelling and Morton H. Halperin, *Strategy and Arms Control* (New York: Twentieth Century Fund, 1961).

20. Allison, *Essence of Decision: Explaining the Cuban Missile Crisis.*

21. Ibid., p. 30.

22. Jaw-ling Joanne Chang, *United States-China Normalization: An Evaluation of Foreign Policy Decision Making* (Denver: Graduate School of International Studies, University of Denver, 1986), p. 50.

23. See Robert Keohane and Joseph Nye, *Power and Interdependence: World Politics in Transition* (Boston: Little, Brown, 1977), Chapter 1.

24. Chang, *United States-China Normalization,* pp. 49–50.

25. Stephen D. Krasner maintained that because high-level decisionmakers perceive their roles as protecting and promoting national security interests, they act upon their autonomous set of preferences. See Krasner, *Defending the National Interest: Raw Materials, Investment, and United States Foreign Policy.*

26. Amos Perlmutter, "The Presidential Political Center and Foreign Policy: A Critique," *World Politics* 27 (October 1974), p. 93.

27. For good discussions on the evolution of the NSC and the roles of State and the CIA in foreign policymaking, see Zbigniew Brzezinski, "The NSC's Midlife Crisis," *Foreign Policy,* no. 69 (Winter 1987/88), pp. 80–99; Theodore C. Sorensen, "The President and the Secretary of State," and Robert M. Gates, "The CIA and American Foreign Policy," *Foreign Affairs* 66, no. 2 (Winter 1987/88), pp. 215–230, 231–248.

28. See Sorensen, "The President and the Secretary of State," p. 234.

29. Allison, "Conceptual Models and the Cuban Missile Crisis," and Halperin, *Bureaucratic Politics and Foreign Policy.*

30. Allison, *Essence of Decision,* p. 176.

31. John Spanier and Eric Uslaner, *American Foreign Policy Making and the Domestic Dilemmas,* 4th ed. (New York: Holt, Rinehart and Winston, 1985), p. 178.

32. Pastor, *Congress and the Politics of U.S. Foreign Economic Policy 1929–1976,* p. 32.

33. Jerel A. Rosati, "Developing a Systemic Decision-making Framework: Bureaucratic Politics in Perspective," *World Politics* 33 (January 1981), p. 245.

34. Perlmutter, "The Presidential Political Center and Foreign Policy: A Critique," p. 95.

35. Robert J. Art, "Bureaucratic Politics and American Foreign Policy: A Critique," *Policy Science* 4 (December 1973), pp. 467–490.

36. Stephen Krasner, "Are Bureaucracies Important? (Or Allison Wonderland)," *Foreign Policy*, no. 7 (Summer 1972), p. 165.

37. See I. M. Destler, *Presidents, Bureaucracies, and Foreign Policy* (Princeton: Princeton University Press, 1972), and Glen H. Snyder and Paul Diesing, *Conflict Among Nations: Bargaining, Decision-making, and System Structure in International Crises* (Princeton: Princeton University Press, 1977).

38. Pastor, *Congress and the Politics of U.S. Foreign Economic Policy 1929–1976*, p. 33.

39. Robert Dahl, *Congress and Foreign Policy* (New York: Norton, 1950).

40. James A. Robinson, *Congress and Foreign Policy Making: A Study in Legislative Influence and Initiative*, rev. ed. (Homewood, Ill.: Dorsey Press, 1967), p. 180.

41. John F. Lehman, *The Executive, Congress, and Foreign Policy: Studies of the Nixon Administration* (New York: Praeger, 1976), p. 220.

42. Pastor, *Congress and the Politics of U.S. Foreign Economic Policy 1929–1976*, p. 51.

43. See Frans R. Bax, "The Legislative-Executive Relationship in Foreign Policy: New Partnership or New Competition?" *Orbis* 20 (Winter 1977), p. 7.

44. Arthur Maass, *Congress and the Common Good* (New York: Basic Books, 1983), p. 13.

45. Pastor, *Congress and the Politics of U.S. Foreign Economic Policy 1929–1976*, p. 53.

46. Ibid.

47. Ibid., p. 54.

48. Ibid., pp. 49–57.

49. David Mayhew, *Congress: The Electoral Connection* (New Haven: Yale University Press, 1974), p. 51.

50. Gary Jacobson, *The Politics of Congressional Elections* (Boston: Little, Brown, 1987), pp. 216–217.

51. Richard F. Fenno, *Congressmen in Committees* (Boston: Little, Brown, 1973).

52. See Richard Fenno, "The Internal Distribution of Influence: The House," in David B. Truman, ed., *The Congress and America's Future*, 2d ed. (Englewood Cliffs, N.J.: Prentice-Hall, 1973), pp. 63–90; John Kingdom, *Congressmen's Voting Decisions* (New York: Harper and Row, 1973).

53. Bax, "The Legislative-Executive Relationship in Foreign Policy: New Partnership or New Competition?" p. 884.

54. Krasner, "Are Bureaucracies Important?" and Art, "Bureaucratic Politics and American Foreign Policy: A Critique."

55. For example, the bureaucratic politics model and the congressional model all focus on the analysis of one single institutional politics, its inputs and policy outcomes.

56. Michel P. Sullivan, *International Relations: Theories and Evidence* (Englewood Cliffs, N.J.: Prentice-Hall, 1976), p. 272.

57. Theodore Lowi, "American Business, Public Policy, Case Studies and Political Theory," *World Politics* 16 (1964), pp. 676–715.

2

Taiwan Relations Act: A By-Product of Normalization?

With the normalization of Sino-U.S. diplomatic relations in 1978, the United States severed its official relations with Taiwan, but thus also pledged to continue its unofficial ties with Taiwan. In 1979, the U.S. Congress passed the Taiwan Relations Act, which aimed to govern future commercial, cultural, and other relations between the United States and the people of Taiwan.

There are two important policy provisions in the TRA. First, the act declared that the peace and security of the Western Pacific were in the interests of the United States and that any nonpeaceful effort against Taiwan, including boycotts and embargoes, would be considered a threat to the peace of the Western Pacific and of grave concern to the United States. Second, it provided for arms sales to Taiwan, and Congress and the president would determine the types and quantities of defensive arms and services to be provided to Taiwan. The act also required the president to inform the Congress promptly of any threat to Taiwan's well-being.[1]

The TRA was important for its policy implications. It became a controversial issue in U.S.-China relations because of two key provisions concerning security and arms sales, which China regarded as violating the principles of the normalization communiqué. The TRA posed a policy dilemma for U.S. decisionmakers: The implementation of the TRA, especially the arms sales, would have to affect relations with the People's Republic of China. The TRA also offers a good case study of U.S. China policymaking in the post-normalization era. The passage of the TRA represented an important change in the making of China policy. It signified congressional assertiveness in China policymaking. Congress, by revising the Taiwan legislation proposed by the executive, established its role as a China policymaker. In this chapter I utilize the three decisionmaking models to analyze and explain the making of the TRA. Three issues are addressed here: How did the TRA come into being? Which theory can best explain the terms and content of the TRA? What can account for congressional assertiveness in the policymaking process?

U.S. Taiwan Policy: The Executive Process

When President Carter took office in January 1977, one of his administration's foreign policy goals was normalization of relations with China. According to NSC head Zbigniew Brzezinski, the United States "wanted to initiate talks with the PRC . . . and to establish full diplomatic relations by 1979."[2] In his memo to the president on April 15, 1977, Secretary of State Cyrus Vance also suggested that "in terms of our strategic position, normalization is highly desirable."[3]

Normalizing relations with China was a key strategic consideration of the Carter administration. Like the previous administrations, the new administration saw that a genuinely cooperative relationship between the United States and the PRC would greatly enhance stability in Asia, and that, more generally, it would help maintain a world strategic posture favorable to U.S. interests. In his speech at Notre Dame in May 1977, President Carter stated explicitly:

> It is important that we make progress towards normalizing relations with the People's Republic of China. We see the American-Chinese relationship as a central element of our global policy, and China as a key force for global peace. We wish to cooperate closely with the creative Chinese people on the problems that confront all mankind.[4]

Given its goal for normalization of relations with China, the administration still had to resolve the Taiwan problem. The president noted that there was a need to "find a formula that can bridge some of the difficulties that still separate us."[5] This required a different approach from previous administrations' positions on Taiwan. The Chinese government had insisted that the U.S. government accept three conditions for normalization: cessation of diplomatic relations with Taiwan; withdrawal of U.S. military forces from Taiwan; and abrogation of the U.S.-Taiwan defense treaty signed in 1954. The Carter administration faced the dilemma from the beginning of how to accept the three conditions in order to normalize relations with China and at the same time avoid the possible political repercussions of appearing to abandon Taiwan.

Preparing U.S. Taiwan Policy

The first comprehensive China policy study conducted during the Carter administration came out of an extensive interagency memorandum on China drafted for the president—Policy Review Memorandum (PRM-24)—in May 1977. It was prepared by the State Department, the National Security Council, and the Defense Department as a China policy recommendation to the president.[6]

This study recommended that "the United States establish diplomatic relations with the PRC and terminate formal governmental relations with Taiwan. Without diplomatic relations with Taipei, the defense treaty and the United States military presence would be terminated."[7] At the same time, the study suggested that the United States continue to have economic, social, and other unofficial relations with Taiwan and terminate its defense treaty with Taiwan on one year's notice. Furthermore, the study proposed two more conditions: that the United States would continue to sell selective defensive arms to Taiwan after the termination of the treaty, and that China must state its intent to seek a peaceful solution to the Taiwan issue.[8] At the end of June, Secretary Vance chaired a Policy Review Committee meeting to consider the PRM-24 recommendation on China. His position, in favor of a slower and more deliberate pace, prevailed over Brzezinski's position to move rapidly toward normalization. Differences of opinion emerged from the meeting between Vance and Brzezinski and, to a lesser degree, Harold Brown, secretary of defense in two areas: security relations with China and the Taiwan question.[9] On the grounds of mutual strategic concerns about the Soviet Union, Brzezinski felt that the United States should make a commitment to normalization when Vance went to Beijing in August. Given the strategic importance of U.S.-PRC relations, he was also ready to "deemphasize" the links with Taiwan.[10]

On June 27, the Policy Review Committee recommended to Carter that the United States establish diplomatic relations in the near future, provided it would not endanger Taiwan's security. The United States must also maintain economic and cultural relations with Taiwan and continue to provide Taiwan with "carefully selected defensive weapons."[11]

On July 30, in preparation for Vance's August trip to Beijing, President Carter decided at a meeting attended by Vance, Brzezinski, Brown, Richard Holbrooke, and Michel Oksenberg, to go for normalization, provided Vance could obtain from Beijing the following assurances: first, the United States could continue to maintain unofficial economic, cultural, and other relations with Taiwan; second, the United States could sell selective, defensive arms to Taiwan; and third, the United States could make a unilateral, uncontested statement upon normalization regarding its expectation for a peaceful settlement of the Taiwan issue.[12]

To demonstrate U.S. sincerity, Carter instructed Vance to prepare a draft communiqué to be issued in Beijing and to begin negotiating if Beijing responded favorably to his presentation. However, the U.S. position on future U.S.-Taiwan relations was still somewhat ambivalent at that time. In his presentation to the Chinese leaders, Vance stated that "it would be necessary for U.S. government personnel to remain in Taiwan under an informal arrangement."[13] In response to Vance's presentation, Chinese leader Deng Xiaoping responded with strong criticism, stating that it was a retrogression from Ford's statement to normalize relations in accordance with the Japanese formula.[14]

It was not surprising that Vance's trip resulted in no progress. For one thing, it appeared during that period that the Carter administration had a tough battle with the Senate over the approval of the Panama Canal treaties. President Carter, warned by Vice President Mondale and presidential assistant Hamilton Jordan, developed second thoughts as to the possible consequences of compromising on the Taiwan issue.[15] He was concerned that it would jeopardize the vote on the treaties. In his last-minute instruction to Vance, Carter shifted slightly his position on normalization, authorizing Vance to proceed more slowly and press for more Chinese concessions on Taiwan.[16] As a result, Vance, already favoring a slower, more deliberate pace toward normalization, decided not to push hard on normalization.[17] After his return from China, Vance recommended to Carter that the United States should not move any faster on normalization than the U.S. political situation would actually allow.

Despite the lack of progress during Vance's visit and the administration's preoccupation with the Panama treaties and with the Soviet Union, the United States was still exploring alternatives to the Taiwan issue. Secretary Vance asked State Department legal adviser Herb Hansell to work closely with Holbrooke on the arrangements that would govern U.S.-Taiwan relations in the postnormalization era.[18]

Rehearsing Taiwan Policy on a Broader Stage

Over the next few months, three developments occurred that tended to favor normalization: lack of progress in SALT talks, the Soviet expansion in Africa, and the approval of the Panama Canal treaties. Internationally, Soviet actions in the Horn of Africa strengthened Brzezinski's position on cultivating good relations with China in the strategic context. Domestically, as passage of the treaties was nearing in mid-March, Carter approved a long-debated Brzezinski trip to China.[19] The United States informed China of Brzezinski's acceptance of the invitation one day after the first treaty was approved by the Senate, and the actual date for his visit was set on the day following the approval of the second treaty.[20]

With the ratification of the Panama Canal treaties in March and April, the State Department was ready to set the normalization process in motion. On May 10, Vance, joined by Brown and Brzezinski, sent a memorandum to the president outlining the U.S. position on the Taiwan issue. Vance stated in his memoirs:

> We were prepared to "close down our embassy in Taipei, terminate the U.S.-ROC mutual defense treaty, and withdraw our remaining military personnel and installation." We would insist on continuing selective arms sales to Taiwan for defensive purposes, terminate all official

relations, and remove all U.S. government representation; we would insist that we retain economic, cultural, and other unofficial ties with Taipei, and would also publicly reaffirm the American interest in a peaceful resolution of the Taiwan issue.[21]

President Carter approved the Taiwan policy and privately told Brzezinski on May 12 that he would like to move quickly toward normalization. In the president's May 17 instruction, Brzezinski was authorized to convey to his Chinese counterparts that the United States would accept the three basic Chinese conditions regarding normalization and reaffirm the five points previously made by Nixon and Ford.[22] Because of State Department reservations, Carter had dismissed as premature these same five points, which in early 1977 Brzezinski had urged the president to reaffirm. Brzezinski was also authorized to make two counterconditions: (1) that "at the time of normalization the United States will make a unilateral statement calling for a peaceful settlement of the Taiwan question by the Chinese themselves and that there will have to be an understanding with the Chinese that such a statement would not be contradicted; and (2) that the United States will continue to provide Taiwan with access to military equipment for defensive purposes."[23]

Brzezinski's visit turned out to be more successful in establishing strategic relations with China than in normalizing diplomatic relations. The Chinese leaders seemed more interested in his strong position against the Soviet threat than in normalization. They embraced his world views and strategic thinking. However, he did test the Chinese reaction to a unilateral U.S. statement expressing hope for a peaceful resolution of the Taiwan issue. He was told by Deng Xiaoping that each side could express its own opinion, and that how and when China resolved the Taiwan issue was an internal Chinese affair.[24]

At this stage, a compromise appeared possible: either the United States could continue to sell arms to Taiwan without obtaining public Chinese assurance of their intent to resolve the Taiwan issue peacefully, or the United States would stop arms sales, reciprocated with a Chinese declaration of peaceful intent. Chinese Premier Hua Guofeng told Brzezinski that China could not accept arms sales and commit itself to a peaceful resolution at the same time because it might result in a two-Chinas solution.[25]

Deciding U.S. Taiwan Policy

Upon Brzezinski's return, the United States made several important moves toward normalization. On June 13, Vance sent detailed negotiation instructions to President Carter for approval. He recommended that normalization should precede efforts to seek Senate ratification of SALT II, and that the best target date for normalization would be mid-December. On June 20, a special meeting, attended only by Carter, Vance, Brown,

Brzezinski, and Jordan, was held to set the negotiating agenda. It was decided that the United States would aim for December 15; that the United States would explore broader options in its relations with Taiwan, such as a trade mission or a military sales mission; that Ambassador Leonard Woodcock would be the sole negotiator in the process; and that Woodcock, as a way out of the dilemma, would explore the possibility of giving one year's notice to Taiwan before terminating the defense treaty.

For the first time, the United States decided to put the one-year's notice to Taiwan on the negotiation agenda. On August 17, Brzezinski, in a meeting with Chief Liaison Officer Chai Zemin, hinted at the approach that the United States subsequently adopted regarding the termination of the defense treaty with Taiwan. Between July and December, Woodcock conducted a series of negotiations with the Chinese, gradually laying out U.S. positions on Taiwan. In the meantime, two other channels were opened: Brzezinski continued his regular meeting with Han Xu and then met with Chai Zemin on global strategic issues; Holbrooke opened a third channel through which Chinese complaints about U.S. arms sales to Taiwan were delivered. On September 19, President Carter met with Chai, stressing again arms sales to Taiwan and a noncontradicted statement on a peaceful resolution of the Taiwan issue. This insistence and a simultaneous U.S. foreign policy diversion of seeking normalization with the Vietnamese left China unsure of the seriousness of the U.S. intention on normalization. To break the subsequent stalemate in the negotiation, President Carter accepted the National Security Council's recommendation to submit a draft communiqué on normalization, and advanced the date from January 15 to January 1 for normalization.[26] Woodcock presented a draft of the joint communiqué on November 2 and a few days later told his counterparts that the United States would terminate the defense treaty with Taiwan with one year's notice. On December 4, China tabled a second draft in response to the first one. On December 13, Deng entered into the negotiation, accepting the invitation to visit the United States in early 1979. In response to the treaty termination with one year's notice, leaving the treaty in effect in 1979, Deng requested that the United States stop arms sales during that year. On December 14, Woodcock conveyed Carter's willingness to stop arms sales in 1979.[27]

However, the two sides differed deeply on the issue of arms sales beyond the one-year moratorium. While the United States insisted that the sales would go on after 1979, China responded that arms sales infringed upon Chinese sovereignty and could not be accepted. On the eve of the announcement, Brzezinski proposed to China through Woodcock:

> Recognizing Chinese sensitivities on this matter, we will not make a formal statement but will respond to the inevitable question . . . in the following fashion: Within the agreement to normalize, the United States has made it clear that it will continue to trade with Taiwan, including the restrained sale of selective defensive arms, after the

expiration of the defense treaty, in a way that will not endanger the prospects for peace in the region. The Chinese side does not endorse the U.S. position on the matter, but it has not prevented both sides from agreeing to normalize relations.[28]

In agreeing to normalize relations, both the United States and China deferred their disagreements on the sensitive subject of arms sales to Taiwan. Thus, normalization was finally achieved. Throughout the negotiation, the Taiwan issue had been the main obstacle. For the United States, the political process demanded that the Carter administration make acceptable Taiwan policies upon normalization. The Carter administration made three "counterconditions" in an attempt to cope with domestic constraints, namely: that the United States would make a unilateral statement at the time of normalization concerning the peaceful future of Taiwan; that the United States would continue to sell arms to Taiwan; and that the United States would maintain economic, cultural, and other relations with Taiwan on an unofficial basis.

The first two aimed largely at satisfying the U.S. political process, at least as Beijing saw them, since they were separately stated by the U.S. government and were not written in the normalization communiqué. The Beijing government viewed the second countercondition as incomprehensible because Beijing had been making peace overtures to the Taiwan authorities since 1977; moreover, Beijing believed that U.S. arms sales to Taiwan would make the Taiwan regime only more intransigent.[29] However, the Beijing government may have recognized the political intricacy that the Carter administration was facing at home and tacitly taken the U.S. statements as a way out of the normalization dilemma. Therefore, Beijing may have expected that after normalization, along with the PRC's intent to respond to U.S. expectations for a peaceful resolution, the United States would gradually stop arms sales to Taiwan. The third "countercondition," which Beijing regarded as the Japanese formula and accepted without controversy, became the basis for the administration to develop a comprehensive policy governing postnormalization U.S.-Taiwan relations. It was known as the Taiwan legislation. The Taiwan legislation was created by the administration for several reasons. First, in order to set up a nongovernment entity to conduct unofficial U.S.-Taiwan affairs, congressional legislation was needed to fund and staff the agency that would manage economic, cultural, and other unofficial relations with Taiwan. Second, a law was required "to indicate that previous agreements (except the Defense Treaty) with Taiwan remained in force and to exempt the people on Taiwan from requirements that certain formal agreements, programs, or transactions between the United States and a foreign entity must be with a nation, state, or government."[30]

The State Department organized a special task force, known as the China Working Group, to draft a major legislative proposal immediately after the announcement. The drafting process involved a wide range of intergovernmental consultation and legal specialists in the Defense, Justice, Treasury, State, and Transportation departments. On January 26, 1979, the administration sent the proposed legislation to Congress along with a message from President Carter urging the Congress to enact it "as promptly as possible."[31]

The proposed legislation was a three-page text with a four-page section-by-section analysis. The administration described three fundamental purposes of the bill. First, it would confirm the continued eligibility of the people on Taiwan to participate in programs and activities that under U.S. law were to be carried on with foreign governments. Second, it would provide for the execution of such programs and activities on an unofficial basis through the American Institute in Taiwan and the corresponding instrumentality that the United States expected to be established by the people of Taiwan. Third, it would establish funding, staffing, and administrative relationships for the institute.[32] Here the term "people on Taiwan" was used to show a relationship that was not a government-to-government one and that applied to both the authorities and the inhabitants on the islands of Taiwan and the Penghus (the Pescadores).

The proposed legislation clarified the application of laws of the United States to the people on Taiwan in a situation of no diplomatic relationship (sections 101–103). It specified that laws, regulations, and orders that required maintaining diplomatic relations with the United States would continue to apply to the people on Taiwan and would provide for the continued conduct of programs and transactions. These provisions were intended to confirm the continued eligibility of the people on Taiwan under the Arms Export Control Act, Atomic Energy Act of 1954, the Export-Import Bank Act, the Foreign Assistance Act of 1961, and the Trade Act of 1974.

The proposed legislation also contained provisions facilitating the new nongovernmental relationship with the people on Taiwan (sections 201–205). Specifically, it called for the establishment of a nonprofit, private corporation named the American Institute in Taiwan—the AIT (sections 104–105). Programs, transactions, and other relations were conducted and executed by or through this institute. Government funds would be appropriated for the institute to carry out these functions, and it would be staffed by personnel separated from government services but eligible for reinstitution with full career benefits after they left the institute. Reciprocally, the United States would permit an instrumentality as a counterpart to the AIT, to be established in the United States by the people on Taiwan (sections 106–107).

Approving U.S. Taiwan Policy:
The Congressional Process

From the beginning of the Carter administration, Congress had been consulted and involved in normalization. The administration actively sought support and ideas from members of Congress who endorsed the normalization process. During the preparation of the PRM-24, Holbrooke started an intensive series of consultations with key members of Congress on the Taiwan issue. The recommendation of the United States, which sought assurances from Beijing regarding a peaceful Taiwan solution, reflected congressional conditions on the termination of the defense treaty with Taiwan.[33] Although Congress was consulted on the treaty termination, some members of Congress felt strongly that the administration should act in accordance with the termination provisions of the treaty.[34]

Prior to Vance's mission to Beijing in August 1977, the State Department cooperated with Senator Edward Kennedy (D-Mass.) in sending a signal to Beijing that the administration was prepared to accept Beijing's three preconditions. On August 15, Kennedy made a well-publicized speech before the World Affairs Council in Boston that was in line with the administration's policy as set forth in PRM-24.[35]

The Congress, which had not been frequently consulted during the period between July and December, was actively concerned with the terms of normalization and was eager to play a role in the process. However, President Carter and his chief advisers agreed that secret negotiations would be the best way to prevent leaks that might damage normalization efforts.

Congressional Call for Consultation

On July 20, Senators Robert Dole (R-Kan.) and Richard Stone (D-Fla.), together with eighteen Senate cosponsors, proposed an amendment to the fiscal year 1979 Security Assistance Authorization bill, S. 3075. Congress approved the amendment stating that it was the sense of Congress that there should be prior consultation on any proposed policy change affecting the treaty with Taiwan.[36] The amendment registered Congress's intention to play a role in the formulation of new Taiwan policy. The original proposal was put forth in stronger form and was modified after the Senate debate to be a nonbinding resolution.

However, the administration was by no means sure that the negotiations would be successful, especially when China's final position on continued U.S. arms sales was unknown. The administration felt it necessary to ignore the congressional amendment, deciding instead to conduct negotiations in secrecy.[37] Congress, obviously disturbed by the lack of consultation during the final month, took issue with the executive on the future security relationship with Taiwan. Even before the submission of the administration's Taiwan legislation bill, the Congress started its deliberations on Taiwan on January 15, 1979. Six measures were proposed in the Senate by Senators Dole, Stone, John Danforth (R-Mo.), and Dennis DeConcini (D-Ariz.) to stress certain continuities in diplomatic and military relations with Taiwan.

As a countermove, on January 22, Senators Kennedy and Allan Cranston (D-Calif.) sponsored a resolution reaffirming U.S. interest in Taiwan's security. Representative Lester Wolff (D-N.Y.), chairman of the House Subcommittee on East Asia and Pacific Affairs, had agreed to sponsor an identical resolution in the House. The resolution was drafted after the two senators had consulted with the administration. It was meant as a countermeasure to congressional conservatives who were trying to block Carter's decision on normalization. The aim of Kennedy and Cranston was to give members of Congress a chance to demonstrate their concern about Taiwan without simultaneously voting for legislation that might undo the administration's agreements with China.[38]

President Carter was very concerned about any resolution dealing with Taiwan. He expressed his opposition by stating that "I really do not believe that any resolution is needed."[39] But the State Department held a slightly different view on the Kennedy-Cranston resolution. A department spokesperson said that the resolution "would not cause insurmountable problems." Later in the day, the White House issued its own statement, reaffirming that "the position of the administration is that a resolution is not necessary."[40]

A few days later, Senator John Glenn (D-Ohio), chairman of the Senate Subcommittee on East Asia, and Senator Frank Church (D-S.D.), chairman of the Foreign Relations Committee, warned of impending congressional action on the Taiwan security issue.[41] It became clear to the administration that any congressional move directly linking U.S. interests to the security of Taiwan would violate the principles of normalization and thereby be unacceptable to the Chinese government. Facing mounting congressional demands for an official statement of support for Taiwan's security, President Carter, on January 26, the day the administration submitted its legislation to the Congress for approval, publicly warned at a news conference that he would veto any congressional legislation that "would contradict or that would violate the agreements" with China.[42]

The Congressional Goal and the Process

It became clear that in formulating Taiwan policy Congress retained different goals and priorities from those of the administration. Each had different objectives in the Taiwan legislation. The administration viewed Taiwan policy from a broader, more strategic perspective of U.S-PRC relations. Its priority was normalization, and Taiwan policy was conducted within the framework of the normalization communiqué. The administration bill clearly reflected this approach. Congress, on the other hand, was more concerned with Taiwan policy per se. The Congress wanted to give its priority to the security of Taiwan and the arms sale. The approval process provided the Congress an opportunity to realize its objectives. As Senator Jacob Javits stated, "The legislation proposed by the administration to implement its approach was only a bare skeleton; it was left to Congress to consider what concrete undertakings were required to make it work."[43]

Senate actions and processes. Despite the presidential warning, Congress opened hearings on the proposed legislation with a strong disposition to revise the administration bill. On February 5, at the Senate Foreign Relations Committee hearings, Senator Church said that the proposed legislation did not address the Taiwan security issue and was "woefully inadequate." He warned that it would be "substantially revised."[44] Church worked with Senator Glenn on a statement drafted in the form of a resolution expressing their concern about the security of Taiwan. On the same day, Senator Javits told Warren Christopher, deputy secretary of state, and Brown that "I am prepared to forgo it [normalization with Beijing], hot as I am for it," if Beijing refused to accept a statement of U.S. support for Taiwan security.[45]

The administration tried to reassure members of Congress that there was no security problem as far as Taiwan was concerned.[46] However, the Congress fundamentally disagreed with the executive on the approach to Taiwan security. Congress was determined to develop a policy clearly restating U.S. interests in Taiwan policy.[47]

In the Senate Foreign Relations Committee, Senator Javits proposed an amendment stating that an attack on Taiwan would be "a common danger to the peace and security of the people of Taiwan and the United States in the Western Pacific."[48] This language was substantially drawn from the U.S.-Taiwan defense treaty affirming U.S. interests in Taiwan security. The amendment also pledged U.S. actions to protect its interests in the region.

Church presented the draft to Christopher, who strongly opposed the language of the amendment. Church was called to the White House on February 8 and was informed by the president of his strong concern about the language.[49] Thus, Church concluded publicly that the amendment had been "hastily drawn up" and was unacceptable. He then suggested a revision that "the words that we find to express that agreement should not conflict with any understanding" between the United States and China.[50]

Interaction between executive officials and Church finally produced a compromise on the security provisions. On February 22, the committee adopted a modified Church-Javits amendment stating that it was the policy of the United States

> 1a. to maintain extensive, close, and friendly relations with the people on Taiwan;
> 2a. to make clear that the United States' decision to establish diplomatic relations with the PRC rests on the expectation that any resolution of the Taiwan issue will be by peaceful means;

3a. to consider any effort to resolve the Taiwan issue by other than peaceful means a threat to the peace and security of the Western Pacific area and of grave concern to the United States; and

4a. to provide the people on Taiwan with arms of a defensive character.

In order to achieve the objectives of the section,

1b. the United States will maintain its capacity to resist any resort to force or other forms of coercion that would jeopardize the security or social or economic system of the people on Taiwan; and

2b. the United States will assist the people on Taiwan to maintain a sufficient self-defense capability through the provision of arms of a defensive character; and

3b. the President is directed to inform the Congress promptly of any threat to the security of Taiwan and any danger to the interests of the United States arising therefrom.[51]

The compromise amendment eliminated the language directly spelling out U.S. interests in the security of Taiwan. Instead, it substituted "a common danger to the peace and security of the people of Taiwan and the United States" with "a threat to the peace and security of the Western Pacific area and of grave concern to the United States." The new provision softened the tone of the Javits amendment. And it delinked U.S. security from that of Taiwan and instead linked Taiwan security with "security of the Western Pacific." This change reflected the concern of the executive and most members of Congress that there was a need to draw a line between conveying seriousness with which such efforts should be viewed by the United States and making an actual commitment by linking U.S. security with Taiwan security.

Another deviation of this security provision from the administration's Taiwan policy was a written guarantee of arms sales to Taiwan. Although Congress agreed to the administration's position that the removal of U.S. forces and installations from Taiwan would not significantly affect the U.S. regional military posture, it wanted the United States to provide Taiwan with a sufficient self-defense capability by providing arms of a defensive nature. Some members on the Foreign Relations Committee were critical of the administration's one-year freeze on the arms sales to Taiwan and believed that a provisional guarantee would limit the impact of the one-year freeze.[52] In face of congressional concern, the administration did not object to a written guarantee and worked with members of Congress, especially Church and Javits, on the arms sales provision.

The committee approved two similar bills proposed by Senators Dole and Stone to grant representatives of Taiwan privileges "comparable to those provided to missions of foreign countries" in the United States. Dole's bill called for the president to extend to any principal office of Taiwan established in the District of Columbia the same privileges and immunities as enjoyed by other diplomatic missions. Stone's bill called for granting diplomatic immunity and privileges to all the offices representing Taiwan in the United States. The administration had strongly opposed both bills on the ground that they would be inconsistent with the unofficial character of U.S. relations with the people on Taiwan since January 1, 1979.[53] The administration initially planned to give the Taiwan agents diplomatic privacy and exemption from customs taxes and taxes on personal income. But they would not have complete immunity from criminal prosecution.

The Senate committee's clearance of its bill S. 245 did not entirely remove the anxiety of executive officials who were responsible for the Taiwan legislation. Although it was rare for the Senate to reject the committee's recommendation on the floor, the executive officials were still concerned about the possibility of serious amendments by conservative members of the Senate.[54]

The floor debate focused on the issues of security commitments to Taiwan and Taiwan's future status. The administration had earlier been able to head off similar arguments during the committee consideration of S. 245 and had seen the committee's unanimous approval of the bill as a sign the bill would sail through the floor without difficulty.

However, Senator Charles H. Percy (R-Ill.) offered his amendment, which had been rejected by the committee, and managed to attract supporters from moderate Republicans and Democrats. The amendment explicitly linked U.S. security interests with the security of Taiwan. Senator Church commented that the Percy amendment brought us back very close to the phraseology in the 1954 mutual defense treaty and "would place in jeopardy the new relationship we seek with mainland China."[55]

But Church's warning did not prevent a motion to table the amendment from being defeated 45-49, which meant the amendment would be brought to a floor vote. This sent a clear signal to the administration that it would be directly confronted by the Congress over the issue if the amendment were to be adopted. Walter Mondale, who had served in the Senate before becoming vice president, and White House congressional liaison chief Frank Moore were quickly called in to lobby some wavering members. In the meantime, Senator Church warned before the vote that "if it is the object of the Senate to undermine and place in jeopardy normalization of relations with mainland China, let it be clear to everyone that is what they are doing with this vote."[56] Glenn joined Church, pointing out that the amendment "creates the serious risk of the United States being pulled into a war not of our own choosing."[57]

Key senators' positions and the intense lobbying of administration officials helped turn the Senate around. The final 42-50 vote on the amendment was achieved when several senators (five Republicans and two

Democrats) who had opposed the tabling motion decided to go along with the administration request.[58]

House actions and processes. The House Foreign Affairs Committee finished its deliberation on a companion bill (H.R. 2479) on February 28, which was formally reported (H. Rept. 96-26) on March 3.

The committee version was drafted by senior committee members and aides in consultation with State Department representatives and was released publicly on February 22. The bill was similar to S. 245 as reported by the Senate Foreign Relations Committee. Both bills expressed U.S. concern about Taiwan's security.

The House version of the Kennedy-Cranston resolution (S. J. Res. 31) was sponsored by Congressmen Wolff, Stephen Solarz (D-N.Y.), and other cosponsors. The committee had earlier defeated an amendment proposed by Congressman Dan Quayle (R-Ind.). That amendment stated that hostile action against Taiwan would be a threat to the "security interests of the United States."[59] Other members opposed that suggestion. Congressman Solarz made it clear that "the one interest we do not have [in Taiwan] is a security interest."[60] Still other members were concerned that such language would lead to presidential usurpation of power. Wolff commented that Quayle's amendment reminded him of the 1965 Gulf of Tonkin resolution, which was used by President Johnson as the legal basis for waging the Vietnam War.[61]

The amendment was also opposed by the State Department, which worked closely with the House Foreign Affairs Committee on the Taiwan legislation. Douglas J. Bennett, Jr., assistant secretary of state for congressional relations, pointed out that the Quayle amendment "has Gulf of Tonkin overtones. The term security interest . . . seems to create a commitment to take action" if the situation arises.[62]

After working with the State Department on the security issue, the House committee produced a final version H.R. 2470 as reported by the committee. It contained several revised provisions that were slightly different from the Senate bill. First, it linked the peace and stability of Taiwan with U.S. political security and economic interests. Second, it specified that any use of "force, boycott, or embargo to prevent Taiwan from engaging in trade with other nations, would be a threat to the stability of the Western Pacific area and of grave concern to the United States." Third, it recommended that, in the event of a threat to the security of Taiwan, both the president and Congress should jointly determine, in accordance with constitutional processes, appropriate U.S. action in response. Fourth, the committee bill ensured that Taiwan could retain legal possession of all its property in the United States.[63]

The House floor debate reflected a similar pattern of conservative members attempting to change the committee stance on Taiwan security and the future Taiwan status in U.S.-Taiwan relations. The House rejected two

Republican amendments reaffirming the 1954 U.S.-Taiwan defense treaty and substituting an official U.S. liaison office for the proposed nongovernmental institute as the channel for future U.S. dealings with Taiwan.[64]

Two modified amendments regarding arms sales guarantees to Taiwan were adopted on the House floor. The original amendment was intended to give Taiwan special treatment in arms sales. The amendment by Ken Kramer (R-Colo.) guaranteeing Taiwan access to weapons "incorporating the highest available technology" was replaced by an amendment proposed by Richard C. White (D-Tex.), requiring the United States to make available to Taiwan "modern military equipment and services."[65]

Another amendment, by Paul Findley (R-Ill.), was approved by voice vote, replacing that of Edward J. Derwinski (R-Ill.), which called for the exemption of Taiwan from the normal U.S. arms sales review process. Findley's amendment ensured that Congress would receive military assessment of Taiwan's defense needs but did not exclude proposed arms sales from the normal review process.[66]

On March 13, both Houses passed their respective committees' bills; the final vote was 90-6 in the Senate and 345-55 in the House. Both Houses rejected conservative efforts virtually to restore the government-to-government relationships that existed before the recognition. On March 8, both Houses again defeated amendments that would have affected normalization with Beijing. Congressional conservatives, however, did manage in the process to pass some amendments regarding future U.S. relations with Taiwan.

Conference action. With the help of the floor managers, Congress passed the Taiwan legislation. The two versions were identical in many respects. The Conference Committee took actions on March 19 and 20 to incorporate the two measures into one authorization bill. The conferees carefully skirted controversial language by omitting or softening most provisions in the House- and Senate-passed versions opposed by the administration. Specifically, the administration wanted the bill to make no formal security commitment to Taiwan and to retain relations with Taiwan on a strictly unofficial basis.

The conference version on U.S. security assurances for Taiwan incorporated Senate language, expressing concern for Taiwan, and House language, concerning future U.S. response on behalf of Taiwan. The conference retained a Senate provision that the United States would regard "any effort to determine the future of Taiwan by other than peaceful means, including boycotts or embargoes, a threat to the peace and security of the Western Pacific and of grave concern to the United States."[67] The conference version also employed the House language stating that "the President, and the Congress shall determine, in accordance with Constitutional processes, appropriate action by the U.S. in response to any such danger."[68] After other modifications,[69] the conference report on H.R. 2479 was approved by the House on March 28 by a 339-50 vote and the Senate on March 29 by an 85-4 vote. On April 10, 1979, President Carter signed the TRA law.

An Analysis

Although the new TRA granted the authority requested by the administration to conduct unofficial relations with Taiwan,[70] its content was significantly enriched in comparison with the original bill proposed by the administration. The original bill did not contain any provision regarding the security of Taiwan. The Congress not only added the security provisions but also attached to the TRA new provisions concerning arms sales to Taiwan that the original bill did not mention.[71] It clearly bore the congressional imprint of assertiveness and compromise between the executive and Congress. The TRA also signified that the Congress, by incorporating U.S.-Taiwan interests into policies, played a role of balancing the executive's foreign policy objectives.

Intellectual Origin of the TRA: The Bureaucratic Role

The TRA as enacted did not alter the basic intention of the administration in the original legislation. It granted what the administration sought from Congress, namely, the authority to carry out future U.S.-Taiwan relations on an unofficial basis.

How the United States would continue its relations with Taiwan after normalization had been a research subject in the Ford administration. The United States closely watched how Japan dealt with its relations with Taiwan when it established diplomatic relations with China in September 1972. Japan ended diplomatic relations with Taiwan, recognized Beijing as the sole legal government of China, and respected the PRC claim that Taiwan is part of China.[72] But it continued its economic, cultural, and other relations with Taiwan through private organizations staffed by retired Foreign Service people.[73]

In 1975, the United States conducted the first comprehensive exploration of what U.S.-Taiwan relations would be in the postnormalization era. A series of papers was produced, facilitating "the ultimate source of the Carter administration's omnibus legislation proposal with regard to Taiwan."[74] The study, by Charles W. Freeman, analyzed for the first time the legal and legislative aspects and implications of U.S. derecognition of Taiwan. Based on the "Japanese formula," the study examined the concept of private U.S. representation in Taiwan and specified the nature and problems of such a corporation. It proposed that the United States could set up a "U.S. Interchange Association" entrusted with foreign economic policy matters. Such a private corporation might have the following general powers:

economic policy matters. Such a private corporation might have the following general powers:

> (a) the right of succession; (b) the right to a corporate seal; (c) the right to sue or be sued; (d) the right to transact such business as may be authorized in the articles of incorporation; (e) the right to make contracts and incur liabilities; (f) the right to hold real and personal property and to dispose of it; (g) the right to borrow money; (h) [the right to] establish offices at such places in China [Taiwan] as it deems advisable.[75]

The Freeman study raised some problems regarding a private U.S. organization with a purpose similar to the Japanese Interchange Association (JIA). First, congressional delegation of important executive and legislative functions to a private body was needed in order to perform some duties similar to consular functions: handling of visas and passports, and notarization. Further congressional amendments to U.S. domestic laws, governing U.S. foreign economic relations, were needed to ensure Taiwan's eligibility for U.S. economic assistance from such government agencies as the Overseas Private Investment Corporation (OPIC) and the U.S. Agency for International Development (USAID). Second, funding and staffing of a private corporation could be a problem without special legislation. There was no general legislative authority by which the United States government could provide operating funds to a private corporation. To staff such a corporation with people retired, or "on leave," from the Foreign Service would have required a legislative authorization of their salaries, accumulation of "home leave," and retirement benefits.[76]

After surveying the feasibility of the Japanese model for U.S.-Taiwan relations, Freeman concluded that copying the model would not work with the U.S. case, because complications involving congressional actions might give those opposing U.S.-PRC normalization the opportunity to disrupt the process at the expense of U.S.-Taiwan relations. Freeman reasoned:

> While the United States could establish a "U.S. Interchange Association" or its equivalent in Taipei, this would require amendments of a considerable body of current legislation, and offer the relevant congressional committees with numerous opportunities to attack any U.S.-PRC normalization of relations based on the Japanese formula. This in itself would be enough to raise serious doubts about the viability of such an arrangement for the United States. It would inject a question into the domestic political process which is difficult to answer—why give up representation in both Peking and Taipei for representation in Peking alone?[77]

As a U.S. government official on leave, Freeman laid down a foundation on which the U.S. government could take a position on the Taiwan issue. In another unpublished paper, he comprehensively explored the legal framework of U.S. economic relations with Taiwan in trade, communications, investment, nuclear cooperation, and military coproduction. After surveying current U.S.-Taiwan economic relations, he concluded that "with adequate prior consultation with both the Congress (which would have to amend a considerable body of legislation), most of the substance of the economic relationship could indeed be preserved," provided that the "Taiwan authorities" were recognized as a legal entity.[78]

Freeman's papers were important documents, not only in that they were widely read by government officials, but also in that they represented U.S. government efforts to find a solution to the Taiwan issue at that time, in case negotiations for normalization were seriously under way. The fact that the papers were completed before President Ford's visit to China in 1975 implied particular policy significance, since a major topic of discussion during the president's meetings with the Chinese leaders would be the Taiwan issue in normalization.

Furthermore, Freeman's study anticipated an important congressional role in the political process. The complication of establishing a private corporation to carry out economic, cultural, and other relations with Taiwan would inevitably invite various congressional amendments to continue relations with Taiwan on an unofficial basis. Finally, and most important, Freeman's study formed a legal base on which the Carter administration quickly proposed its Taiwan legislation in an urgent period of time.

The Rational Actor Explanation

In the early Carter administration, U.S. China policy suffered from lack of explicit, clearly agreed-upon objectives. There were strong differences within the administration about the ultimate objectives of U.S. policy. Although major officials reached a consensus on normalization with China, Vance and Brzezinski differed sharply on the goal of strategic cooperation with China in the context of U.S.-USSR relations. President Carter's initial motivations in developing the new relationship with China remained unclear. Despite his political sensitivity regarding the potentially favorable domestic repercussion of his new China initiatives, the president acted cautiously to avoid upsetting his other major foreign policy goals. China policy thus remained subject to Carter's policy priorities and objectives, rather than to U.S. Taiwan policy.

It took a change in the international situation, foreign policy priorities, and strong advocacy by cabinet members to shape U.S. China policy objectives. With the changing international power structure and Soviet expansionist activities in the 1970s, the choice of whether or not the United States should develop strategic cooperation with China became a hotly debated issue among U.S. policymakers. The domestic dispute on U.S.-China strategic cooperation had been profound and consequential. Some policymakers believed that an improved Sino-U.S. relationship could enhance broader U.S. foreign policy interests, especially in the context of Soviet global strategy. Others advocated an "evenhanded policy" toward both China and the USSR.[79]

When the Soviets invaded Afghanistan in 1979, U.S.-Soviet relations underwent a steady decline, which prompted an increasingly strong perception in the United States of a growing menace posed by Soviet military power. At the same time, the Chinese leaders repeatedly stressed their opposition to Soviet global expansion.[80] Under those circumstances, members of the Carter administration who favored closer ties with China, including security ties, gained an upper hand in China policymaking. The idea of using China to counterbalance Soviet expansion became more attractive. Improving U.S.-Chinese relations was once again a high priority on President Carter's agenda. Brzezinski, with his persistent anti-Soviet views, influenced the president as he moved from his evenhanded U.S. policy, supported by Vance, toward closer ties with China and against the Soviet Union.[81]

Another China policy objective was the stabilizing of Asian affairs. Better Sino-U.S. relations could serve as a balance of forces in Asia, favorable to the United States and its allies and friends in the region, and help stabilize the situation on the Korean peninsula. As Deputy Secretary Warren Christopher stated, "Full and normal relations will allow us to work more effectively towards a stable system of independent nations in Asia."[82]

The U.S. economic objective of its China policy was largely based on the economic benefits other countries had derived from having diplomatic relations with China and the economic gains the United States would likewise enjoy. One important indicator was trade. Japan's trade with China increased by 63 percent in 1974 as a result of Japan's decision to normalize relations with the PRC in 1972.[83] Sino–West German trade rose 73 percent in 1973, one year after the two countries established diplomatic relations.[84] In the meantime, due to the lack of diplomatic relations, U.S.-PRC trade was subject to changes in political relations between the two countries. Sino-U.S. trade increased sharply in the first two years after Nixon's visit. Yet Sino-U.S. trade declined sharply in 1975 and 1976, when there was a lack of progress toward normalization and U.S.-Soviet détente.

Trade was also used by China as a tool to press for normalization. When China's grain harvests improved after the mid-1970s, the Beijing government reduced imports from the United States, while maintaining imports from Canada and Australia, which had diplomatic relations with China.[85] In light of these factors, the United States set up its objective in such a way to "enable American business to deal on an equal footing with other suppliers as China moved towards modernization."[86]

The objectives of U.S. China policy necessarily established a framework for defining future U.S.-Taiwan relations. In order to pursue its broader objectives, the United States had to sever its official ties with Taiwan and start a new relationship on an unofficial basis so that it could maintain economic, cultural, and other relations with Taiwan. The proposed Taiwan bill was the Carter administration's engineering to facilitate this new relationship with Taiwan.

Another issue regarding U.S. Taiwan policy is the security issue. Both sides were aware of this sensitive issue during normalization and tried to prevent the issue from obstructing the efforts toward normalization. Because of the primary goal of normalization, both sides developed calculated alternatives to the problem: the Beijing government decided not to push on the issue for a settlement; the U.S. government, on the other hand, made an announcement that the United States would stop selling arms to Taiwan for one year.

Bureaucratic Factors—Can They Explain the Outcome?

Normalization of Sino-U.S. relations was what the Carter administration wanted. The question was when and how, given the unresolved Taiwan issue. Bureaucratic politics played an important role in addressing the two questions, bureaucratic players laying out the groundwork for resolving the Taiwan problem. A special task force was organized by the State Department to recommend policy options for continuing U.S. relations with Taiwan and to draft the executive Taiwan legislation. The Freeman papers provided a legal framework for U.S.-Taiwan relations after normalization. Freeman's emphasis on the congressional authorization of such a new relationship with Taiwan inspired members of Congress and, in a way, facilitated congressional assertiveness in making Taiwan policy. Bureaucratic modification of the Japanese formula for maintaining future unofficial relations with Taiwan and three proposed conditions for normalization paved the way for presidential China policymaking.

Bureaucratic politics was important in implementing China policy. Initial bureaucratic fissures over strategic cooperation with China and lack of presidential action gave State, which positions itself more favorably than other bureaucratic agencies in conducting diplomacy, more leeway to advance its policy preference. In the normalization process, State's manipulation of the Taiwan issue affected the timing of normalization.

The bureaucratic players, however, did not differ much on the Taiwan policy principles laid out in the normalization communiqué. Nor did bureaucratic politics affect the final outcome of the TRA. Secretary Vance and National Security Council adviser Brzezinski disagreed on playing the China card and on the timing of normalization, but they both endorsed the president's decision to comply with China's three conditions on Taiwan. Vance, after using his discretion to cling to U.S. maximum positions on the Taiwan issue, supported the arrangements to resolve that issue.

Least expected was the position of the Department of Defense on the Taiwan issue. When some members of Congress pushed for the guarantee of

Taiwan security, Secretary of Defense Brown testified that there was no possibility of any military danger to Taiwan security. His testimony was intended to help the State Department argue for the proposed Taiwan legislation. It attested to the fact that there were no bureaucratic divisions over the administration's Taiwan policy.

The Interactive Policy Process: The Congressional Role

In the normalization process, the Congress had been concerned with the way the administration conducted the negotiations and the agreement reached on the Taiwan issue. The Congress had passed the Dole-Stone amendment calling for consultation with the Congress, and some members of Congress had expressed their discontent with the secretive nature of the negotiations.

Another issue was that the Congress shared the executive goal of normalization but had different emphases on U.S. China policy. It perceived normalization as mainly a matter of bilateral relations. The Congress tended to articulate its interest in Taiwan security more than in the strategic implication of normalization. Some members of Congress were even concerned with a stronger China posing a threat to its Asian neighbors.[87]

Some members brought up some substantive issues with the executive on U.S.-Taiwan policy. The security of Taiwan was their principal attention. They did not disagree with Secretary Brown's testimony that the severing of U.S. military relations would not significantly change either the U.S. regional military position or global strategy, but insisted that a Chinese threat to Taiwan security would have "severe impact on America's other allies and friends throughout Asia. They claimed that hostilities could escalate and spread to other parts of the region."[88] Those members' position influenced the executive's bargaining with the Congress, and the final outcome evinced a compromise on the security issue.

Most members of Congress were also interested in Taiwan's economic development, and they regarded Taiwan as a showcase of effective U.S. economic aid to the Third World. From 1949 to 1965, Congress had provided Taiwan with $1.7 billion in grants, loans, and food aid.[89] U.S. investors had provided $1,924 million in capital investment and contributed 44.1 percent of the total foreign capital to Taiwan development needs.[90] They held that "on Taiwan the United States had demonstrated a willingness and a capacity to contribute significantly to the economic development and industrialization of a less-developed community."[91]

Congressional discontent with lack of consultation in the later stage of the normalization process and different emphases on foreign policy objectives shaped in a way the decisionmaking environment in which the executive proposed its China policy. The executive constantly looked over congressional shoulders for policy clues. In the TRA case, the executive accepted Beijing's three conditions on normalization with a few modifications on its policy toward Taiwan in order to pursue U.S. China policy objectives and attend to congressional interests in Taiwan at the same time.

These modifications also displayed a shared Taiwan policy objective among U.S. policymakers. Both the executive and members of Congress supported the following positions in order to maximize U.S. Taiwan interests. First, the United States did not terminate the U.S.-Taiwan defense treaty immediately after normalization, but rather kept the treaty for another year in accordance with the provisions of the treaty. Second, the United States publicly stated that it expected the Taiwan issue to be settled peacefully—an alternative to a U.S. demand of a written guarantee from Beijing regarding Taiwan security. Third, the United States would continue to make available to Taiwan "selected defense weaponry" on a restricted basis after a one-year moratorium on arms sales to Taiwan in 1979.[92]

Differences between the Congress and the executive in U.S. China policy centered on how to deal with U.S.-Taiwan relations after normalization. This became clear as the Congress viewed as insufficient the Taiwan legislation proposed by the administration, which enabled the United States to maintain unofficial relations with Taiwan. The administration contended that the legislation contained all the provisions necessary for the United States to carry out relations with Taiwan on an unofficial basis. The Congress disagreed and intended to take advantage of the congressional approval process to insert its priorities and preferences into the new legislation. As a result of the interaction in the process, the Congress and the executive came up with the final outcome, which bore some congressional marks.[93]

Conclusion

According to the rational actor model, the United States would define its China policy goals in broader strategic, political, and economic contexts while trying to maximize its Taiwan interests. The making of the TRA reflected the rational actor approach. The TRA was finally approved within the framework of the normalization communiqué, and in the meantime, it addressed U.S. Taiwan interests. The United States chose to delink its security relations with Taiwan to pursue its broader strategic interests in its new China policy. But it maintained unofficial relations with Taiwan. However, the policymaking process pointed out that the TRA was not made by a unitary actor. There was an obvious division within the U.S. government on the TRA. Congress sought to amend the executive proposal by stressing Taiwan security and arms sales. The rational actor model was seriously qualified in two respects. One is that the model does not address the importance of the governmental processes. When foreign policymaking involves more political institutions than the executive decisionmaking elites, the model misses the substance of different viewpoints that emerge from the government process. Although the final outcome is consistent with the model's prediction, the model did not account for the actual making of the content of the TRA which was largely shaped by the interbranch policy process. In the case of the TRA, though the executive (the president and his advisers) was able to define the goals of foreign policy and select the best alternative to maximize U.S. interests, it could not just make the policy without the policy being seriously amended in the process. The Congress, with different policy concerns and priorities, did not agree entirely on the executive Taiwan policy.

The other aspect is that the TRA represented a policy outcome different from the Taiwan legislation initially proposed by the executive. The TRA incorporated what the executive had proposed, but it also took into account congressional preferences on arms sales to Taiwan. The Congress saw the initial executive proposal as inadequate in maintaining U.S. Taiwan policy goals. The Congress quickly moved to raise its concerns over Taiwan security and managed to use the interbranch policy process to address the problem. On the other hand, the executive, through consultations, persuasions, and even a veto threat, used the process to prevent any extreme measures. On the whole, the TRA manifested a policy process of interaction and compromise between the Congress and the executive that fashioned the overall legislation, especially the security provisions.

The bureaucratic model, emphasizing the importance of the bureaucratic process in Taiwan policymaking, is only partially confirmed in this case. Bureaucratic differences over policy priorities were a factor in the timing of normalization. It accounted for Vance's use of his discretion in delaying the normalization process. The bureaucratic process was also important in proposing Taiwan policy options and Taiwan legislation. Bureaucratic expertise and research, as residual factors, can also help decisionmakers to choose and formulate policies when the right circumstances arise.[94] In the TRA case, the Freeman study was obviously a factor in influencing the draft of the Taiwan legislation soon after the announcement of normalization.

The bureaucratic politics model lost its explanatory power, however, once policymaking moved out of the bureaucratic process. Bureaucratic preferences became largely irrelevant in the interbranch policy process since they could not have had any impact on the outcome of the TRA.[95] Bureaucratic influence is also subject to the degree of presidential attention and control. In cases where presidential attention is not present, or low, the bureaucracy can bring matters to the president's attention and influence presidential policymaking by policy recommendation. Thus, presidential interests and attention are the important intervening variables that may strengthen or weaken bureaucratic effectiveness in influencing policymaking. The case of the TRA confirmed Krasner's assertion that bureaucratic influence in foreign policymaking is a function of presidential attention.[96]

The interbranch politics model, predicting that U.S. Taiwan policy would be the outcome of a compromise between the Congress and the executive, is more useful in explaining the policy outcomes. The Congress did not comply with the administration's initial proposal but rewrote, revised, and amended the executive bill. The Congress was able to stress its interest in Taiwan security and arms sales, but was not able to go so far as to link U.S. security interest with Taiwan's security, due to its own diverse views and the strong executive opposition. The security provisions were carefully drafted through close negotiations between the Foreign Relations Committee and the State Department. Once the committee language was agreed upon by the administration, the key committee members, including the committee chair, the ranking Republican member, and the congressional leaders from both parties managed the floor debate, guarding any potential amendments to alter the agreed language. These floor managers worked very closely with the administration's congressional liaison representatives on every provision being amended or added. The Percy amendment on the floor was a typical example of how the process worked.

The merit of the interbranch politics model lies in its inclusion of two political institutions and the policy process. The model goes beyond the rational actor model and the bureaucratic politics model to catch the ascending congressional role "not only in redefining American foreign policy in Asia after the Vietnam War, but in dealing with other important diplomatic questions as well."[97] This institutional predisposition preceded congressional goals and preferences in U.S. Taiwan policy different from those of the administration. Congressional priorities were obtained in a substantial interactive process in which the Congress was able to initiate its Taiwan security efforts, counterproposals, and amendments to the administration's initial Taiwan legislation.

The interbranch politics model proposes that U.S. foreign policy is an outcome of an interactive policy process between Congress and the executive. The TRA confirmed this proposition by suggesting that the notion of an assertive Congress is not necessarily synonymous with frictions and conflicts between Congress and the executive in foreign policymaking.[98] As the TRA process demonstrated, conflict between the executive and Congress over Taiwan security occurred within certain prescribed limits. The president retained his constitutional veto power to guard the principles of the normalization communiqué. The Congress, rather than challenging that power, chose to work out its differences with the executive within those limits. The TRA case proved that U.S. foreign policy processes provide opportunities for Congress to interact, conflict, and most often cooperate with the executive in formulating U.S. foreign policy.

In sum, the rational actor model is useful in defining the policy boundary of the TRA, based on the goals of U.S. China policy. The bureaucratic politics model provides little insight, since the policy was made from the top down; the presidential control of U.S. Taiwan policy left little room for bureaucratic influence. The interbranch politics model is the most useful in explaining and understanding the terms and content of the TRA (see Figure 2.1).

Figure 2.1 Dynamics of Creating the Taiwan Relations Act

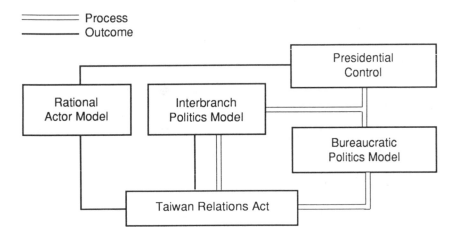

Notes

1. United States, *Taiwan Relations Act*, Public Law 96-8 (Washington, D.C.: Government Printing Office, 1979).

2. Zbigniew K. Brzezinski, *Power and Principle: Memoirs of the National Security Adviser* (New York: Farrar, Straus, Giroux, 1983), p. 54.

3. Cyrus R. Vance, *Hard Choices: Critical Years in America's Foreign Policy* (New York: Simon and Schuster, 1983), p. 199.

4. Department of State, *U.S. Policy Toward China, July 15, 1971–January 15, 1979*, Selected Documents no. 9 (Office of Public Communication, Bureau of Public Affairs, 1979), p. 32.

5. Ibid.

6. Oksenberg, "A Decade of Sino-American Relations," pp. 175–195.

7. Brzezinski, *Power and Principle*, p. 200.

8. In addition to Oksenberg's account, Brzezinski and Vance also discussed the content of the PRM-24. See Brzezinski, *Power and Principle*, p. 197; Vance, *Hard Choices*, p. 77.

9. Brown was more interested in Sino-U.S. security cooperation to strengthen U.S. defense. Interview with Brown by Alexander Moens in Moens, *Foreign Policy Under Carter: Testing Multiple Advocacy Decision Making* (Boulder: Westview Press, 1990), p. 114.

10. Oksenberg, "A Decade of Sino-American Relations," p. 181.

11. Vance, *Hard Choices*, p. 78.

12. Oksenberg, "A Decade of Sino-American Relations," p. 182.

13. Vance, *Hard Choices*, p. 81.

14. Oksenberg, "A Decade of Sino-American Relations," p. 182. The Japanese formula refers to the Japanese government agreeing to sever its diplomatic relationship with Taiwan in order to establish diplomatic relations with China, but Japan would continue its economic relations with Taiwan through a private organization.

15. Brzezinski, *Power and Principle*, p. 20.

16. Jimmy Carter, *Keeping Faith* (New York: Bantam Books, 1982), p. 191.

17. Before going to China, Vance was given some leeway in choosing whether the United States should adhere to its maximum position on the Taiwan issue. He used his discretion in the negotiations. See Vance, *Hard Choices*, P. 82.

18. Hansell then produced a study of alternatives in 1978, which provided the framework for the administration's Taiwan legislation. The study was done independently of the negotiations. See also Vance, *Hard Choices*, p. 83.

19. The State Department opposed a visit by Brzezinski on two grounds: (1) a visit by the president's national security adviser would send the Soviets a sensitive signal of a possible Sino-U.S. alliance against the Soviets; (2) the United States had not finished formulating a detailed position on Taiwan policy. See Vance, *Hard Choices*, pp. 114–115. Underlying the State opposition is the fact that the State Department never likes NSC staff to get involved in diplomatic travels and negotiations.

20. Oksenberg, "A Decade of Sino-American Relations," p. 184.

21. Vance, *Hard Choices*, p. 115.

22. During his visit to China in 1972, President Nixon made five points regarding U.S. policy toward Taiwan and China, namely that (1) the United States will acknowledge the Chinese position that there is one China and that Taiwan is a part of it; (2) the United States will not support a Taiwan independence movement; (3) as the United States leaves Taiwan, Taiwan will not be under any foreign power's influence; (4) the United States will support any peaceful solution to the Taiwan situation and the United States will not support Taiwan in any military action against China; and (5) the United States will seek normalization and try to achieve it.

23. For details of the instruction, see Brzezinski, *Power and Principle*, Annex.

24. Ibid., p. 218.

25. Ibid., pp. 218–219.

26. Ibid., p. 229.

27. Oksenberg, "A Decade of Sino-American Relations," p. 188.

28. Brzezinski, *Power and Principle*, p. 231.

29. Since 1978, the Beijing government had adopted a fundamental change in its approach to the Taiwan issue, speaking of "peaceful reunification" rather than "liberation." This new policy was officially approved at the Third Plenary Session of the Eleventh Chinese Communist Party Congress in December 1978.

30. Michel Oksenberg, "Congress, Executive-Legislative Relations and American China Policy," in Kenneth W. Thompson, *The President, the Congress, and Foreign Policy* (Lanham, Md.: University Press of America, 1986), p. 216.

31. U.S. Congress, House, *Relations with Taiwan: Message from the President of the United States*, House Document 96-45 (Washington, D.C.: Government Printing Office, 1979), p. 1.

32. U.S. Congress, Senate, Committee on Foreign Relations, *Taiwan: Hearings Before the Committee on Foreign Relations*, 96th Cong., 1st sess., 1979, p. 15.

33. Vance, *Hard Choices*, p. 77.

34. Warren Christopher, in reply to Representative Robert J. Lagomarsino's question, confirmed that the executive consulted with Congress during the entire

first two years. See Congress, House, Committee on Foreign Affairs, *Taiwan Legislation: Hearings Before the Committee on Foreign Affairs, United States House of Representatives*, 96th Cong., 1st sess., 1979, pp. 19–20.

35. According to Robert Downen, the Department of State discussed the content of the speech with Kennedy in advance. See Downen, *The Taiwan Pawn in the China Game: Congress to the Rescue* (Washington, D.C.: The Center for Strategic and International Studies, Georgetown University, 1979), footnote 30. See Murrey Marder, "State Department and Kennedy Discussed China Speech," *Washington Post*, August 17, 1977, p. 17.

36. The text of Amendment No. 3264 can be found in the *Congressional Record*, July 25, 1978, p. S22571.

37. For reasons the administration conducted negotiations in secrecy, see Oksenberg, "Congress, Executive-Legislative Relations and American China Policy," p. 215.

38. John M. Goshko, "Two Senators Urge Giving a Security Pledge to Taiwan," *Washington Post*, January 23, 1979, p. 11.

39. John M. Goshko, "President Warns Hill On Taiwan," *Washington Post*, January 27, 1979, p. 9.

40. Edward Walsh, "Resolution on Taiwan Stirs Struggle," *Washington Post*, February 2, 1979, p. 14.

41. Senator John Glenn was quoted by the *Washington Post* that he would make the issue of Taiwan security his "principal focus of interest" during Senate committee hearings. Senator Church, who was asked to sponsor the administration bill, also warned that he would do all he could "to bring about committee approval of a strong statement of national policy [on Taiwan security] to be incorporated in the legislation." See John M. Goshko, "Glenn Says China Pledge On Taiwan Is Essential," *Washington Post*, January 25, 1979, p. 21; "President Warns Hill On Taiwan," p. 1.

42. Ibid.

43. Jacob K. Javits, "Congress and Foreign Relations: The Taiwan Relations Act," *Foreign Affairs* 60, no.1 (Fall 1981), p. 58.

44. Robert G. Kaiser, "Senators Insist U.S. Give Strong Support to Taiwan," *Washington Post*, February 6, 1979, p. 15.

45. Congress, Senate, *Taiwan*, p. 29.

46. Both Deputy Secretary Christopher and Defense Secretary Brown testified from the political and military points of view that it was not realistic for the PRC to resolve the Taiwan issue by force. See Congress, House, *Taiwan Legislation*, p. 4.

47. Michael Frost, "Taiwan's Security and United States Policy: Executive and Congressional Strategies in 1978–1979," *Occasional Papers in Contemporary Asian Studies*, No. 4 (School of Law, University of Maryland), 1982, p. 29.

48. *Congressional Quarterly Almanac*, 1979, p. 105.

49. Downen, *The Taiwan Pawn*, p. 45.

50. *Congressional Quarterly Almanac*, 1979, p. 105.

51. Ibid., pp. 105–106.

52. Congress, Senate, *The Taiwan Enabling Act*, p. 14.

53. Congress, House, *Taiwan*, p. 56.

54. Senator Percy asserted that he would introduce his amendment on the floor if it were rejected by the committee. See Congress, Senate, *The Taiwan Enabling Act*, p. 30.

55. *Congressional Quarterly Almanac*, 1979, p. 110.

56. Mary Russell, "Bill on Taiwan Ties Survives Early Tests in Senate and House," *Washington Post*, March 9, 1979, p. 2.

57. *Congressional Quarterly Almanac*, 1979, p. 110.

58. With regard to future U.S. relations with Taiwan, some members tried to amend the administration's position on nonofficial relations with Taiwan. Senator Gordon J. Humphrey (R-N.H.) sponsored an amendment that would have created a liaison office in Taiwan similar to the one the United States had in Beijing from 1975 to 1979. The amendment drew criticism from proponents for normalization. Republican Senator Javits put it simply: "If you want to normalize relations with the PRC, you cannot vote for this amendment" (*Congressional Quarterly Almanac*, 1979, p. 110). Humphrey's amendment was tabled without further action.

While rejecting the two most sensitive issues on Taiwan security and Taiwan's future status, the senator approved other amendments by voice vote. Some of them were opposed by the administration. One amendment was proposed by Ernest F. Hollings (D-S.C.) to establish a Joint Commission on Security and Cooperation in East Asia. The commission was to monitor operation of the new institute and U.S. policies toward Taiwan. Despite the administration's opposition, the amendment was passed in the Senate. See Robert G. Kaiser, "House and Senate Adopt Taiwan Bills," *Washington Post*, March 14, 1979, p. 10.

Senator David L. Boren (D-Okla.) proposed another amendment, granting permanent ownership of the old Taiwanese embassy in Washington, D.C., to Taiwan. Earlier Christopher had stated in his testimony that the embassy property rightly belonged to China (see Congress, Senate, *Taiwan*, p. 24). In light of the Senate's unusual intention to determine the ownership of real property, Church and Javits offered a substitute amendment stating that the ownership question should be settled by the courts. But the amendment was tabled and the Boren amendment was adopted by voice vote.

Two other amendments concerned presidential dealings with arms sales. Dole's amendment required the president to make an annual report to Congress on arms sales and transfers to Taiwan. Humphrey's amendment required the president to notify Congress thirty days before granting any license for commercial arms sales to China. The rest of the amendments specified some detailed guarantees for Taiwan. The Hollings amendment intended to prevent Taiwan from being expelled or excluded from membership in international organizations. Jesse Helms (R-N.C.) proposed five technical amendments to ensure the provision of services of U.S. citizens and businesses in Taiwan. James A. McClure (R-Idaho) proposed to permit Taiwan to retain all of its fourteen consular offices in the United States despite State Department plans to allow Taiwan to keep only eight offices.

59. *Congressional Quarterly Almanac*, 1979, p. 107.

60. Ibid.

61. Congressman Findley also expressed his concern about section 2 of H. J. Res. 167, which was strikingly similar to Article 5 of the Mutual Defense Treaty. See Congress, House, *Taiwan Legislation*, pp. 32–33.

62. *Congressional Quarterly Almanac*, 1979, p. 107

63. Ibid., p. 109

64. Dan Quayle's amendment on a U.S. liaison office was rejected by a vote of 172–182, and Ken Kramer's amendment on Taiwan security was defeated by a 149–221 vote. See also *Congressional Quarterly Almanac*, 1979, p. 114.

65. Ike Skelton (D-Mo.) opposed Kramer's amendment, pointing out that no U.S. ally had such a guarantee of unlimited access to the most advanced weapons. Lester Wolff ensured that the committee bill on H.R. 2479 precluded the executive from selling Taiwan only obsolete equipment. See *Congressional Quarterly Almanac*, 1979, p. 114.

66. Ibid. The House defeated one attempt to include the security of the two islands located about ten miles off the China coast. Mickey Edwards (R-Okla.) proposed an amendment concerning the security of Jinmen (Quemoy) and Mazu (Matsu), which the abrogated U.S.-Taiwan Defense Treaty did not even cover.

The House further adopted eight amendments, of which three dealt with Taiwan security. Lagomarsino's amendment required the president to inform Congress of any threats to Taiwan, which would be viewed as a threat to the Western Pacific and U.S. interests. Quayle's amendment proposed that the United States would maintain its capacity to resist any coercion that would endanger the security of Taiwan. The amendment by George Hansen (R-Idaho) assured Taiwan of a U.S. law withholding U.S. corporations from respecting any economic boycott of a friendly country. Two amendments contained the same language as the Senate amendments, allowing Taiwan to keep all its offices in the United States and establishing a joint commission to oversee the AIT. Another amendment by Congressman Derwinski asserted "the preservation of the human rights" of the people on Taiwan "as a commitment of the United States" (*Congressional Quarterly Almanac*, 1979, p. 116).

67. *Congressional Quarterly Almanac*, 1979, p. 116.

68. See also Downen, *The Taiwan Pawn*, p. 48.

69. The conference modified other major provisions opposed by the administration. Executive officials pointed out that the House bill title, "The United States–Taiwan Relations Act," would be interpreted to mean an official relationship between the United States and Taiwan. The committee altered the title to the "Taiwan Relations Act." Furthermore, the committee made three changes regarding the AIT. The House bill did not specify the AIT, instead referring to a "designated entity." The new version utilized the AIT "or such comparable successor" agency designated by the president. The conference version changed a reference in the House bill from performing "consular" duties by employees of the AIT to those duties "as if" they were consular functions. The administration strongly opposed a House provision barring use of any federal funds for the institution unless they were authorized and appropriated by Congress. The conference committee eliminated the provision on the basis of the administration's argument that it would impede the institute and make it impossible for government agencies to contract with the institution without prior approval of Congress.

The conference committee dropped the Senate concept of creating a separate joint commission of twelve members of Congress to oversee the AIT. Instead, the conference committee invested the Foreign Relations Committee with oversight authority. The committee reached compromise on the terms "the people on Taiwan," used by the Senate bill, and "Taiwan," referred by the House bill, incorporating both terms into the final bill. The administration had preferred the Senate language over the House language because it sounded less official.

70. President Carter claimed that "the Act contains all of the authority" that he had requested. See the White House press release, April 10, 1979, *Weekly Compilation of Presidential Documents*, vol. 15, no. 15 (Washington, D.C.: Office of the Federal Register, 1979), p. 640.

71. The administration proposal initially contained seventeen sections and four subsections. The TRA has eighteen sections and thirty-five subsections. Congress created nine entire sections and added or revised twenty-seven subsections. In the congressional process, approximately 100 amendments were introduced by the Senate and thirty-five by the House. Twenty-two amendments were called up and acted upon in the Senate and twenty in the House. The Congress

totally adopted twenty-six amendments: Senate 17, House 9. See Downen, *The Taiwan Pawn*, Appendix 3, p. 65.

72. For a detailed study of the Japanese formula, see Gene T. Hsiao, "The Sino-Japanese Rapprochement: A Relationship of Ambivalence," in Hsiao, ed., *Sino-American Detente and Its Policy Implication* (New York: Praeger, 1974). See also David Nelson Rowe, *Informal "Diplomatic Relations": The Case of Japan and the Republic of China, 1972–1974* (Hamden, Conn.: Shoestring Press, 1975).

73. Robert G. Sutter accounted for different international approaches to the PRC claim to Taiwan. See his *The China Quandary: Domestic Determinants of U.S. China Policy, 1972–82*, footnote 20, Chapter 3.

74. Interview with Charles W. Freeman, deputy assistant secretary of state for African affairs, Washington, D.C., July 27, 1987. In my interview, Freeman disclosed that he was the one who did the study at the Harvard Law School while he was on leave from the State Department in 1974–1975. His study became the intellectual basis for the TRA. Mr. Freeman has been a China expert in the State Department, working on various aspects of U.S. relations with China and Taiwan. He accompanied President Nixon to China in 1972 as his principal interpreter and was recalled to serve on the Taiwan Working Group to handle the passage of the Taiwan legislation and the negotiations with Taipei's special emissary, Yang Hsi-k'un, on the actual arrangements for U.S.-Taiwan relationships through the TIT and the Coordination Council for North American Affairs (CCNAA).

75. See Charles Freeman, "The Japanese Model: Could U.S. Relations with Taiwan Also Be Conducted Through 'Private' Incorporated Associations?" (an unpublished paper, East Asian Legal Studies, Harvard Law School, March 17, 1975), pp. 18-19. I would like to thank Mr. Freeman for letting me use his papers for this research. His papers on the subject, as I was told, were widely read and had great influence in the State Department.

76. Ibid., pp. 15–31.

77. Ibid., pp. 35–36.

78. Freeman, "Legal/Economic Consequences of Derecognition for American Economic Relations with Taiwan" (an unpublished paper, East Asian Legal Studies, Harvard Law School, March 3, 1975), p. 56.

79. According to Oksenberg, Brzezinski advocated a pro-China policy while Secretary Vance maintained an evenhanded foreign policy. See Oksenberg, "A Decade of Sino-American Relations."

80. *People's Daily* (in Chinese), August 17, 1982.

81. Sutter, *The China Quandary*, p. 7.

82. Prepared statement by Warren Christopher, Congress, Senate, *Taiwan*, p. 19.

83. See prepared statement of Dwight H. Perkings in Congress, House, Committee on Foreign Affairs, Subcommittee on Asian and Pacific Affairs, *Normalization of Relations with the PRC: Practical Implications*, 95th Cong., 1st sess., September, 20, 21, 28, 29, October 11 and 13, 1977, p. 289.

84. Ibid.

85. Ibid., p. 288.

86. Warren Christopher's statement, Congress, Senate, *Taiwan*, p. 19.

87. Congress, Senate, *The Taiwan Enabling Act*, p. 4.

88. Ibid., p. 13.

89. Department of State, "Economic and Commercial Relations with Taiwan," *Department of State Bulletin*, 79, no. 2023 (Office of Public Communication, Bureau of Public Affairs, February 1979), p. 27.

90. James Gregor, "The United States, the Republic of China, and the Taiwan Relations Act," *Orbis* 24 (Fall 1980), pp. 611–612.

91. Ibid., pp. 614–615.
92. Some members were critical of the administration's several normalization arrangements. First, the administration did not obtain a written pledge from China that it would not take military action against Taiwan. Second, the administration agreed to a one-year moratorium on new arms sales to Taiwan in 1979. Third, Congress felt that "the language of the December 15, 1978, communiqué went slightly beyond that of the 1972 Shanghai Communiqué in recognizing China's claim to sovereignty over Taiwan. In the Shanghai Communiqué, the United States "acknowledges that all Chinese on either side of the Taiwan strait maintain there is but one China and that Taiwan is a part of China. The United States Government does not challenge that position." In the normalization communiqué, the United States "acknowledges the Chinese position that there is but one China and Taiwan is part of China." The latter recognized China's claim. See Congress, Senate, *The Taiwan Enabling Act*, pp. 8–9.
93. Congressional alterations of the executive legislation were reflected in *The Taiwan Enabling Act* drafted by the Senate Foreign Relations Committee. First, the act defined the phrase "the people on Taiwan" as the governing authority as well as the people governed by it. Second, the act provided the legal standing of the people on Taiwan to sue and be sued in U.S. courts, and the protection of property rights of entities and persons in both countries. Third, the act, with regard to congressional oversight of the American Institute in Taiwan, the private instrumentality established to conduct U.S. relations with the people on Taiwan, provided for reporting agreements made by the institute in a manner that satisfies requirements of the Case Act. It also specifies that agreements made by the institute are subject to the same congressional notification, review, and approval requirements as if such agreements had been made by or through a department or agency of the United States. Fourth, the act authorized and requested the president to provide extensive privileges and immunities, as appropriate, to members of the counterpart instrumentality, subject to reciprocal privileges and immunities being granted to the members of the American Institute in Taiwan working on that island. See Congress, Senate, *The Taiwan Enabling Act*, pp. 7–8.
94. James C. Thomson, Jr., "On the Making of U.S. China Policy, 1961–69: A Study in Bureaucratic Politics," *China Quarterly* 50 (April-June 1972), pp. 220–243.
95. President Carter rejected a bureaucratic recommendation to veto the TRA after the Congress passed the bill. Instead, Carter issued a statement regarding the implementation of the TRA. Interview with Roger Sullivan, former assistant secretary of state in the Carter administration, Washington, D.C., August 7, 1987.
96. Krasner stated that "the ability of bureaucracies to independently establish policies is a function of Presidential attention. Presidential attention is a function of Presidential values." See Krasner, "Are Bureaucracies Important?" p. 168.
97. Cecil Crabb, Jr., "An Assertive Congress and the TRA: Policy Influence and Implications," in Louis W. Koenig, James C. Hsiung, and Kin-yuh Chang, eds., *Congress, the Presidency, and the Taiwan Relations Act* (New York: Praeger, 1985), p. 97.
98. For example, the renowned constitutional scholar Edward S. Corwin once remarked that the U.S. constitutional system extends an "invitation to struggle" to the presidency and Congress for control over foreign policy. See his *The President: Office and Powers*, 4th ed. (New York: New York University Press, 1957). See also Cecil V. Crabb, Jr., and Patt M. Holt, *Invitation to Struggle: Congress, the President, and Foreign Policy* (Washington, D.C.: Congressional Quarterly, 1980).

3

U.S. China Trade Policy
and China's MFN Status

The U.S.-China trade agreement signed in 1979 was the first bilateral trade agreement aimed at the promotion of trade between the two countries. The agreement was a pivotal document in normalizing U.S.-China economic relations. Specifically, it granted most-favored-nation status to each country, protected mutual industrial interests, and facilitated business services as bilateral economic relations developed.[1] The agreement represented an important transformation of U.S. China economic policy after normalization from one of treating China as part of its general restrictive trade policy, governing the East-West economic relations, to one that considered China a friendly country.

Furthermore, the trade agreement implied that the United States intended to strengthen the new Sino-U.S. relationship through economic linkages. Lastly, by granting China MFN status, the agreement marked a significant U.S. foreign policy move to closer U.S.-China ties in the U.S.-PRC-USSR strategic context. This chapter discusses the initial conditions that gave rise to a trade agreement and addresses the following questions: What are the factors that made the United States change its foreign economic policy toward China? Why did the United States extend MFN relations to China, but not to the Soviet Union?

U.S. Economic Policy Toward Socialist Countries

Benjamin J. Cohen defined U.S. foreign economic policy as "the sum total of actions by the nation-state intended to affect the economic environment beyond the national jurisdiction." Later, he added that foreign economic policy can also be part of a nation's total foreign policy and serve the same foreign policy objectives.[2] But this definition tended to separate foreign from

Portions of this chapter are reprinted with permission from the *Journal of Northeast Asian Studies*, vol. 9, No. 1 (Spring 1990). Copyright ©1990 by the Institute for Sino-Soviet Studies, George Washington University.

domestic economic policy and failed to take into account the interplay between domestic political processes and economic conditions. Robert A. Pastor defined U.S. foreign economic policy more comprehensively by referring to it as "the totality of U.S. Government actions intended to affect the international economic environment either directly or by adjusting the way the U.S. economy relates to it."[3]

The above definitions, however, are more relevant to U.S. foreign economic policy toward Western Europe, Japan, and developing countries than to socialist countries. Since the 1930s, the United States had, for the most part, viewed trade with the West in basically economic terms. Pastor surveyed U.S. foreign economic policy from 1929 to 1976 and concluded that "U.S. foreign economic policy has been coherent and consistently liberal."[4] Since the Smoot-Hawley Tariff Act, which represented the peak of U.S. protectionism, the United States had generally committed itself to a liberal trade policy that served U.S. interests foremost but also the economic well-being of the Western world.

When it came to trade with socialist countries, however, the United States had tended to adopt a "carrot and stick" policy aimed at affecting the international political environment. As a result, U.S. foreign economic policy has customarily been subordinated to broader political objectives and often used as a tool to advance those foreign policy goals. For a brief period after the Second World War, U.S. trade policy toward the Eastern European bloc was adopted to influence the foreign policy of some countries like Hungary, Czechoslovakia, Poland, and Romania toward pro-West policies. When those policies failed, the United States switched to a more restrictive trade policy to isolate and weaken the Eastern bloc.

There were several laws that used economic policies as weapons against hostile countries. During both World War I and World War II, the United States passed legislation to control or cut off exports of certain commodities. The deterioration of East-West relations in the postwar era also brought additional legislative controls on East-West trade.

Trading with the Enemy Act. The Trading with the Enemy Act of 1917 was originally intended to restrict trade during wartime. It permanently empowered the president to control all transactions involving the transfer of funds between Americans and foreigners in time of war or declared national emergency. President Truman invoked this act in 1950 to impose a trade embargo against China and North Korea.[5]

Export Control Act. The Export Control Act was passed in 1940 and revised in 1949. It delegated to the president the power to ban or restrict exports as necessary in order to advance U.S. foreign policy or national security interests or to deal with domestic shortages and inflation. Administered by the Commerce Department through a licensing system, the act was extended through the 1950s and 1960s. It was substantially revised in 1969 and renamed the Export Administration Act.[6]

Mutual Defense Assistance Control Act. In 1951, Congress passed more restrictive legislation: the Mutual Defense Assistance Control Act, dubbed the "Battle Act" after Representative Laurie C. Battle. This act aimed to punish countries that traded with socialist countries. It forbade U.S. aid to any third country shipping arms to socialist nations and directed the president to suspend aid to nations shipping specified "strategic" commodities to those countries the president found it contrary to the national interests to trade with. This act also constrained the president's flexibility to conduct foreign economic policy.

Under the Battle Act, the United States established three categories of items subject to security controls:

Category A: twenty-one classes of war materials, including "arms, ammunition, implements of war, and atomic energy materials," deemed to be of such strategic importance as to require complete embargo;

Category B: 260 items of "primary strategic significance," including petroleum, transportation equipment, and equipment used in the production of war materials, also subject to total embargo; and

Category C: some machine tools, raw materials, and construction and electrical equipment of secondary strategic importance, subject to lighter controls than imposed on the other two categories.[7]

In addition, exporters who received government subsidies, such as wheat farmers, had to apply for special permission to trade. The United States also passed various foreign aid bills, as well as amendments to the Agricultural Trade Development and Assistance Act of 1954, to bar the government from providing foreign economic or military aid, credit guarantees, or similar benefits to socialist countries.

The 1974 Trade Act. The United States had invoked different trade acts to regulate its trade relations with socialist countries. In the 1962 Trade Act, Congress directed the president to suspend any trade benefits to "any country or area dominated or controlled by communism."[8] Despite the fact that it established a procedure linking trade concessions to emigration, the 1974 Trade Act was by far a less restrictive act regarding trade with socialist countries.[9] It authorized the president to negotiate three-year bilateral trade agreements with socialist countries. It also delegated to the president greater discretion in negotiating trade with socialist countries. Although the Jackson-Vanik amendment prohibited the U.S. government from entering MFN relations with communist countries that did not allow free emigration, it empowered the president to waive such emigration requirements if he found that the country would "substantially" promote freedom of emigration and if he had received "assurances" that the country's practices would "henceforth lead substantially to freedom of emigration."

Background of U.S.-China Economic Relations

U.S. economic relations with the People's Republic of China were of secondary importance, subject to the change of political atmosphere surrounding international as well as bilateral relations. There were three periods in the development of U.S.-China economic relations. The first two decades after the founding of the People's Republic saw the United States using its economic means as U.S. foreign policy toward China. At the outbreak of the Korean War in 1950, President Truman invoked the Trading with the Enemy Act of 1917 against China. This trade policy was further reinforced by the U.S. "containment" policy toward Chinese communism in the 1950s. China was excluded from a reappraisal of U.S. policy on communist trade in the early 1960s when the Kennedy administration began to encourage a "détente" with the Soviet Union.[10] The same administration entertained and rejected a "food-for-peace" policy that might have eased China's alleged "aggressiveness" during its "three-year-natural-calamity." In the mid-1960s the United States relaxed restrictions on scholars traveling to China, a policy that the China specialists at the China Desk under the Far East Bureau had sought for several years.[11] With the change in international environment, the Nixon administration actively pursued a policy of improving U.S. relations with China in the late 1960s. At the same time, the United States started changing its economic policy toward China. In July 1969, President Nixon began to ease regulation of travel of U.S. citizens to and trade restrictions with China. In June 1971, he dismantled the two-decade trade embargo against China. The United States removed blocks on exports of a wide variety of nonstrategic goods to China and on commercial imports from the mainland.

The second phase of U.S.-China economic relations emerged in the early 1970s as a result of the improved Sino-U.S. relations. Nixon's historic visit in 1972 led to the resumption of formal U.S.-China trade. Despite a common belief that trade would develop at a gradual rate and in relatively small volume, Sino-U.S. trade experienced rapid growth, from $4.9 million in 1971 to $933.8 million in 1974, an eighteenfold increase. Concomitantly, U.S. exports increased from none in 1971 to total exports of $819.1 million in 1974. Meanwhile, Chinese exports to the United States grew steadily from

$4.9 million in 1971 to $114.7 million in 1974. During this period, the United States had a trade surplus of $704.4 million.

From 1975 to 1977, U.S.-China trade declined, due in part to economic improvement in China and in part to political circumstances. China increased its agricultural output in 1975, reducing its demands for agricultural commodities such as wheat and soybeans. China also used trade to express its dissatisfaction with the lack of progress in normalization. Instead of purchasing U.S. wheat, China signed agreements with Canada and Australia. Consequently, U.S.-China trade dropped by almost half between 1974 and 1977; U.S. exports to China dropped from $303.6 million in 1975 to $171.3 million in 1977, while Chinese exports to the United States increased slightly from $158.4 million in 1975 to $201 million in 1976, then stagnated around the 1976 level. Chinese exports to the United States during this period consisted largely of textiles and apparel, antiques and art crafts, bristles and feathers, fireworks and nonferrous metals. U.S. exports to China included aluminum and equipment for oil drilling and exploration, in addition to grain and cotton. China also bought ten Boeing aircraft and eight ammonia plants.

The third period began in 1978 with a new surge in U.S.-China trade, more than doubling that of the previous year to over $1 billion. U.S. and Chinese exports went up to $823.6 million and $324.1 million, respectively. Resumption of U.S. agricultural purchases by the PRC contributed three-quarters ($614 million) of the total exports, including wheat ($291 million), cotton ($157 million) and corn ($118 million) (see Figure 3.1).[12]

Figure 3.1   U.S.-China Trade, 1971–1986

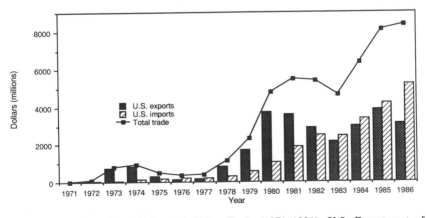

Sources: National Council for U.S.-China Trade (1971–1981); U.S. Department of Commerce (1982–1986)

Two factors were primarily responsible for this increased trade activity. One was the establishment of diplomatic relations with China. The other was the Chinese economic reform that led to the open-door policy. The former permitted U.S. business people to conduct business in China with U.S. government help.[13] The latter provided new prospects for increasing imports of industrial products, advanced technology, grains, and other raw materials from the United States.

Large numbers of U.S. business people went to China in 1978 to explore possible business opportunities. Letters of intent were signed for several large transactions. The Fluor Corporation signed an agreement for a proposed $800 million complex to mine and process copper. Beijing ordered three Boeing 747 SP planes, with options on two more—a deal worth $250 million. An agreement was also concluded to sell and later bottle Coca-Cola. The U.S. Steel Corporation agreed to set up an iron ore processing plant worth about $1 billion. Bethlehem Steel made a deal for more than $600 million. Pan American Airlines, through its subsidiary Intercontinental Hotels, negotiated a $500 million agreement to build luxury hotels.[14] Despite the rapid increase of Sino-U.S. trade, however, some remaining problems hindered further development of bilateral economic relations. The foremost was high tariffs imposed by the United States on imports from countries like China that did not have MFN relations with the United States. For example, China's exports to the United States could have been 30 percent higher in 1976 had China been granted MFN status.[15] Another problem was that the Export-Import Bank Act of 1945, as amended, prohibited the bank from conducting any credit transactions (export credits and credit guarantees) involving a socialist country, except in cases where the president considered that restriction contrary to national interests. This ruled out Export-Import Bank financing for any business transactions between the two countries. These problems had a general impact on the bilateral trade, reducing China's exports to the United States and weakening China's ability to purchase U.S. goods, since its imports were largely financed by exports. Moreover, these problems restricted the United States in competing with Japan and Western Europe for a market share in China.

Executive Perception and Initiation of China Trade

The economic reforms introduced in China in 1978 greatly enhanced U.S. perceptions of the benefit of developing closer economic ties with China. The administration perceived the reform in two significant terms: pragmatism and economic opportunity.

U.S. interests would appear to be best served by successful reforms. Pragmatic reform was aimed at making economic progress in China by "opening the Chinese door" to the outside world. Most pragmatic Chinese leaders supported an open-door foreign policy toward the West, because maintaining good relations with the United States and other Western countries would help obtain technology and financial investment. In this sense, pragmatism replaced ideology.

Chinese economic reforms also enhanced the U.S. perception of new economic opportunities in China. The Third Plenum of the Eleventh Central Committee of the CCP decided to shift its "working gravity" from emphasizing politics to promoting economic development. China also committed itself to achieving the "four modernizations" by the year 2000.[16] Although no one knew the size of the potential Chinese market, China had to import much of the needed capital and technology from the West in order to achieve its goals of modernization. Of the four modernizations, agriculture alone required $650 billion.[17] Even in the short run, China's imports would appear to be significant. According to Commerce Department estimates, Chinese real imports would increase at the rate of 12 to 15 percent annually, with accumulated imports in the 1979–1985 period reaching $115 to $130 billion (at 1978 prices).[18]

These U.S. perceptions prompted further questions: What did Chinese reform mean to the United States in terms of trade? What should the United States do?

Using as a basis the trade trend from 1971 to 1978, the Commerce Department outlined prospects for U.S. exports to China in 1979. U.S. exports to China could rise 70 percent in 1979 to $1.4 billion, up from a total of $818 million in 1978. Agricultural exports would increase 30 percent and be valued at $750 million. Nonagricultural exports were expected to rise 165 percent for a total of $650 million. Thus, the total volume of U.S.-China trade in 1979 could reach $2 billion, almost double the volume in 1978. Using these projections, the Commerce Department estimated that U.S. exports to China could reach $3.5 billion in 1985 and imports about $1.5 billion. U.S. exports to China could total $15 billion and imports from China $6 billion, over the period 1979–1985 (see Figure 3.2).[19]

The Commerce Department's figures were substantially lower than the figures projected by the National Council for U.S.-China Trade, a semiofficial organization established in 1973 in the absence of U.S.-China economic relations.[20] It estimated that the U.S. share in China's imports would double by 1985 to about 16 percent from the 1978 level of 8 percent, and U.S. exports to China would reach about $5 billion in 1985 and total $22 billion over the 1979-1985 period.[21]

In terms of specific fields in which U.S. business could get involved, Commerce Department officials believed that the United States could expand its business activities beyond traditional agricultural products to "hotel construction, iron ore development, non-ferrous metals, petroleum,

Figure 3.2   U.S. Exports to China, 1979–1985

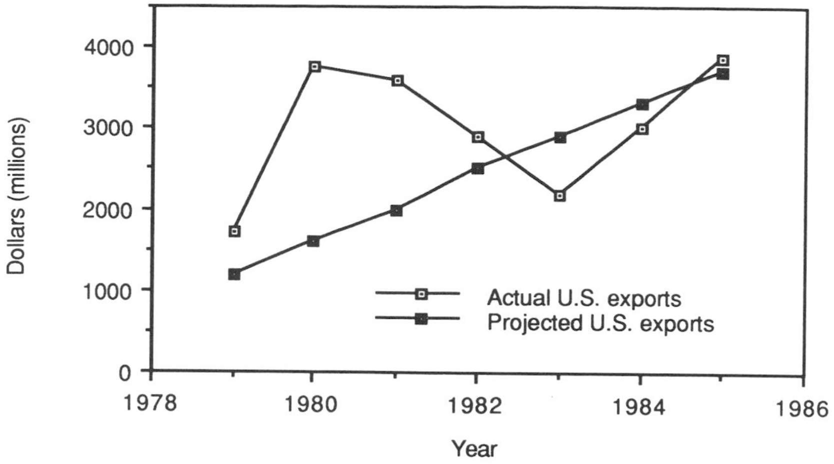

Source: U.S. Department of Commerce (1979)

water transport, electric power, coal, transportation equipment including aircraft and helicopters, communications equipment, and other machinery."[22]

Prospects for increasing U.S.-China trade, however, rested on the basis of normal economic relations between the two countries. Without it, U.S.-China trade encountered artificial trade barriers set up by each country's discriminatory trade policies. The United States was mainly responsible for such trade barriers because it had adopted a restrictive trade policy toward the socialist countries in the postwar era. As the international environment changed, this restrictive trade policy reduced business opportunities in China. For example, a Commerce Department study pointed out that "without recourse to U.S. government loan and loan guarantee programs, American firms will be at a competitive disadvantage with Japanese and West European suppliers." [23]

Furthermore, without MFN treatment, China's exports to the United States would be greatly limited, which in turn reduced U.S. exports to China. However, the Jackson-Vanik provisions of the Trade Act of 1974 precluded MFN tariff treatment to Chinese goods and the use by China of U.S. Export-Import Bank loans unless a presidential waiver on Chinese emigration was granted. The study suggested that a Sino-U.S. trade agreement be negotiated and that all those commercial barriers be removed "if the United States was to maximize its trade with China."[24]

Executive Initiation of the Trade Agreement

In initiating a trade agreement with China, the United States had two specific objectives. One was to protect U.S. business interests by providing U.S. business people with patent, trademark, and copyright assurance. The other was to regularize bilateral trade relations by safeguarding against perceived potential market disruption by Chinese goods.

After extensive negotiations and exchanges of draft agreements, a general trade agreement between the United States and China was officially initiated by Secretary of Commerce Juanita Kreps in Beijing in May 1979.[25] Since China was regarded as a nonmarket economy or a communist country, it was subject to a long list of requirements specified in the U.S. Trade Act of 1974.[26] Specifically, section 405 of the act requires that any bilateral commercial agreement must contain provisions designed to protect U.S. economic and national security interests. First the provisions must include safeguard arrangements providing for prompt consultation whenever actual or potential imports cause or threaten to cause market disruption. In case of perceived disruption, it authorizes the imposition of import restrictions to prevent such disruption. Second, the act requires arrangements for the protection of industrial rights and processes, trademarks, patents, and copyrights and the promotion of trade. Third, it requires a provision for dispute settlement as well as consultations to review the operation of the agreement. Fourth, it requires the negotiation of other commercial arrangements that will promote the purposes of the Trade Act. Fifth, it requires a provision for the termination or suspension of the agreement at any time for national security reasons. The other provisions could not restrict the rights to protect national interests.

Section 405 also limits the duration of such an agreement to an initial period of not more than three years, renewable for successive periods not to exceed three years. Section 402(a) stipulates that if any nonmarket economy country denies its citizens the right to emigrate or imposes more than a nominal fee on emigration or as a consequence of the desire to emigrate, MFN tariff treatment shall not be extended to the goods of such country.

All of the requirements touched on political, economic, and technical issues. They presented a legal framework for the executive to reach an agreement. The negotiation was conducted in such a way as to cope with the different Chinese system as well as congressional requirements. Chinese negotiators, for example, did not understand why the United States insisted that a copyright, trademark provision be included in the agreement, since China did not have laws concerning those matters. The negotiators spent eleven days working through the details of U.S. patent law and trade policies, which, according to one of the U.S. principal negotiators, C. L. Haslam, the Commerce Department's general counsel, the Chinese found "baffling, complex and legalistic."[27]

The original draft presented to China was a long and detailed document that went beyond even what the 1974 Trade Act required. In spite of Chinese preference for a short, principle-guarding trade agreement, the U.S. version was long and detailed.[28] The slow progress of the negotiations caught Secretary Kreps's attention when she arrived in Beijing on May 9, 1979. She immediately instructed her delegation to reexamine the draft and exclude nonessential details.

The revised draft kept those provisions dealing with emigration policy and patent protection required by the Trade Act, including those guarding against "market disruption." With the new draft, the negotiation focused on the issue of industrial rights. According to a member of the U.S. negotiating team, Beijing found it difficult to accept provisions dealing with U.S. patents since China did not have patent law.[29] The negotiations were virtually stalemated by the intransigence of both sides in their positions. Kreps predicted that she might end her six-day trip without an agreement. On May 11, Deng Xiaoping intervened in the negotiations and told the U.S. delegation that China would soon establish an institution to protect patents, including foreign patents.[30] Deng's assurance solved the problem, and the negotiators started working out the final version. Just before Secretary Kreps left China for Hong Kong on May 14, the United States and China reached an agreement on trade.

Bureaucratic Preferences in the Process

The State Department, the Treasury Department, and the Commerce Department were all involved in developing a U.S.-China economic framework. It was generally agreed that the United States should resolve the assets-claims issue and the textile issue before reaching a trade agreement with China.

The assets-claims issue involved Chinese assets blocked in the United States and U.S. private claims against the PRC. The origin of the assets-claims issue dated to the U.S.-PRC confrontation in Korea. The U.S. government froze all Chinese dollar-denominated accounts and other assets on December 17, 1950, after PRC military "volunteers" went across the Ya-lu River. Subsequently, on December 29, 1950, the Chinese government issued a decree declaring seizure of U.S. property in the PRC.[31]

In 1966, the Foreign Claims Settlement Commission, pursuant to the International Claims Settlement Act of 1949 as amended, undertook a census of claims by U.S. citizens for losses resulting from PRC nationalization of property and other assets after October 1, 1949. The commission adjudicated a total of 384 claims having a value of $196.9 million.[32]

The Treasury Department, responsible under the Foreign Assets Control Regulations for keeping control over those assets, evaluated the frozen

Chinese assets in June 1970. It estimated that their total value amounted to $76.5 million.[33]

Negotiations on the assets claims had started in the early 1970s. The settlement of the issue was important for bilateral trade. Without settlement, any Chinese-owned property, such as ships and airplanes brought into the United States, would be subject to attachment by U.S. private claimants through court orders. China sought to settle the matter by paying an amount roughly equivalent to the amount of the frozen assets it had already collected outside the United States and transferring the assets blocked in the United States to the U.S. government. However, the United States considered the amount less than desirable and felt that Congress would probably reject it.[34]

Settling the assets-claims issue was a priority of the Commerce Department after normalization and was the sole purpose of Secretary of Treasury Michael Blumenthal's visit to China in February 1979. He attached great importance to the settlement preceding normalization of bilateral trade and other commercial relations.[35] The agreement was reached in March and was officially signed by Commerce Secretary Kreps during her visit in May.[36]

U.S.-China textile trade was another issue in developing bilateral economic relations. Since the U.S. textile industry had been facing strong international competition, the Carter administration had worked out Orderly Market Arrangements (OMA) with other Asian textile export regions and countries.

The United States had suffered from a lack of effective coordination in formulating and implementing its East-West trade policy in the past. President Carter sought to address this problem by establishing the United States Trade Representative (USTR) as a new institution; its responsibilities would include coordinating East-West trade policy and conducting East-West trade negotiations. The president's Reorganization Plan #3, which founded the USTR, was submitted to the Congress on September 25, 1979, for approval. When it became effective, the USTR would play a central role in the future development of economic relations between the United States and the PRC.[37]

Before the founding of the USTR, the Office of the Special Representative for Trade Negotiations was responsible for coordinating U.S.-China economic relations. The Special Trade Representative (STR) was charged with the task of trade negotiation and trade policy coordination. In developing a framework of U.S.-China economic relations, it had been primarily concerned with U.S.-China textile trade. It had preferred to reach an agreement with China on restricting textiles before any general trade agreement was initiated.[38]

Informal consultation on textile exports to the United States had been conducted with Chinese officials in 1978, prior to normalization. The STR

Figure 3.3   U.S. Imports from China, 1974–1985

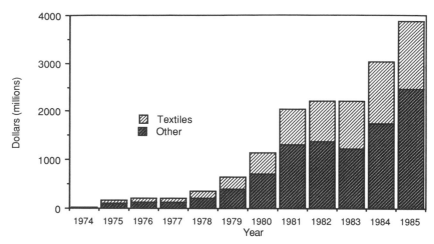

Sources: U.S. Department of Commerce, 1982–1985; Commodity Trade Statistics, Series d United Nations, 1974–1981

was concerned with the rapid growth rate of textile imports from China, especially with those imports shifting to some of the most import-sensitive apparel product categories (see Figure 3.3).

The United States and China entered into formal negotiations on a textile agreement after the normalization of relations. The United States sought specific limits or quotas on a number of product categories and the establishment of a consultative mechanism to prevent future disruptive trade in other product categories. China opposed the number of specific limits and the proposed levels of those limits and it responded that high U.S. non-MFN tariffs created an adequate restraint on Chinese textile trade. Given the size of its domestic textile industry and the short period in which its textile exports to the United States had been permitted to develop, China actually had a very small share of the U.S. market. According to a Chinese trade official, Chinese exports of textiles "comprise only a little more than 1 percent of total U.S. textile imports."[39]

When four rounds of formal negotiations failed, the United States, on May 31, 1979, imposed unilateral restraints (under section 204 of the Agricultural Act) on five apparel product categories: cotton gloves, cotton knit shirts, cotton knit blouses, cotton trousers, and synthetic-fiber sweaters.[40] On October 29, 1979, the United States extended unilateral limits on Chinese textile imports in two additional sensitive product categories: woven cotton blouses and synthetic-fiber coats.

The intensive textile trade negotiations and the unilateral U.S. actions limiting Chinese textile imports represented the preferences of STR and other U.S. agencies to strike a textile agreement with China before a general trade agreement was initiated. When such efforts failed, the Carter administration had to alter its priorities and began negotiations on a trade agreement.

The U.S.-China trade agreement was officially signed on July 7, 1979, by U.S. Ambassador Leonard Woodcock and Chinese Foreign Trade Minister Li Qiang, two months after its initiation on May 14 by Kreps and Li Qiang. The trade agreement remained to be approved by Congress, however.

There were divisions within the administration as to whether the United States should proceed with the trade agreement independent of reaching a similar agreement with the Soviet Union. In principle, the Carter administration had adopted an evenhanded foreign policy toward both the Soviet Union and China. Secretary of State Vance, particularly, felt that it would be a grave diplomatic mistake to establish MFN relations with China without having such relations with the Soviet Union.[41]

Officials who were in favor of an evenhanded policy preferred to accord MFN status to both China and the Soviet Union more or less simultaneously. They urged the government to delay submitting the trade agreement for congressional action until the government reached an agreement with the Soviets.[42] However, this approach had been complicated by Moscow's refusal to make explicit assurances about its emigration policy on the ground that it was an internal matter. Moreover, some congressional leaders were thought to oppose granting MFN to the Soviets for various reasons.[43]

In essence, after China had compromised on the trade agreement, the administration had to decide whether U.S. MFN relations with China would depend on the status of U.S. relations with the Soviet Union. The debate within the administration on the MFN issue delayed the submission of the agreement for congressional approval by more than three months. China openly complained about the delay and made it an issue in Sino-U.S. relations.[44]

Congressional Approval and the Policy Process

The Agreement on Trade Relations between the United States and the People's Republic of China granted most-favored-nation status to each country, protected mutual industrial interests, and facilitated business services as bilateral economic relations developed. The Carter administration formally submitted the agreement to the Congress for approval on October 23, 1979. Using a loophole in the Jackson-Vanik amendment that delegated to the president the authority to waive the emigration requirements, President Carter removed the obstacle to developing favorable trade relations with China. In his letter to the Speaker, Carter viewed the agreement as providing a "nondiscriminatory framework for our bilateral trade relations, and thus strengthening both economic and political relations."[45]

Statutory Requirements and Congressional Concerns

According to the Trade Act of 1974, Congress placed a number of requirements and limitations upon the president's authority to extend MFN trade relations with non-market economy countries. First, it had to be negotiated under the provisions of section 405, which set forth the requirements for bilateral commercial agreements with non-market economy countries. Second, it had to fulfill the requirement of section 402 concerning emigration policy. Third, it had to go through the approval procedures required by sections 405(c), 407, and 151.

Title IV sets up the framework for the president. Section 405 delineates the requirements regarding the content of the agreement (granting MFN, safeguards against market disruption, suspension or termination for reasons of national security, settlement of commercial disputes, and protection of patents).

Title IV imposes conditions on the delegation of authority to the president to enter into such agreements. Sections 402(a) and 402(b) stipulate that the United States should not grant any country MFN treatment or government credits, credit guarantees, or investment guarantees if the president determines that such a country (1) denies its citizens the right or opportunity to emigrate; (2) imposes more than a nominal tax on emigration, or on the visas or other documents required for emigration, for any purpose or cause; or (3) imposes more than a nominal tax, levy, fine, fee, or any charge on any citizen as a consequence of the desire of such a citizen to emigrate to the country of his or her choice.

Section 402(c) provides the president with temporary authority to waive the emigration requirements of sections (a) and (b) for any country if a report is sent to Congress that the president (1) has determined that such a waiver would promote the objectives of free emigration, and (2) has received assurances that future emigration practices of the country would substantially lead to freer emigration. This authority was initially granted for an eighteen-month period, and the act provides for successive twelve-month extensions upon recommendation of the president, unless a disapproval resolution is passed by either House within sixty days after the termination date of the waiver.[46]

Section 407 requires the president to submit the text of a trade agreement to both Houses of Congress. A resolution is followed by request in each House. Such resolution is subject to the fast-track procedures of section 151; the committees of jurisdiction are subject to an automatic discharge if they have not acted on the resolution within forty-five legislative days of its introduction; Congress should vote on the final passage within fifteen legislative days after the committee either reports the resolution or the resolution is discharged from further consideration.

In accordance with the implementation procedures of section 151 of the Trade Act of 1974, a concurrent resolution, House Concurrent Resolution 204, was introduced in the House and referred to the Committee on Ways and Means on the same day the president transmitted the agreement to Congress. An identical resolution, Senate Concurrent Resolution 47, was introduced in the Senate and referred to the Committee on Finance. Congressional approval of the concurrent resolution would remove prohibitions on Chinese participation in U.S. government programs extending credit or credit guarantees, or investment or investment guarantees, as provided in section 402 of the Trade Act.

There was, however, a considerable division of opinion within the Congress on three essential issues of the trade agreement. First, there was strong protectionist sentiment against imports of Chinese textiles among some members of Congress. Even before the submission, the administration was concerned with possible opposition to the agreement from members of Congress representing textile-producing districts. Secretary Kreps reportedly acknowledged that the administration might not be able to present the agreement to Congress until a textile agreement had been signed.[47] The opposition of textile interests had been forestalled by U.S. unilateral imposition of nonpreferential textile import quotas on five categories of Chinese textiles on May 31 and October 29.

Second, there were different views among some members of Congress regarding the policy of granting MFN status to China without giving the Soviet Union the same treatment at the same time. Two key members of Congress, Senator Henry Jackson (D-Wash.) and Representative Charles A. Vanik (D-Ohio), whose amendment barred MFN and Export-Import Bank credits to non-market economy countries that did not allow freedom of emigration, split over the administration's China policy. Jackson wanted immediate action on approving the trade agreement on the grounds that China, apart from being a strategic friend, had complied with the emigration requirements while the Soviet Union had not.[48] Vanik, on the other hand, preferred granting MFN status to both China and the Soviet Union at the same time. There were two reasons for his "evenhanded" trade policy. First, instead of demanding assurances from the Soviet government about the emigration policy, he pointed out that existing emigration levels were sufficient for Congress to grant MFN status.[49] Second, Vanik argued that it was a dangerous political game to "play the so-called China card and play either of these major powers against each other."[50]

The third issue was whether China's emigration practices qualified it for MFN status under the Jackson-Vanik amendment. Some members of Congress were skeptical about China's emigration policies and pressed the executive to produce the evidence regarding Chinese assurances about their future emigration policy. Congressman Richard T. Schulze demanded Congress be shown the Chinese statements before the agreement could be acted upon.[51]

Congressional Action

The Subcommittee on Trade of the Ways and Means Committee held a public hearing on House Concurrent Resolution 204 on November 1, 2, and 29. Another hearing was held by the Subcommittee on International Trade of the Committee on Finance on Senate Concurrent Resolution 47 on November 15. Testimony, written statements, and correspondence in favor of the trade agreement came from the departments of Commerce, State, and the Treasury, the Office of the Special Representative for Trade Negotiations, some members of Congress, trade associations, and individual corporations engaged in East-West trade.

On November 13, the House Ways and Means Committee approved by a 24-8 vote the resolution acceding to the trade agreement. The Senate Finance Committee, after the hearing, decided to delay further action regarding emigration matters. On December 14, the committee met with Deputy Secretary of State Warren Christopher in closed session to discuss the assurances that the United States had received from the Chinese government regarding the emigration policy. On December 18, the committee approved the trade agreement without dissent.[52] The Finance Committee reported the resolution on January 10, 1980, and the Ways and Means Committee on January 17, 1980. In neither case was the resolution amended.

Congressional floor debates on the trade agreement in both Houses centered on three issues: relations between the United States and China in light of the Soviet invasion of Afghanistan, the disruption of U.S. markets, and China's emigration policy.[53] Other members of Congress expressed their opposition to the administration's position on China immigration policy and the plan to extend $2 billion in credit to China.[54]

Congress approved the trade agreement by overwhelming majorities; the House voted 294-88 on January 24, and the Senate voted 74-8 on the same day.

An Analysis

There have been in the history of East-West trade two different perceptions of and motivations for the linkage between economics and politics. While the East has promoted economic cooperation with the West with the goal of gaining economic benefits from closer ties, the West has tended to be more concerned with political goals.[55] In a world of increasing interdependence, however, it may be too simple for one to make such a distinction "because political and economic considerations are often inextricably intertwined, and no country could emphasize one factor to the exclusion of the other."[56] Nevertheless, the United States regarded economic interdependence as a means to an end and sought to use economic cooperation to obtain political advantages.

During the Nixon administration, the United States adopted the "strategy of linkages" in conducting foreign policy toward communist countries. As former Secretary of State Henry Kissinger explained, "We have . . . sought to move forward across a broad range of issues so that progress in one area would add momentum to the progress of other areas."[57]

The Carter administration basically followed the same strategy; while normalizing diplomatic relations with China, the United States also sought to improve relations in other areas such as trade, culture, technology, and education. Both the United States and China hoped that improvements in areas other than diplomatic relations would lead to institutionalization of bilateral relations and thus enhance the overall relationship between the two countries. One prominent China scholar pointed out that "trade and other economic links are at the cutting edge today in the development of U.S.-China relations, and the success or failure of the two countries in their efforts to build lasting economic ties will have a major influence on long-term political and strategic relationships."[58]

U.S. Economic Policy Goals Toward China

An important foreign policy objective for the Carter administration after normalization was the development of a comprehensive and institutionalized economic relationship with China. Warren Christopher, deputy secretary of state, stated it clearly: "Diplomatic relations alone do not automatically insure the development of a normal and mutually beneficial relationship. Thus, our task is clear: We must find new ways to build a new relationship in tangible and practical ways."[59]

Developing healthy economic relations with China would help serve U.S. foreign policy objectives. The Carter administration saw that an economically strengthened China would contribute to the stabilization of Asian affairs as well as a balanced U.S. global strategic posture. As President Carter stated, "We have not entered this new relationship [with China] for any short-term gains. We have a long-term commitment to a world community of diverse and independent nations. We believe that a strong and secure China will play a cooperative part in developing that type of world community."[60] Moreover, economic interdependence between the United States and China would lead to cooperation in other areas and strengthen the overall relationship. President Carter made it explicit that developing economic relations with the PRC would "give further impetus to the progress we have made in our overall relationship" since normalization.[61]

Vice President Walter Mondale, during his visit to China in August 1979, explained the U.S. goals of developing further economic relations with China. In his public speech at Beijing University, Mondale attached great importance to economic cooperation, linking it to the political and strategic interests of the two countries:

> We must press forward now to widen and give specificity to our relations. The fundamental challenges we face are to build concrete political ties in the context of mutual security, to establish broad cultural relations in a framework of genuine equality, and to forge practical economic bonds with the goal of mutual benefit. . . . What we accomplish today lays the groundwork for the decade ahead. The 1980s can find us working together—and working with other nations—to meet world problems. Enriching the global economy, containing international conflicts, protecting the independence of nations—these goals must also be pursued from the perspective of our bilateral relationship. The deeper the relationship, the more successful that worldwide pursuit will be.[62]

After normalization, leaders of both nations became more concerned with the economic dimension of U.S.-China relations.[63] A sound framework for economic relations remained to be established. Both governments realized that early removal of trade barriers and establishment of official trade relations would best serve the interests of both countries. Mondale related trade with bilateral national interests as follows:

> In trade, our interests are served by your expanding exports of natural resources and industrial products. And at the same time your interests are served by the purchases you can finance through these exports.
> As you industrialize, you provide a higher standard of living for your people. And at the same time our interests are served—for this will increase the flow of trade, narrow the wealth gap between the developed and the developing world, and thus help alleviate a major source of global instability.[64]

There were several specific advantages the United States hoped to gain in normalizing U.S.-China economic relations. First, expanded trade could help reduce the U.S. trade deficit. In contrast to the U.S. trade deficit with other Asian trade partners such as Hong Kong, Taiwan, and South Korea, U.S.-China trade from 1972 to 1979 had resulted in a U.S. surplus of $3.1 billion.[65] In 1979 alone, the United States had a favorable balance of trade with China at $1,124.2 million—a remarkable increase of 225 percent from 1978.[66] Nevertheless, there remained room for potential improvement in U.S. exports. Special U.S. trade negotiator Robert S. Strauss pointed out that "Japan probably sells China six or seven times as much as we do;

Europe probably five or six times as much as we do, and they were opening the gap."[67] Though the trade volume was still small, U.S. officials felt that normalizing relations could help the United States reduce its $30 billion trade deficit.[68]

Normalization of economic relations could also stabilize bilateral trade, especially agricultural purchases by China. Due to both political reasons and the lack of trade agreements, U.S.-China agricultural trade had been very unstable from 1972 to 1978. In contrast, China agreed to purchase a total of 7.5 million tons of wheat from Australia and 8.4 to 10.5 million tons from Canada from 1980 to 1983.[69] Hinting at a trade agreement with the United States, China told Robert Bergland, secretary of agriculture, during his visit in 1978 that it would like to purchase 5 to 6 million tons of grain from the United States each year if the United States was a reliable supplier.[70] Bergland predicted that agricultural exports to China, which topped $600 million in 1978, would increase further in 1979, to $1 billion.[71]

Another benefit was that it would permit the U.S. government to provide official credit financing for U.S. exports to China. Treasury Deputy Assistant Secretary for Trade and Investment Policy Gary C. Hufbauer noted the importance of export credit financing for U.S. trade in China: "If U.S. exporters are to be competitive with foreign exporters in this extremely important market for Western goods, then it is imperative that the U.S. Government also make available appropriate export financing."[72] The United States lagged considerably behind other Western countries in this respect. In 1979, China had negotiated export credits with France for $7 billion, Great Britain for $5 billion, Canada for $1.9 billion, and Italy for $1 billion. In addition, China and Japan had agreed on a united $2 billion resource development loan, to be financed by Japan's Export-Import Bank. China had also approached Japan for about $3.5 billion in aid loans to finance nine development projects.[73]

The Bureaucratic Role in the Process

Given the administration's goals and interests in developing economic relations with China, bureaucratic agencies were responsible for translating these goals and interests into actual policies. They had their own agenda in creating an economic framework for economic relations with China. The administration initially adopted a strategy consisting of a step-by-step policy process. In a private interview with a government official, Barnett revealed that the U.S government viewed the process as "starting with a solution to the assets and claims problem, then proceeding to an agreement on trade in textile, followed by negotiation of a general trade agreement, after which would come agreement on maritime and aviation links and other matters."[74] It was agreed that an early settlement of textile disputes was preferable or even essential to reaching a trade agreement. However, the importance and complexity of the issue for both countries altered bureaucratic preferences for the agenda. After the asset-claim settlement, the Commerce Department was actually pushing for a trade agreement, while the STR preferred a textile agreement first.

Bureaucratic interests and preferences were important in affecting the negotiations. The STR had been persistently pursuing a textile agreement before trade negotiations and even more so when the administration altered its agenda and decided to go ahead with the negotiations. In fact, U.S. Special Trade Representative Robert Strauss recommended to the president the imposition of textile quotas on five apparel product categories soon after the initiation of the trade agreement. The U.S. imposition of such quotas on imports of Chinese textiles recommended by the STR was also seen as connected with the initiation of the trade agreement.

Another bureaucratic influence was the U.S. officials' views on U.S. foreign policy. Different views within the administration on U.S.-PRC-USSR triangle relations caused a policy debate over U.S.-China economic relations.[75] Some officials felt that U.S. foreign economic policy toward China should parallel that toward the Soviet Union. They saw improving economic relations with China as "playing the China card" to gain greater leverage against the Soviet Union. Secretary Vance, some Soviet specialists at State, and officials from the East-West trade bureau of the Commerce Department argued that the United States should grant MFN status to both countries at about the same time. "A skewed foreign policy," as Vance had argued, would bring about serious consequences in U.S.-Soviet relations.[76] State officials first sought to hold up U.S. efforts to negotiate a trade agreement in early 1979, hoping to reach a trade agreement with the Soviets by trying to obtain Soviet guarantees on its emigration policy at the U.S.-Soviet summit.[77] When this failed, they explored the sentiment of some members of Congress to delay submitting the trade agreement.

Perception of the influence of a "third country" was also a factor in U.S.-China economic policy process.[78] In the case of developing bilateral trade relations, perceptions of Soviet reactions by both China and the United States affected the negotiations and the policy process. China was believed to have compromised in the trade negotiation in May 1979 because it perceived such a move as a counterbalance to a possible Soviet gain in improving relations with the United States as a result of the Carter-Brezhnev summit in June.[79] The United States, on the other hand, was trying to balance its improving economic relations with China with efforts to seek a trade agreement and SALT agreement with the Soviet Union.

In the face of the decline in U.S.-Soviet relations over SALT and Soviet combat troops in Cuba, however, the Carter administration substantially altered its China policy. The United States decided to move ahead in developing further economic relations with China. During his visit to

Beijing in August, Vice President Mondale announced several measures adopted by the administration to improve U.S.-China economic relations.[80]

First, President Carter decided to provide China with U.S. technical services under the terms of section 607(a) of the Foreign Assistance Act of 1961, as amended.[81] This would allow U.S. government agencies to furnish services and commodities on an advance-of-fund or reimbursement basis to China. Second, Mondale pledged to China that the United States would provide China with up to $2 billion in Export-Import Bank credits over the next five years on a case-by-case basis. This would help increase U.S.-China trade. Third, Mondale promised China that the administration would seek investment guarantees from the Overseas Private Investment Corporation (OPIC) for U.S. businesses wishing to invest in China. Lastly, Mondale affirmed to China that the administration would send the long-delayed trade agreement to the Congress and work with supporting members of Congress to gain approval.

Explaining Congressional Behavior

In the congressional approval process of the trade agreement, some members of Congress initially managed to delay the approval process, but Congress subsequently approved the trade agreement overwhelmingly. Why did some members of Congress first successfully delay the process and why did the Congress finally accept the agreement? Two factors were responsible. One was the bureaucratic-congressional coalition for an "evenhanded" foreign policy. The other was the Soviet invasion of Afghanistan.

In developing economic relations with China, some members of Congress, together with members of the executive branch, were concerned with the problem of maintaining a balance in U.S. foreign policy toward Beijing and Moscow. Throughout most of 1979, some leading members of Congress strongly urged the administration to extend MFN status to both China and the Soviet Union. For example, one of the key authors of the Jackson-Vanik amendment, Congressman Vanik, advocated such parallel policy. Senator Adlai E. Stevenson even proposed an amendment to the Jackson-Vanik amendment that might enable the United States to grant MFN status to both China and the Soviet Union.[82] This approach was in compliance with the stance taken by some members of the administration. Secretary Vance was able to exploit congressional sentiment to advance his evenhanded policy toward the Soviet Union. The coalition among officials of the two government branches advocating an evenhanded policy first slowed down the process of negotiating a trade agreement with China and then delayed the submission for congressional approval after the agreement was signed.

Another coalition among members of Congress and the executive that affected the process involved the issue of textile imports. This coalition first encouraged the administration to reach a textile agreement with China before it initiated a trade agreement. When it appeared unlikely to do so, the coalition pressed the administration to take some action on Chinese textile imports. The administration did indeed take unilateral action on Chinese textile imports one week after it submitted the trade agreement to Congress.[83]

The Soviet invasion of Afghanistan in December 1979 had a notable impact on U.S.-China policymaking. It not only strengthened the position of people like Brzezinski and Jackson, who advocated closer U.S.-China ties to gain greater leverage against the Soviet Union, but also changed the perceptions of those who had tended not to distinguish China from the Soviet Union in policymaking and had regarded China and the Soviet Union as the same. The beginning of the new decade saw a shift in policy debate among U.S. policymakers from whether or not the United States should conduct an evenhanded policy toward the Soviet Union to how the United States should deal with Soviet expansionism. The administration formally broke away from its past evenhanded policy and moved toward closer political, economic, and security ties with China. Congress, allied with the administration in face of a foreign policy crisis, approved the long-delayed trade agreement by an overwhelming majority.

Conclusion

Both political and economic factors were important in the formulation of U.S. China economic policy. Politically, the United States regarded normalization of bilateral economic relations as important in strengthening and institutionalizing U.S.-China relations and as serving U.S. foreign policy objectives. Economically, the United States viewed normalizing U.S.-PRC economic relations as beneficial to reducing the U.S. trade deficit, increasing U.S. exports, and establishing U.S. share in the Chinese market. Chinese economic reforms provided tremendous business opportunities for the West to gain access to the Chinese market.

The rational actor model correctly predicted that the United States would develop economic relations with China by extending MFN treatment for U.S. foreign policy goals. The newly normalized Sino-U.S. relations were still fragile, and the passage of the TRA in early 1979 caused a chill in the relationship. It was thus urgent for both countries to make a move to normalize economic relations in order to consolidate the relationship. In this context, developing economic relations was seen as a means to advance foreign policy goals. The United States had used economic means to reach its political objectives since World War II, and the Carter administration made it clear that normalizing economic relations with China would serve U.S. foreign policy interests.

Bureaucratic factors greatly affected the foreign economic policymaking process as well as policy contents. The bureaucracy had expertise and was charged with responsibilities for economic policy recommendations and negotiations. Many foreign economic matters involved technical issues, and bureaucrats were influential in the recommendation and formulation of specific foreign economic policies. This was true for textiles, for example, where the ultimate imposition of quotas on Chinese textile imports evidenced bureaucratic importance in the policy process.

Bureaucratic coalitions with some members of Congress also affected the policy process, if not the outcome, in this case. The delay in submitting the agreement to Congress and in securing approval showed the effect of such a coalition. In the present case, such a coalition was formed largely around the political issue of whether or not the United States should extend MFN status to both China and the Soviet Union at about the same time.

The bureaucratic role in making East-West trade policy, however, was limited by the fact that East-West trade was subordinated to presidential priorities given to other areas, such as security concerns in East-West relations. Very often the bureaucracy was instructed to provide expertise in technical economic matters, make policy recommendations, and carry out negotiations. In making U.S. China economic policy, the bureaucratic role was limited largely for two reasons. One was that it was attached to U.S. foreign policy goals, which the president controlled. The other was the fact that U.S.-China economic relations were new, and a lot of areas had not been institutionalized. Very often, bureaucrats could not decide an apparently economic matter and had to involve high-level political leaders.[84]

The interbranch politics model predicts that China policy would emerge from the interactive process between the executive and the Congress. This was true with the decision to extend MFN status to China. The legislative branch set up the legal framework for foreign trade negotiations. Trade legislation provided guidelines for the executive to reach trade agreements. The executive was actively seeking congressional input in the process. It was trying to build a coalition with some leading members of Congress to gain their approval. Noticeably, the administration worked closely with Senator Jackson on the timing of the submission and on obtaining congressional support for presidential initiatives on normalizing U.S.-China economic relations. The interbranch interactions centered also on the issue of Chinese emigration policy. Deputy Secretary Christopher assured some members of Congress on the issue in his public testimony and in private consultation.

Presidential leadership in the process ensured congressional support for the MFN decision. The trade case provided a good illustration of how presidential factors affected the policy process and outcome in two aspects.[85] First, President Carter used his formal power—power to enter into executive agreements with foreign countries—to authorize negotiations with China on trade. He then took the lead in the process by sending his letter to the

Speaker of the House and his message to Congress. Second, President Carter's use of a loophole in the Jackson-Vanik amendment to waive the emigration requirement, and his persuasiveness in the process, also ensured the approval of the agreement.

Decisionmakers' calculation of a "third country's" influence also affected the U.S. China economic policymaking process. For example, the policy process and decisions to delay negotiations were interlinked with the state of U.S.-Soviet relations. Changes either in U.S.-Soviet or Sino-Soviet relations could have had perceptual and psychological effects on U.S. policymakers in China policymaking.

International events can influence U.S. China policymaking in three ways. First, they can affect the pattern of interbranch interaction in the policy process, giving the executive more leverage in China policymaking. Second, serious international events can also help change policymakers' perceptions of U.S. strategic interests. Third, they can alter congressional alignments on certain issues. For example, the Soviet invasion of Afghanistan resulted in the shift of many members of Congress from maintaining an "evenhanded" foreign policy toward both China and the Soviet Union to supporting the executive's China initiatives. In an international crisis, members of Congress tend to rally around the president and comply with the executive's priorities. In the trade case, normalizing economic relations with China was made the executive priority after Mondale's visit to China. Congress did not quite comply with that priority until the Afghanistan event.

In sum, the rational actor model is most helpful in understanding the rationale of U.S. initiation of the trade agreement that granted MFN status to China. The bureaucratic politics model and the interbranch politics model are useful in explaining the terms and contents of the agreement (see Figure 3.4). The three models are not mutually exclusive; rather they supplement each other once a broader consensus on U.S. China economic goals was achieved.

Figure 3.4   The Decisionmaking Process for China Trade Policy

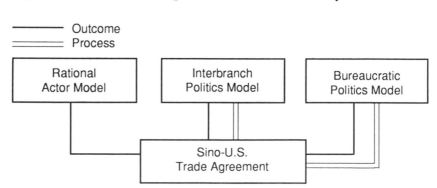

Notes

1. For the full text of the trade agreement, see U.S. Congress, House, *Agreement on Trade Relations Between the United States and the People's Republic of China: Communication from the President of the United States Transmitting Proclamation Extending Non-discriminatory Trade Treatment to the Products of the People's Republic of China, Together with Related Reports, Pursuant to Section 407 of the Trade Act of 1974*, House Document 209, 96th Cong., 1st sess., 1979.

2. Benjamin J. Cohen, ed., *American Foreign Economic Policy: Essays and Comments* (New York: Harper and Row, 1968), pp. 1, 10.

3. Pastor, *Congress and the Politics of U.S. Foreign Economic Policy*, p. 12.

4. Ibid., p. 5.

5. Congress, House, Subcommittee on International Trade and Commerce of the Committee on International Relations, *Trading with the Enemy: Legislative and Executive Documents Concerning Regulation of International Transactions in Time of Declared National Emergency*, 94th Cong., 2nd sess., 1976.

6. United States, *An Act to Extend the Authorities Under the Export Administration Act of 1979, and for Other Purposes*, Public Law 98–207 (Washington, D.C.: Government Printing Office, 1983).

7. Congressional Quarterly Almanac, *Trade: U.S. Policy Since 1945* (Washington, D.C.: Congressional Quarterly, 1984), p. 103.

8. *Congressional Quarterly Weekly Report*, March 3, 1979, p. 357.

9. The text can be found in *Trade Act of 1974*, Public Law 93–618, *United States Statutes at Large*, vol. 88, part 2 (Washington, D.C.: Government Printing Office, 1976).

10. Congressional Quarterly Almanac, *Trade: U.S. Policy Since 1945*, p. 101.

11. Thompson, "On the Making of U.S.-China Policy."

12. Congressional Quarterly Almanac, *Trade: U.S. Policy Since 1945*, p. 124.

13. One of the main reasons that Japan and Western Europe were able to explore the Chinese market successfully was that their governments played an important role in financing their trade with China. Realizing that the United States lagged behind Japan and Western Europe, many U.S. businesses were eager to have official relations with China.

14. William Clarke, "Commercial Implications of Normalization," *The International Trade Law Journal* 5, no. 1 (Fall-Winter 1979), p. 95.

15. *Congressional Quarterly Weekly Report*, March 3, 1979, p. 359.

16. The Four Modernizations Program was first put forth by Premier Chou En-lai in 1975 as a program to modernize agriculture, industry, national defense, and science and technology. After Chou's death and the downfall of the "Gang of Four," a revised outline of the program was announced by Premier Hua Guofeng and approved by the Fifth National People's Congress in March 1978. Again, in December 1978, the Central Committee of the CCP revised the order of economic priorities—agriculture, light industry, and heavy industry—which had been the official policy since the early 1970s, but not always carried out. The new program called for reducing the share of state investment in heavy industry and increasing investment in agriculture and light industry. For further reading on the PRC's economic policy, see Congress, Joint Economic Committee, *China Under the Four Modernizations: Selected Papers Submitted to Joint Economic Committee*, 97th Cong., 2nd sess., 1982.

17. Congress, Senate, Subcommittee on Foreign Agricultural Policy of the Committee on Agriculture, Nutrition, and Forestry, *Agricultural Trade with the People's Republic of China and Taiwan: Hearing Before the Subcommittee on*

Foreign Agricultural Policy of the Committee on Agriculture, Nutrition, and Forestry, 96th Cong., 1st sess., March 13, 1979, p. 23.

18. Congress, House, Subcommittee on Trade of the Committee on Ways and Means, *United States–China Trade Agreement: Hearings Before the Subcommittee on Trade of the Committee on Ways and Means, House of Representatives,* 96th. Cong., 1st sess., 1979, p. 17.

19. Ibid., p. 49.

20. The Council was set up to promote U.S.-China economic relations and help provide business information concerning both countries.

21. Ibid., p. 17.

22. Hobart Rowen, "U.S. Signs Pact to Grant China Favored Status," *Washington Post,* July 8, 1979, p. 1. Another Commerce Department paper studied the development of projects in some of the areas necessary for the four modernizations. It suggested that U.S. business might be involved in the years to come in major construction projects such as mines and processing facilities for nonferrous metals and minerals, including aluminum, chrome, cobalt, molybdenum, phosphate, and tin; coal mines, both open pit and shaft; iron ore mines; steel mills; ports; railroads and electrification of lines; thermal power plants (1,000MW and above); and hydroelectric power plants and dams. Also suggested were manufacturing facilities for electronic components; agricultural chemicals; construction materials, including cement, timber and wood products, insulation materials, plastics and synthetics used in construction; transportation equipment and assembly, including locomotives, railcars, and trucks; construction equipment and vehicles; agricultural equipment; and consumer products, including small appliances and specialty products. See Congress, House, *United States-China Trade Agreement,* p. 17.

23. Gary R. Teske, Hedija H. Kravalis, and Allen J. Lenz, "U.S. Trade with China: Prospects Through 1985," *Business America* (February 12, 1979), p. 6.

24. Ibid., pp. 6–7.

25. Prior to 1951, the United States had MFN relations with all countries. After the outbreak of the Korean War, Congress withdrew MFN treatment from all socialist countries but Yugoslavia. In 1960, President Eisenhower restored MFN relations with Poland. In 1974, Congress passed the Trade Act Title IV of the Trade Act of 1974 authorizing the president to extend, under certain conditions, nondiscriminatory (MFN) tariff treatment to the products of countries not receiving such treatment, which excluded Yugoslavia and Poland. The only socialist nations that entered MFN relations with the United States under the provisions of Title IV were Romania and Hungary.

26. The Trade Act of 1974 was first introduced by the Nixon administration as the Trade Reform Act in 1973. After being substantially changed by the Ways and Means Committee, it was approved by the Congress in December 1974 and was signed by President Ford on January 3, 1975.

27. Kenneth H. Bacon, "U.S. China Initial Accord to Widen Trade But Benefits Are Not Expected for a While," *Wall Street Journal,* May 15, 1979, p. 8.

28. A. Doak Barnett, *China's Economy in Global Perspective* (Washington, D.C.: Brookings Institution, 1981), p. 522.

29. Jay Mathews, "Kreps Hopeful on Claims Accord, Doubtful on Sino-U.S. Trade Pact," *Washington Post,* May 10, 1979, p. 37.

30. Interview by author with a Commerce Department official who participated in the negotiation (name unattributable), Washington, D.C., July 16, 1987.

31. For further reading, see John R. Garson, "The American Trade Embargo Against China," in Alexander Eckstein, ed., *China Trade Prospects and U.S.*

Policy (New York: Praeger for the National Committee on United States–China Relations, 1971).

32. See Congress, House, *United States–China Trade Agreement*, pp. 20–22.

33. See "Claims-Assets Settlement," *China Business Review* 6, no. 1 (January-February 1979), pp. 50–51. This figure was the early estimate. The final estimate on the assets in 1979 totaled approximately $80.5 million. See Congress, House, *United States–China Trade Agreement*, p. 21.

34. Congress had insisted on a settlement that would pay a minimum of about forty cents on the dollar to U.S. claimants in previous cases involving socialist countries such as Czechoslovakia.

35. See Hobart Rowen, "Blumenthal, in China, Foresees Closer Trade Ties" and "U.S. Closer to Trade Treaty with China," *Washington Post*, February 25, p. 24, March 3, 1979, p. D8.

36. Under the agreement, China would pay an amount equal to the value of Chinese assets blocked in the United States totaling $80.5 million; the U.S. government would then pay U.S. claimants about forty-one cents on the dollar. The procedures in the agreement were highly advantageous to the United States since China agreed to pay cash to the U.S. government first. Then it had to collect the frozen assets by itself, most of which would probably have to be settled through U.S. courts. For Text of Claims/Assets Agreement, see Congress, House, *United States–China Trade Agreement*, p. 55.

37. Testimony by Ambassador Reubin O'D Askew, special representative for trade negotiations; see Congress, House, *United States–China Trade Agreement*, pp. 127–132.

38. Barnett, *China's Economy in Global Perspective*, pp. 518–519.

39. Jay Mathews, "China and U.S. Initial Accord Aiding Trade," *Washington Post*, May 15, 1979, p. 20.

40. Before the United States took unilateral action, U.S. Special Trade Representative Robert Strauss presented China a U.S.-termed textile agreement as an ultimatum. He gave the Chinese three days to accept or reject the U.S. position. He indicated that if it were rejected, he would advise President Carter to take action. See "Strauss Holds Little Hope for Chinese Textile Pact," *Washington Post*, May 29, 1979, p. D7.

41. Rowen, "U.S. Signs Pact to Grant China Favored Status," p. 1.

42. In fact, this was on President Carter's agenda at the Soviet-U.S. summit in June 1979. But Carter failed to obtain from Soviet President Leonid I. Brezhnev an explicit assurance on continued Jewish emigration. See John M. Goshko, "Carter Will Seek Favored Status For China Trade," *Washington Post*, July 4, 1979, p. 22.

43. Don Oberdorfer, "U.S. Moves to Grant Soviets Trade and Tariff Benefits," *Washington Post*, May 17, 1979, p. 1; Bernard Gwertzman, "U.S. Seeking Pledge Soviet Union Won't Curb Rate of Emigration," *New York Times*, May 18, 1979, p. 1. See also U.S. Congress, House, Subcommittee on Asian and Pacific Affairs of Committee on Foreign Affairs, *Playing the China Card: Implications for United States-Soviet-Chinese Relations: Report Prepared for the Subcommittee on Asian and Pacific Affairs of Committee on Foreign Affairs, U.S. House of Representatives*, 96th Cong., 1st sess., 1979, pp. 20–21.

44. The specific remarks made by Deng Xiaoping to Senator Jackson on the trade agreement indicated that China had trade a high priority in Sino-U.S. relations. See Jay Mathews, "Jackson Says Peking Dissatisfied About Trade Status," *Washington Post*, August 25, 1979, p. 18.

45. *Weekly Compilation of Presidential Documents*, vol. 15, no. 42, December 15, 1979, p. 2000. The trade agreement contained four major

provisions: ending discriminatory tariff treatment and granting most-favorable-nation status to each other; facilitating business activities, including the stationing of business representatives and the establishment of business offices and improvement in the conditions under which these offices operated; providing for reciprocal and equivalent protection of patents, trademarks, and copyrights; and settling bilateral commercial disputes, including market disruption due to rapidly rising imports and promoting trade and other commercial arrangements.

46. Such disapproval actions can be country specific, i.e., the resolution may disapprove the extension of the waiver authority in general or with regard to one or more specific countries.

47. Hobart Rowen, "U.S. to Hold China Treaty Until a Textile Pact Is Secured," *Washington Post*, May 16, 1979, p. 1.

48. Mathews, "Jackson Says Peking Dissatisfied About Trade Status"; Robert Parry, "China Pact Hits Snag on Emigration," *Washington Post*, November 2, 1979, D2.

49. Robert G. Kaiser, "Trade Benefits for Russia, China Eyed," *Washington Post*, January 5, 1979, p. 8; Parry, "China Pact Hits Snag on Emigration."

50. Vanik made the remark in his opening statement at the House hearing on the trade agreement. See Congress, House, *United States–China Trade Agreement*, p. 2.

51. Parry, "China Pact Hits Snag on Emigration."

52. It was said that Deng Xiaoping silenced Carter by replying to his question that China could send 10 million immigrants to the United States to satisfy its immigration policy.

53. Senator Goldwater cautioned against playing the "China card" to counter the Soviet Union. He stated that "communist China is no proven friend that can be counted on to rescue the United States from the threat of the Soviet Union." Senator George McGovern asserted that the United States should not appear to be committing itself to defending China in all confrontations between China and the Soviet Union.

Proponents argued to the contrary that approving the trade agreement would punish the Soviet Union for its invasion of Afghanistan. Guy Vander Jagty maintained that any improvement of U.S.-PRC relations would be "a greater deterrent to continued Soviet aggression than the Olympic boycott and the grain embargoes combined" (*Congressional Quarterly Almanac*, 1980, p. 357).

On the issue of potential market disruption, Congressman Robert Bauman argued that China wanted to buy U.S. technology while flooding the U.S. market with consumer goods (*Congressional Quarterly Weekly Report*, February 2, 1980, p. 310). Senator William Roth counterargued that the agreement provided "important protection for domestic industry against potentially unfair competition from low-priced imports such as textile or footwear from China" (p. 310). Congressman Larry McDonald opposed the agreement on the ground that the district he represented would "be grievously hurt by imports of textiles and carpets" from China (Congress, House, *United States–China Trade Agreement*, p. 148).

54. Congress, House, Committee on Ways and Means, *Approving the Extension of Nondiscriminatory Treatment to the Products of the People's Republic of China*, H.R. 96-733, 96th Cong., 1st sess., 1979, p. 11. Bauman asserted that the United States had no assurances from China that the Jackson-Vanik amendment would be observed. He complained about the way the executive handled the issue, stating that "we have only the statement of the Carter administration that confidential assurances have been given, so confidential that

Congress cannot see them" (*Congressional Quarterly Weekly Report*, February 2, 1980, p. 310)

55. See F. D. Holzman and R. Legvold, "The Economics and Politics of East-West Relations," in C. F. Bergsten and L. B. Krause, eds., *World Politics and International Economics* (Washington, D.C.: Brookings Institution, 1975), pp. 275–322.

56. Rosalie L. Tung, *U.S.-China Trade Negotiations* (New York: Pergamon Press, 1982), p. 20.

57. Quoted by Holzman and Legvold in "The Economics and Politics of East-West Relations," p. 294.

58. Barnett, *China's Economy in Global Perspective*, p. 495.

59. Congress, Senate, Subcommittee on International Trade of the Committee on Finance, *Agreement on Trade Relations Between the United States and People's Republic of China: Hearings Before the Subcommittee on International Trade of the Committee on Finance*, 96th Cong., 1st sess., November 1979, p. 28.

60. *Pacific Basin Quarterly*, December 1979, p. 4.

61. "Chinese Trade Pact Is Sent to Congress," *New York Times*, October 24, 1979, p. 1.

62. Walter Mondale's speech at Beijing University, *Department of State Bulletin* 79, no. 2031 (October 1979), p. 11.

63. When Chinese leader Deng Xiaoping visited the United States in January, he spent most of his time meeting business leaders and visiting major plants in such industrial cities as Atlanta, Houston, Seattle, and Los Angeles. His trip was widely hailed by the U.S. press as "Deng's American Business Trip. " Both Vice Premier Deng and President Carter engaged in the process of expanding and institutionalizing economic, scientific, and technological cooperation. As a result, U.S. and Chinese leaders signed several new agreements on January 31, 1979. Except for a cultural agreement and an agreement on consular relations, the remaining agreements called for cooperation in agriculture, energy, space, health, environment, earth science, and engineering, and for broad educational and scientific exchanges of students, scholars, and information. See Barnett, *China's Economy in Global Perspective*, p. 518.

64. Mondale's speech.

65. Congressional Quarterly, *Trade: U.S. Policy Since 1945*, p. 125.

66. Ibid.

67. Ibid.

68. Susanna McBee, "Strauss: China Business Needed to Help U.S. Overcome $30 Billion Trade Deficit," *Washington Post*, January 8, 1979, p. 6.

69. Congress, Senate, *Agricultural Trade with the People's Republic of China and Taiwan*, p. 8.

70. Ibid., p. 19.

71. Ibid, p. 7.

72. Congress, Senate, *Agreement on Trade Relations Between the United States and the People's Republic of China*, p. 63.

73. Ibid.

74. See Barnett, *China's Economy in Global Perspective*, footnote 84 in Chapter 5.

75. For background on the "playing the China card" debate and a review of different views on the issue, see Congress, House, *Playing the China Card*.

76. Don Oberdorfer, "Trade Benefits for China Are Approved by Carter," *Washington Post*, October 24, 1979, p. 2.

77. Congress, House, *Playing the China Card*, p. 15. Also see Kaiser, "Trade Benefits for Russia, China Eyed."

78. U.S.-China relations had been susceptible to a third country's influence in the past. U.S.-China relations drastically deteriorated when both countries were involved in the Korean War. The improvement of bilateral relations was again tied to the Vietnam War in the 1960s when there was a relaxation of East-West relations. The normalization process was started largely due to the Sino-Soviet split and, in the course of the process, U.S. China policy was influenced by Soviet behavior and the state of U.S.-Soviet relations. For detailed analysis on the point, see Garrett, "China Policy and the Constraints of Triangular Logic."

79. See Congress, House, *Playing the China Card*, footnote 24, p. 17.

80. Congress, House, Committee on Foreign Affairs, *Executive-Legislative Consultations on China Policy, 1978–79* (Washington, D.C.: Government Printing Office, 1980), pp. 13-16.

81. This section limited such aid to what the United States considered "friendly" countries. China was later officially acknowledged as a "friendly" country by the Reagan administration.

82. For the summary of the Stevenson amendments, see Congress, Senate, *Agreement on Trade Relations Between the United States and the People's Republic of China*, p. 23.

83. Special Representative for Trade Negotiations Askew, in answering Congressman Schulze's question, acknowledged that those quotas on Chinese textile imports were made out of political considerations. Without quotas, the administration would have had a difficult time getting the agreement through Congress. See his testimony in Congress, House, *United States–China Trade Agreement*, pp. 127–139.

84. For example, the trade negotiations came to a standstill when both sides could not reconcile their differences over patent protection, and it was finally solved by Deng's interference. Another example was that U.S.-China textile disputes often caused concerns for the leadership of both countries.

85. There are two theories of presidential power, one emphasizing formal presidential power (the president's constitutional authority), the other stressing informal power (the president's political skill and influence and willingness to invest resources). Both theories suggest that the presidential craft of using constitutional authority and informal power can greatly influence policy processes and outcomes. See Richard M. Pious, *The American Presidency* (New York: Basic Books, 1979); Richard E. Neustadt, *Presidential Power: The Politics of Leadership from FDR to Carter* (New York: John Wiley and Sons, 1980).

4

Arms Sales Crisis and
Crisis Management, 1981–1982

Few issues could have more serious effects on Sino-U.S. relations than arms sales to Taiwan. Despite the fact that the United States shared with China common interests in most areas of international affairs, arms sales to Taiwan remained a major issue of contention in U.S.-PRC relations. Between 1981 and 1982, the decision made by the Reagan administration to sell arms to Taiwan stirred China's concern about a possible change in U.S. Taiwan policy. China reacted strongly to the arms sales decision and the issue was transformed into a crisis threatening the continuation of U.S.-China diplomatic relations. The crisis was finally resolved when the two countries signed a joint communiqué on August 17, 1982. U.S. intentions regarding arms sales are stated in the following exerpt:

> The United States Government states that it does not seek to carry out a long-term policy of arms sales to Taiwan, that its arms sales to Taiwan will not exceed, either in qualitative or in quantitative terms, the level of those supplied in recent years since the establishment of diplomatic relations between the United States and China, and that it intends to reduce gradually its sales of arms to Taiwan, leading over a period of time to a final resolution.[1]

This statement was a compromise in terms of the original intentions of both countries. China initially demanded that the United States establish a specific date by which arms sales to Taiwan would cease. The United States agreed to terminate arms sales, but did not commit itself to ending arms sales to Taiwan on a specified date. How and why did arms sales become an issue affecting U.S.-China relations? How and why did the two countries reach an agreement on the arms sales issue? This chapter will examine the arms sales process and offer some answers to these questions.

U.S.-China Disputes over Arms Sales to Taiwan

U.S. arms sales to Taiwan were an unresolved issue left over from normalization of U.S.-PRC relations in 1978. The Carter administration took a low-key approach to arms sales to Taiwan and tried not to let arms sales affect U.S.-China relations. Arms sales became a sensitive and prominent issue for the Reagan administration and evolved into the first crisis in U.S.-China relations since normalization.

Arms Sales by the Carter Administration

During the normalization process, arms sales to Taiwan had been a sensitive issue for decisionmakers of both countries. The Carter administration was pressured by conservative political forces in Congress to provide Taiwan with security guarantees, and President Carter felt that continuation of arms sales to Taiwan after normalization was a way of not abandoning Taiwan and a necessary condition to win congressional support for his China initiatives.[2] China, on the other hand, insisted that Taiwan was a part of China and matters related to Taiwan were Chinese internal affairs. U.S. arms sales to Taiwan, according to this view, interfered with China's internal affairs and ran counter to U.S. efforts to normalize relations between the two countries.

Because both governments had given normalization high priority, the United States and China reached an understanding on the arms sales issue in the last days of the negotiations. Both countries agreed to disagree on U.S. policy regarding arms sales to Taiwan while normalizing diplomatic relations. Chinese leader Deng Xiaoping, on receiving U.S. negotiator Leonard Woodcock on December 14, 1978, agreed that normalization could proceed even though the two countries disagreed on the issue of arms sales to Taiwan.[3] At the postnormalization news conference, the Chinese leader Hua Guofeng stated: "During the negotiations, the U.S. side mentioned that after normalization it would continue to sell limited amounts of arms to Taiwan for defensive purposes. We made it clear that we resolutely would not agree to this. . . . So our two sides had differences on this point. Nevertheless, we reached an agreement on the joint communiqué."[4]

As compromised, the United States did not state its position on arms sales to Taiwan in the formal U.S. statement issued on December 15, 1978. Instead, the Carter administration stated:

> The United States is confident that the people of Taiwan face a peaceful and prosperous future. The United States continues to have an interest in the peaceful resolution of the Taiwan issue and expects that the Taiwan issue will be settled peacefully by the Chinese themselves.[5]

The Chinese government agreed not to contradict the U.S. statement on the peaceful resolution of the Taiwan issue. Although China refused to make an explicit commitment not to use force to resolve the Taiwan issue, the Chinese government indicated a willingness to use peaceful means by not contradicting the U.S. statement.[6] The subtle change of the Chinese position obviously resulted from Beijing's belief that the U.S. government would reduce and eventually stop selling arms to Taiwan if China continued its peaceful reunification initiatives.[7]

Arms sales to Taiwan during the Carter administration were under close scrutiny by President Carter, due to the priorities given by both countries to strengthen political and economic ties.[8] He clearly did not want arms sales to complicate his normalization efforts. He turned down the recommendation made by the departments of State and Defense in mid-1978 to allow Taiwan to coproduce a new fighter aircraft (designated the F-5G) with the U.S. Northrop Corporation.[9] Instead, he approved a policy that allowed for the coproduction of several dozen more F-5E aircraft in Taiwan from 1980 to 1983.[10]

After normalization, the Carter administration conducted a careful arms sales policy toward Taiwan. On the one hand, it tried not to provoke Beijing by observing the one-year moratorium on arms sales to Taiwan and rejecting Taiwan's request for advanced arms. On the other hand, it transferred more than a billion dollars worth of arms to Taiwan. During 1979, the Carter administration sold Taiwan $800 million worth of arms already contracted for by Taiwan. The United States delivered military equipment and pipelines as well as spare parts and follow-on support for items previously supplied to Taiwan. Those arms included additional F-5E interceptors with improved weaponry, such as precision guided munitions and Maverick missiles.[11]

In 1979, the Carter administration deferred consideration of new arms requests in keeping with the U.S. moratorium. It continued to defer making decisions on requests from Taiwan to purchase advanced FX fighters.[12] However, on January 2, 1980, the administration sent prenotifications to Congress to sell $280 million in arms. The package included an additional battalion of I-Hawk antiaircraft missiles; an improved version of the Sea Chapparral ship antiaircraft missile; TOW antitank missiles; a shipboard weapons fire control system along with 76mm rapid-firing guns; and an improved electronic identification system to safeguard fighter aircraft against antiaircraft fire.[13]

Several members of Congress expressed their concern about the administration's neglect of Taiwan's repeated requests for permission to purchase more advanced U.S. planes. In mid-1980, seven members of the Senate Foreign Relations Committee sent a letter to President Carter, urging him to consider the Taiwan requests.[14] Senator Richard Stone, one of the signers of the letter, asserted on June 12 that the administration, in reply to the letter, had decided to allow U.S. companies to discuss with Taiwan sales of more advanced planes.[15] However, the Carter administration made no decisions on sales of more advanced aircraft to Taiwan, leaving the FX decision a pending issue for the Reagan administration.

Reagan's Campaign Rhetoric

The arms sales issue had been linked with broader U.S. policy toward China, which was often complicated by ideology, emotions, and political reality. The issue was a part of the whole process of China policymaking. U.S. China policy had frequently been an issue in U.S. national elections. In the 1948 presidential election, U.S. China policy was an intensely debated issue as to "who lost China." In the 1980 election, U.S. China policy was again an issue in the presidential debate. This time the debate focused on U.S. Taiwan policy. Presidential candidate Reagan criticized the ill treatment of Taiwan, "an old friend and an ally," and promised that he would restore "official relations between the United States and Taiwan," if he was elected.[16]

Reagan's campaign speeches caused the Chinese grave concern about future U.S. Taiwan policy. The Chinese commentary sharply criticized Reagan's speeches, warning him not to "turn back the clock."[17] As a gesture to reassure the Beijing government of a continuous U.S. China policy under a Republican administration, George Bush, former head of the U.S. liaison office in Beijing, was sent to China.

Bush's visit hardly reassured Beijing of a Reagan presidency's China policy. Candidate Reagan continued to make contradictory statements regarding his position on the Taiwan issue. Just before Bush's departure on August 16, 1980, a news conference was held in Los Angeles in which Reagan expressed his support for Bush's mission. However, when he was asked about U.S. relations with Taiwan, Reagan replied that he thought those relations ought to be conducted on a "government-to-government" basis.[18]

Immediately after Bush's return from his China mission, on August 25, Reagan asserted in a formal statement:

> I felt that a condition of normalization, by itself a sound policy choice, should have the retention of a liaison office on Taiwan of equivalent status to the one we had earlier established at Beijing. . . . I would not pretend that the relationship we now have with Taiwan . . . is not official. . . . It is absurd and not required by the [Taiwan Relations] Act that our representatives are not permitted to meet with Taiwanese officials with fairness and dignity.[19]

The FX Decision by the Reagan Administration

One of Reagan's campaign themes was his promise to carry out the TRA's provisions of arms sales to Taiwan. This immediately became an issue in Sino-U.S. relations because it was perceived by officials of both sides as a test of Reagan's China policy. China was sensitive to arms sales to Taiwan for three reasons. First, Chinese officials regarded such sales as an infringement upon their sovereignty. Second, they saw such sales as an attempt to pursue a two-Chinas policy. Third, they viewed such a move as encouraging Taiwan to resist their peaceful drive for reunification. On the other hand, Reagan's conservative supporters in the administration and the Congress perceived arms sales as a commitment by Reagan to advance their ideological, anticommunist interests. Reagan himself, being an "old friend" of Taiwan, was driven by his ideology and emotion to favor such sales.

Arms sales to Taiwan before the Reagan administration had been a relatively quiet issue. President Carter gave priority to his foreign policy objective of improving relations with China and was reluctant to deal with Taiwan on arms sales. He fulfilled his promise of no arms sales to Taiwan in 1979, and in January 1980 he rejected Taiwan's request for advanced military equipment (including new jet fighters and missiles), although he approved some innocuous arms sales at the same time. His Taiwan policies drew congressional criticism of his administration's implementation of the TRA. Under congressional pressure, Carter approved some arms sales and before leaving office allowed U.S. arms contractors to discuss with Taiwan possible sales of advanced fighters. [20]

As Reagan entered into office, Taiwan's requests for advanced FX planes and other advanced weapons systems worth $96 million were still pending. Neither request had yet been approved or denied by the new administration. Beijing was fully aware of Reagan's position on the Taiwan issue and wanted to take no chance of showing the slightest tolerance on the arms sales issue. China forewarned the United States by downgrading its diplomatic relations with the Netherlands to the level of chargé d'affaires after the Dutch sale of two submarines to Taiwan in February 1981. [21]

To ease Chinese anxiety over Reagan's China policy, Secretary Haig arranged a meeting between Chinese ambassador Chai Zemin and President Reagan shortly after the new administration was formed. Reagan, however, further perplexed the Chinese about his stance on Taiwan by telling the ambassador that he wanted good relations with China but that he would not desert his old friends. [22] This ambiguous statement was later elaborated on by presidential counselor Edwin Meese, who said that the Reagan administration was "committed" to selling advanced weapons to Taiwan. The State Department confirmed this policy as being "standard United States policy." [23]

All those statements encouraged Taiwan to take advantage of the political atmosphere surrounding the administration. Since the decision to approve sales of advanced arms was in the making, Taiwan intended to influence U.S. Taiwan policymaking by refusing to make a choice between the F-5G (Northrop's improved version of the F-5E) and the F-16/J79 (General Dynamics' scaled-down version of the F-16). Taiwan instead informed the U.S. government that it would accept any combination of the two models. [24] Taiwan's repeated requests for advanced arms caused a heated debate among U.S. decisionmakers, which further aroused Chinese anxiety about future U.S. arms sales. Beijing bluntly stated that China opposed arms sales to Taiwan, and nothing could compromise China's position on this issue.[25]

Secretary Haig's visit to Beijing in mid-June 1981 hardly reassured the Chinese leaders of Reagan's Taiwan policy. Deng Xiaoping, in his meeting with Haig on his final day in Beijing, compared U.S. arms sales to Taiwan to the British policy of supplying munitions to the Confederacy during the U.S. Civil War. For the first time, Deng indicated that U.S. arms sales, if they went too far, would have an adverse effect on Sino-U.S. relations.[26] The Chinese had reasons for such a warning, because on the same day Haig met with Deng, Reagan at a press conference again asserted, "I have not changed my feelings about Taiwan," and "I intend to live up to the Taiwan Relations Act."[27]

China's pressure on the Taiwan issue mounted after Haig's trip to Beijing. In July, U.S. Ambassador Arthur W. Hummel, Jr., received a demarche from the Chinese Foreign Ministry indicating that continued U.S. arms sales to Taiwan would cause strong Chinese reaction that could affect U.S.-China strategic relations. In the meantime, China ignored a U.S. offer of possible arms sales.[28] The postponement of a senior Chinese military official's visit to the United States showed that China would not separate its strategic relations with the United States from the Taiwan issue. China solemnly characterized the arms sales issue as "a shadow that hangs over Sino-American relations."[29]

The serious Chinese concern over the arms sales to Taiwan was once again conveyed to President Reagan by Chinese Premier Zhao Ziyang when they attended a summit meeting of North-South leaders at Cancún, Mexico, in October 1981. The Chinese leader made it clear that China wanted a long-term strategic relationship with the United States, but Taiwan was a problem. To assure the United States of China's sincerity in its peace initiatives, Zhao revealed to Reagan that China was taking an important approach in resolving the Taiwan issue. The new Chinese nine-point plan for reunification promised to let Taiwan keep virtually everything intact except its flag.[30]

Reagan did not seem to be impressed by the Chinese initiatives and again reiterated his position on keeping good relations with China and Taiwan as well. However, what was not conveyed to Reagan was that behind the plan, China wanted to resolve the arms sales issue.[31] The proposal was officially put forward by Foreign Minister Huang Hua on October 29 during his visit to Washington. The proposal contained three points: first, the United States must specify the period of time over which it wanted to sell arms to Taiwan; second, such arms sales in any given year should not exceed the level of the Carter years and should decrease year by year; third, the United States should specify a date by which it would terminate arms sales altogether.[32] The Chinese proposal offered a starting point for both countries to reach an agreement on the arms sales issue. On December 4, talks began in Beijing between U.S. Ambassador Hummel and Vice Foreign Minister Zhang.

The Defense Department had conducted an expert study on arms sales in mid-November and concluded that Taiwan did not need the FX fighter planes for its defense needs. Instead, it recommended extension of the F-5E coproduction line in Taiwan.[33] The administration held back the Defense Department recommendation and went ahead with the decision to sell an assortment of spare parts to Taiwan. On December 29, the United States announced that it was going to sell military spare parts worth $97 million to Taiwan.[34] The sale by itself was qualitatively and quantitatively insignificant, and the State Department called it "a routine transaction." However, it took place during the negotiations and before the FX decision. Thus, the decision took on special importance. This "trial balloon" move by the United States caused an exceptionally strong reaction from China. Foreign Minister Huang Hua immediately stated that "the Chinese government resolutely opposes the U.S. sale of weapons to Taiwan." He demanded that the U.S. government "clarify its decision to sell arms parts to Taiwan."[35]

This arms sales decision confirmed Beijing's belief that arms sales were not simply Reagan's campaign rhetoric, but the policy of the administration to enhance U.S.-Taiwan relations. If China did not firmly oppose this arms sale, Chinese officials believed, the United States would soon sell more arms to Taiwan. Therefore, China felt it was time to put an end to the whole issue. A commentary in the official newspaper, *People's Daily*, on December 31 stated: "Not only is the U.S. Government prepared to continue selling arms to Taiwan, it is in fact considering an escalation of this action and has even declared that China has no right to interfere in the matter. In this way the gravity of the problem is increased and, as a result, the problem has now reached a point where it absolutely must be solved."[36] This authoritative commentary restated the Chinese opposition to the arms sale in the strongest terms and pointed out that the arms sale violated the principles of the normalization communiqué and interfered in Chinese internal affairs. The article criticized the United States for not responding to Beijing's peace initiatives by seizing the improved situation on the Taiwan Strait to cease arms sales to Taiwan. It also criticized the United States for escalating the problem of arms sales.[37]

The commentary further challenged U.S. sincerity in developing strategic relations with China. It pointed out that the Chinese government had always viewed and handled Sino-U.S. relations from the angle of global strategy. Now it was a crucial test for the U.S. government to solve the issue of arms sales with a vision of global strategy.[38]

The strong Chinese reaction to the U.S. "test" sent a clear signal that any further sales of arms to Taiwan would result in diplomatic retrogression. The commentary was effective in ending the Reagan administration's maneuver to sell advanced arms to Taiwan. The administration finally reached a decision on the FX fighter planes. The State Department announced on January 11, 1982, that the United States would not sell advanced fighter aircraft to Taiwan. Instead, it would extend the F-5G coproduction line in Taiwan.[39] This decision was actually what the Defense Department had recommended earlier in November.

The FX decision, as viewed by the U.S. government, was a compromise on the arms sales issue. According to the administration's logic, the United States would not sell advanced arms to Taiwan, but it would sell certain arms, including airplanes, in return. However, this logic was rejected by the Chinese government. The center of the issue was not the level of arms sales but the issue of infringing on China's sovereignty by selling arms to one part of the country. Beijing made it clear to U.S. special envoy Assistant Secretary of State John Holdridge, who was dispatched to China to explain the FX decision, that "the whole question of U.S. arms sales to Taiwan is a major issue affecting China's sovereignty. . . . The Chinese government will never accept any unilateral decision made by the U.S. government."[40] China regarded the FX decision as U.S. intent to keep the status quo rather than to resolve the issue of arms sales to Taiwan.

The Crisis and the August 17 Joint Communiqué

The purpose of Holdridge's special trip to Beijing was to continue exploring ways to resolve the arms sales issue. The fact that the sale was announced on the day of Holdridge's arrival in Beijing only made China more determined to press the United States for a solution. Holdridge presented to the Chinese a list of principles that the United States believed could form the basis of an agreement resolving the arms sales issue once and for all. It was apparent that the United States was hoping for an early settlement, preferably before the tenth anniversary of the Shanghai Communiqué. Despite the exchanges of many new drafts of the proposed joint communiqué in the early months of 1982, differences remained large and no agreement could be reached before the communiqué's tenth anniversary.[41] The anniversary of the unresolved arms sales issue was marked by Reagan's initiation of an exchange of letters between Zhao and himself; neither letter mentioned the arms sale or strategic cooperation.[42] In Washington, Ambassador Chai Zemin hosted former President Nixon, whom China had reportedly been planning to invite to Beijing to take part in the tenth anniversary celebration.[43] The low-key celebrations were further highlighted by a Chinese commentary charging that "if the United States insists on a long-term policy of selling arms to Taiwan, Sino-U.S. relations will retrogress."[44]

The tension around the arms sales issue accumulated to a point of crisis for the next two months. President Reagan was under pressure from conservatives in Congress to honor his campaign promises. Conservative senators, like Strom Thurmond, urged the president to supply upgraded fighter planes to Taiwan. Senator Barry Goldwater even threatened to take the issue to the public.[45] In late March, Reagan decided to submit to Congress the transaction of selling $97 million worth of spare parts to Taiwan. The decision came amid a continuing stalemate in the negotiations on arms sales to Taiwan, which had been going on for two and a half months. In response, China hardened its position by threatening to downgrade its diplomatic relations with the United States. Deng Xiaoping himself for the first time spoke on the issue in a negative tone. He was quoted as saying, "We cannot accept the U.S. way of handling the Taiwan issue. We have no room for maneuver on this question. If things really cannot go on like this, then relations should retrogress."[46]

The lack of Chinese trust in President Reagan's sincerity in resolving the arms sales issue led to rapid deterioration of Sino-U.S. relations. The negotiations on arms sales was deadlocked. To bring the negotiations back on track, Reagan sent letters to Deng Xiaoping and Zhao Ziyang on April 5. He clearly stressed in the letter to Deng that he would not "permit unofficial relations between the American people and the people of Taiwan to weaken" U.S. commitment to the one-China principle. Reagan also expressed his appreciation for China's initiatives to peacefully settle the Taiwan issue, saying that the United States "fully recognize[s] the significance of the nine-point proposal" for reunification. Then he assured China of his sincerity in resolving the Taiwan issue by proposing to Deng that Vice President Bush visit China to discuss the arms sales problem in late April.[47]

President Reagan's letters were effective in making China change from threatening to downgrade relations to just lodging a protest, when the administration notified the Congress of the transaction of $60 million in spare parts to Taiwan on April 13. In fact, China went out of its way to point out that it had taken note of the three-point explanation and assurance given by the U.S. side: (1) the sale was for spare parts, not arms; (2) the sale was promised before the Sino-U.S. high-level meetings held in Cancún and Washington; and (3) the United States would not consider military transfers to Taiwan while the two sides were continuing their bilateral discussions on a settlement of the question of U.S. arms sales to Taiwan.[48]

The Issue of Terminating Arms Sales

Despite many exchanges of drafts during the negotiations, differences remained large between Washington's position and Beijing's demands as put forward by Zhao Ziyang and Huang Hua at Cancún and Washington. The major point of difference was on the termination of arms sales to Taiwan; China had demanded a specified date.

Some progress had been made on the level of arms sales in the negotiations since December 4, 1981. The State Department assessed that it was unlikely that the Reagan administration would wish to exceed the level of arms sales during the Carter administration, since more than a billion dollars in arms and military equipment had been transferred to Taiwan between 1978 and 1980.[49]

However, the key issue regarding a final date for terminating arms sales remained unresolved. President Reagan and his White House aides had been insisting that the United States would not agree to end arms sales, although the State Department had been more flexible on the issue.[50] Reagan, with National Security Adviser Clark's assistance, revised new U.S. proposals prepared by State Department staff,[51] which were supported by Haig. Reagan toughened the U.S. terms in the proposal before Bush's visit, making no compromise to end arms sales to Taiwan.

Vice President Bush did not take a new arms sales proposal to Beijing. Nevertheless, his mission reaffirmed the Reagan administration's one-China policy, restored Chinese confidence in Reagan's intentions to abide by the normalization agreement, and put the negotiations back on track. Deng placed high hopes on Bush's participation in the issue: "You know China quite well. I sincerely welcome you as an old friend of China. We hope that certain dark shadows and clouds between our two countries will be swept away by your visit here." Bush, in reply to Premier Zhao, promised: "I will go back and prepare to discuss in detail with the President with much better understanding of the depth of the feelings that you have on the positions."[52]

Upon Bush's return from Beijing, the State Department began to prepare a new proposal. Secretary Haig sent President Reagan a memorandum on July 1, recommending that he make a final proposal to the Chinese. It contained three points. First, it proposed that future reduction in arms sales to Taiwan be tied to China's peaceful approach to reunion with Taiwan. Second, it proposed that no specific date be named. Third, it proposed a U.S. statement that "envisioned the goal of an eventual end to arms sales to Taiwan."[53]

The final draft of the communiqué was prepared by the State Department and revised by the president and the NSC. It embraced Haig's three points with the following compromising language on the subject of ending arms sales to Taiwan: "The United States does not seek to carry out a long-term policy of arms sales to Taiwan and affirms the ultimate objective of ending arms sales to Taiwan. In the meantime, it expects a gradual reduction of its arms sales, leading to a final resolution of this difficult issue."[54] With some minor changes, China accepted the proposal. On August 17, the United States and China signed and issued the joint communiqué settling the problem of arms sales to Taiwan.

The Arms Sales Issue: An Analysis

Historical, legal, and political factors were responsible for turning the arms sales issue into an imminent crisis in Sino-U.S. relations during the Reagan administration. The arms sales problem was an inherited issue from the Carter administration and was worsened by the passage of the TRA. Presidential factors further enhanced Chinese suspicion of U.S. intent in its Taiwan policy. Conservative political forces also complicated the policy process and were influential in the Reagan administration's arms sales policy toward Taiwan.

Diplomatic ambiguity in the normalization negotiations may have contributed to the problem of arms sales. Some scholars believed that the U.S. government was trying to convey to the Chinese that there was a linkage between peaceful reunification and arms sales in the negotiations and that the U.S. position was understood by the Beijing government. [55]

The Chinese understanding was shattered by the passage of the TRA in March 1979. The TRA specifically provides for arms sales to Taiwan and clarifies the ambiguity of the linkage between the peaceful resolution and arms sales. It contains no provision reciprocating Chinese peaceful moves by U.S. arms reduction. On the contrary, the TRA contains provisions governing U.S. arms sales to Taiwan that were not mentioned either in the normalization communiqué or in the presidential announcement and the U.S. statement regarding normalization. Section 2(b)(5) of the TRA stipulates: "It is the policy of the United States to provide Taiwan with arms of a defensive character." Section 3 further specifies arms sales procedures. It states: "(a) In furtherance of the policy set forth in section 2 of this Act, the United States will make available to Taiwan such defense articles and defense services in such quantity as may be necessary to enable Taiwan to maintain a sufficient self-defense capability. (b) The President and the Congress shall determine the nature and quantity of such defense articles and services based solely upon their judgment of the needs of Taiwan, in accordance with procedures established by law. Such determination of Taiwan's defense needs shall include review by United States military authorities in connection with recommendations to the President and the Congress."[56]

The passage of the TRA also prompted the Chinese not to take a chance with the United States on the Taiwan issue. They strongly objected to the terms of the TRA regarding security of Taiwan and arms sales. They regarded the TRA as violating the principles of normalization and contradicting the understanding between the two countries on normalization.[57] There was no doubt that China regarded the TRA as a source of problems in Sino-U.S. relations and sought to change the act.[58]

Presidential factors were instrumental in causing tensions around arms sales. These factors included presidential ideology, campaign promises, and political advisers. Being a political conservative and anticommunist, Reagan had long supported Taiwan. He knew, however, that his conviction, often charged with emotion, had to be reconciled with political reality. The interplay between his belief and reality often confused him. Although Bush was trying to convince Beijing that he and Reagan had never proposed any change in China policy and did not intend to do so, Reagan kept making contradictory statements. For example, Reagan reaffirmed his position for official relations with Taiwan at a news conference on August 22.[59] Then two days later, Reagan denied what he had said.[60] Later, Reagan was asked to clarify his position. He replied that he had "misstated" his position on "government-to-government" relations and had meant only that since U.S.-Taiwan relations were governed by the TRA, it was therefore "official."[61]

It was not new to China that conservative Republican presidents were strongly anticommunist. Former president Nixon was perhaps best known for his anticommunist ideology in the 1950s and 1960s. However, since Nixon, U.S. presidents have taken realistic approaches in dealing with the international situation and the U.S. strategic position in the world despite their ideological beliefs. It was Nixon who replaced the ideology with his strategic vision by developing good relations with China. President Reagan was the first U.S. president since Nixon to stress ideology in his China policy during his campaign and the initial period of his administration. His ideology was reflected in his pro-Taiwan speeches and approach. However, the pragmatic nature of the office requires restrained emotion and a strong sense of reality. As his predecessors had done, Reagan had to deal with the reality that China cannot be strategically neglected. Although he tried to match reality with his ideology, he could do it only to a certain extent, since U.S. China policy had been developed on the basis of bipartisan consensus, and he had not attained such bipartisan participation. As a result, in his various speeches, Reagan constantly sent out mixed signals to China regarding his Taiwan policy, and he left the public an impression that he was advocating a two-Chinas policy, which alarmed sensitive Chinese leaders in their dealings with him on the arms sales issue.

The victory of Reagan's presidential bid disappointed the Chinese, who would have felt much better dealing with the Carter administration.[62] Reagan's appointees only confirmed Chinese worries and anxieties. Reagan's selection of top government officials and Republican control of the Senate after the election made Beijing even more uncertain about the new administration's China policy. Reagan appointed Edwin Meese III, James A. Baker III, and Michael K. Deaver as his principal White House aides, who would manage to carry out the president's priorities and protect the president's interests. Alexander M. Haig's appointment as secretary of state was made to add foreign policy experience to the new administration, though Reagan's first choice was George P. Shultz, who was passed over because of his inexperience in foreign policymaking. However, to make sure that his ideology would be blended into foreign policy, Reagan named

William P. Clark as deputy secretary and Richard Allen as his national security adviser.

Reagan's choice of aides increased Chinese suspicion of his Taiwan policy. Most of his appointees, who were capable of having considerable influence on Reagan, were considered to be pro-Taiwanese due to their ideology or previous connections with Taiwan. Reagan's foreign policy adviser, Richard Allen, was co-owner of a consulting firm that had Taiwan as a major client. Michael Deaver, who had been a major Reagan political adviser for sixteen years, was a partner in a firm that was listed with the Justice Department as an agent of Taiwan. He was responsible for placing materials favorable to Taiwan in small-town newspapers around the United States. To balance Secretary Haig's position in foreign policy, William Clark, who had served as Governor Reagan's executive assistant, was named deputy secretary of state. With no background in foreign policy, but being the president's intimate friend, Clark's assignment was "to act as Reagan's watchdog in the State Department."[63] When Allen resigned, he became national security adviser and grew increasingly influential in U.S. foreign policymaking. He was one of the key players in the process of drafting the arms sales agreement. In any administration, top White House aides and certain key members of the cabinet actually manage day-to-day affairs. Therefore, they are a critical factor in policymaking. This was especially so in the Reagan administration because of Reagan's hands-off style and approach to the decisionmaking process.[64]

Reagan's allies in the Senate also footed his ideological approach to foreign policymaking. Reagan's election victory brought fifteen new Republican senators and enabled the Republican party to gain control of the Senate. With the incumbent conservative members, joined by conservative Democrats, the Senate was characterized by "its most right-leaning posture in modern times."[65] The key influential members in the Senate were the majority leader, Howard Baker (R-Tenn.); the chairman of the Foreign Relations Committee, Charles Percy; Frank Murkowski (R-Alaska), who became chairman of the Subcommittee on East Asia and Pacific Affairs; and Jesse Helms (R-N.C.), a member of that subcommittee. Two other members with special relationships to Reagan, Barry Goldwater (R-Ariz.) and Paul Laxalt, were also influential on China policy because of their pro-Taiwan approach to U.S.-China affairs.

Conservative members of Congress, whose support Reagan needed to pass his budget and tax proposals, played a large role in influencing the arms sales to Taiwan. Some members of Congress urged arms sales to Taiwan because they felt that the Carter administration had largely neglected implementing the TRA, and they wanted the executive to adhere to the spirit of the TRA in working with Congress to provide arms to Taiwan. Other members advocated arms sales, including advanced arms, on pro-Taiwan and anticommunist grounds. These people were strong supporters of President

Reagan, and their opinions carried certain weight in the administration's arms sales policy toward Taiwan. For example, a few members of the House Foreign Affairs Committee sent a letter to Reagan on November 17, 1981, urging him to approve the FX sale.[66] Reagan was also pressured by some twenty-five senators to supply upgraded fighter planes to Taiwan.[67] Senator Goldwater pressed even harder by stating his intention to go to the public on the arms sales issue, because he was "profoundly disturbed by the mounting evidence that we do not intend to honor our commitments to [Taiwan]."[68] Those congressional pressures may be residual in terms of influencing the actual decision of arms sales, but they did contribute to the zigzagging of Reagan's arms sales policy during this period. For example, not long after the senators' letter, Reagan decided in March 1982 to go ahead with sales of military spare parts, a decision made during the apex of the arms sales crisis.

Settlement of the Crisis: An Explanation

During the arms sales crisis, several factors came into play and finally led to the August 17 Communiqué. An examination of strategic, bureaucratic, and presidential factors provides an explanation of why the United States reached an agreement with China in settling the arms sales issue.

A Rational Calculation—U.S. Policy Interests

First and foremost, U.S. strategic relations with China carried much weight in the equation of United States-China-Taiwan relationships. After Reagan took office, the administration reevaluated China's strategic importance. It concluded that China's economic and military development limited China's role as a world power; nevertheless, China remained as a regional power with strategic implications. Despite ideological preferences of some U.S. decisionmakers, the U.S. government ultimately had to make a rational choice between supporting Taipei and maintaining good relations with Beijing. Given the administration's foreign policy priorities and international situation at that time, it was in the interests of the United States to resolve the arms sales issue in a way that would allow the United States to maintain its Taiwan policy goals and the consistent and coherent China policy that had been developed over the years.

At the beginning of the Reagan administration, U.S. China policy remained directionless because of strategic reassessment and Reagan's contradictory statements about improving relations with Taiwan. Haig's appointment as secretary of state, however, again placed China policy in the context of U.S.-USSR relations, for Haig was known as pro-Beijing in his dealings with Moscow. Even with dubious feelings about Taiwan, the starting point of the new administration's China policy was based on its strategic considerations. Future China policy would develop along this strategic line. Assistant Secretary of State John H. Holdridge stated that U.S.-China relations should be further developed in the years ahead. This relationship was based on the premise that "China is not our adversary but a friendly, developing country with which, without being allied, we share important strategic interests."[69]

Reagan stated more explicitly in his statement, upon issuance of the communiqué, that strategic relations with China were in U.S. national interests. He stated:

> Building a strong and lasting relationship with China has been an important foreign policy goal of four consecutive American administrations. Such a relationship is vital to our long-term national security interests and contributes to stability in East Asia. It is in the national interests of the United States that this important strategic relationship be advanced.[70]

U.S. strategic interests thus placed certain limits and constraints on the behavior of some U.S. decisionmakers who were in favor of arms sales to Taiwan. First, foreign policy objectives of strategic cooperation with China were greater than those of arms sales to Taiwan. Second, arms sales should not disrupt U.S.-China diplomatic relations. Third, arms sales had to be handled, if they became a serious issue in Sino-U.S. relations, in a way to ensure U.S. international interests.

What were the U.S. potential gains and losses in the arms sales crisis? First of all, it was unclear what kind of gains the United States would obtain from arms sales to Taiwan since the U.S. goal of maintaining a secure and prosperous Taiwan had been enhanced by developing a good relationship with China. Subsequently, China's peaceful Taiwan initiatives also accommodated the U.S. Taiwan policy goal. Second, the United States might weaken Chinese cooperation in confronting Soviet expansion in Afghanistan and Indochina. Third, a deteriorating Sino-U.S. relationship would arouse anxiety among U.S. Asian allies who had maintained good relations with China.[71] Fourth, Sino-U.S. economic, cultural, and commercial relations might be adversely affected.

On the other hand, a prompt solution of the arms sales issue would not entail losses. Taiwan was not threatened in the light of Chinese peaceful offensives. It is unlikely that Taiwan would face a threat from China as a result of resolving the arms sales crisis. On the other hand, resolving the crisis would enable Sino-U.S. relations to continue developing on the foundation of previous efforts. Assistant Secretary Holdridge representatively assessed the significance of an arms sales solution in the following manner:

> Removal of the arms question as a serious issue in U.S.-China relations will help to ensure that both countries can continue to cooperate on mutually-shared international objectives, e.g., deterring Soviet

aggression in East Asia and removal of Vietnamese troops from Kampuchea. It will ease fears by American friends and allies that the general peace and stability in the Asia/Pacific region could be undermined. By defusing the difficult issue of arms sales, we will open the way for an expansion of U.S.-China relations in a broad range of economic, cultural, scientific and technological areas as well as in people-to-people contact.[72]

Bureaucratic Preference and Influence

Bureaucratic factors played a positive role in resolving the arms sales crisis. Bureaucratic agencies, particularly the State Department, strongly expressed their preferences for settling the arms sales issue. They tried to translate their preferences into policy by bringing their arguments to presidential attention, by recommending policy alternatives, and by arousing public opinion on the issue. Bureaucratic players were able to insert their influence in the policy process by skillfully stressing the linkage between the arms sales issue with the possible downturn of Sino-U.S. relations and by forming an alliance with some key figures in the U.S. government.

Secretary Haig was perhaps the single most effective figure responsible for settling the arms sales issue. He was widely credited for convincing President Reagan to turn down Taiwan's request for the FX fighter planes. He was directly in charge of arms sales negotiations and preparing drafts of the communiqué. In fact, his influence was so persistent and pervasive on the issue that many opponents in Congress felt that he had manipulated President Reagan in making the deal with the Chinese.[73] Haig's effectiveness in influencing the arms sales policy stemmed from his strong inclination toward developing cooperative relations with China in international affairs.[74] His perception of international affairs and his role in Nixon's China initiatives made Chinese leaders believe that he was "the defender" of U.S. China policy in the Reagan administration.[75]

Under Haig's leadership, the State Department was a strong voice in advocating a better and strengthened relationship with China. Its predisposition on arms sales to Taiwan was that such sales should not jeopardize Sino-U.S. relations and that the United States should reach an agreement to solve the issue. In the arms sales policy process, many bureaucrats who had helped in building a constructive relationship with China were trying to influence U.S. arms sales policy by leaking information. For instance, before the administration made any decision on the FX, a CIA and Pentagon report, concluding that there was no defensive need for Taiwan to purchase such advanced planes, was leaked to the press.[76] The State Department was instrumental in recommending U.S. options in the negotiations and was directly responsible for drafting different versions of the communiqué.[77]

Domestic Constraints: The Presidential Role

The combination of presidential considerations and involvement also contributed to the explanation of the August agreement. Direct presidential involvement helped reduce Chinese doubt of U.S. intentions and make way for the final settlement. While the political pressure to notify Congress of the F-5E arrangements established a deadline for the negotiations, the possible adverse domestic effect of downgrading U.S.-China relations provided Reagan with an incentive to resolve the arms sales issue.

In the arms sales crisis between 1981 and 1982, presidential attention and involvement had been highly visible. Not only did President Reagan use more discretion in commenting on his China policy in public, but he also made efforts to enhance communication with the Chinese. He sent Vice President Bush, Secretary of State Haig, and Assistant Secretary of State Holdridge to Beijing for talks on the arms sales issue. Vice President Bush's trip in late April 1982 bore a special presidential mission to find a way to solve the problem.[78] Presidential correspondence also helped increase direct communications with top leaders in China. They were meant to convey to the Chinese the president's sincerity in his China policy and flexibility in resolving arms sales to Taiwan. Reagan took the initiative to send his letter, observing the tenth anniversary of the Shanghai Communiqué in February 1982, and again he wrote letters to Deng and Zhao in April and Hu in May. Those letters all stressed the importance of maintaining good relations between the two countries, but the April letters were specifically addressed to the arms sales issue. In his letter to Premier Zhao, Reagan for the first time recognized the Chinese nine-point proposal on peaceful unification with Taiwan and indicated that the United States was prepared to expect a decrease in arms sales to Taiwan in light of Beijing's peaceful initiatives in resolving the Taiwan issue. He told Zhao in the letter that the United States "appreciate[s] the policies which your [Chinese] government has followed to provide a peaceful settlement . . . we welcome your nine-point initiative." Reagan specifically suggested that "in the context of progress towards a peaceful solution, there would naturally be a decrease in the need for arms by Taiwan."[79] This suggestion indicated that a peaceful environment around the Taiwan Strait could lead to decreasing arms sales to Taiwan, which thus paved the way for breaking the stalemate in the Sino-U.S. arms sales negotiations.

Why did President Reagan change his position regarding U.S. Taiwan policy? There were two explanations. One was Reagan's political socialization of the office. By virtue of the office, a president must possess a keen sense of reality, on which foreign policy goals can be set forth and pragmatic approaches can be taken to fulfill those goals. The office also requires a president to listen to subordinates' advice and policy recommendations that will best serve foreign policy goals. Reagan had obviously gone through the following political socialization process:

realizing the political reality of Sino-U.S. relations; clarifying his China policy goal; and relying on the State Department to deal with the arms sales issue. The other was the strong Chinese reaction to arms sales to Taiwan. The unusual Chinese commentaries and Deng's comment on possible retrogression of PRC-U.S. relations helped convince the president that China viewed arms sales as a very serious issue. A wrong move by the president could cause grave political consequences.

Two domestic considerations prompted Reagan to seek solutions to the arms sales problem. It became apparent that, as a result of arms sales, the rapid deterioration of Sino-U.S. relations might lead to downgrading the level of diplomatic presence in both capitals. If this happened, it would inevitably become a major issue in U.S. politics, since building such a relationship had gained bipartisan support and national consensus. Whoever was responsible for worsening Sino-U.S. relations would have to bear the political consequences.[80]

Another presidential consideration was the congressional pressure on the sale of promised F-5E planes. Reagan had promised to provide Taiwan with F-5E planes in January. Because of the arms sales crisis, the administration held back the decision to transfer the F-5Es. However, conservatives in Congress, led by Goldwater, pressed Reagan to go ahead with the sale. They urged the administration to send notification of F-5E sales to Congress. Moreover, realizing that the F-5E coproduction line in Taiwan would have to be closed in September 1982, there was an urgent need for Reagan to make a decision on F-5Es. On the other hand, China had already promised to take further actions after the transfer of spare parts to Taiwan. If no agreement on arms sales was achieved, a new F-5E sale would necessarily result in retrogression of Sino-U.S. relations. When George Shultz indicated during the Senate confirmation hearing that he would recommend to the president an early decision on the F-5E,[81] China strongly warned Shultz not to give in to pressure from Washington's Taiwan lobby. The Chinese wasted no time in pointing out that "Sino-American relations would be sabotaged if the views held by Goldwater and his ilk prevail."[82] Taking these domestic factors into consideration, Reagan faced no other alternative but to seek a settlement on the arms sales issue before September.

Conclusion

The issue of arms sales to Taiwan during 1981-1982 preoccupied the attention of leaders of both the United States and China. It became what Beijing called a "time bomb" in Sino-U.S. relations. It started with the FX decision and soon developed into a crisis endangering Sino-U.S. diplomatic relations. Initially, the two governments viewed the issue of arms sales in different ways. The U.S. government under President Reagan saw arms sales as a commitment to the safety of its old friend. The Chinese government, on the other hand, regarded arms sales as U.S. infringement upon its sovereignty and interference in its internal affairs. As a result, U.S.-China relations were greatly restrained and were subject to retrogression if the problem went unresolved. Subsequently, both countries made efforts to increase communication.

The initial conditions that gave rise to the arms sales issue were several. First, historical and legal aspects of arms sales became an imminent issue for the new Reagan administration. The compromises reached between the two countries on arms sales to Taiwan in the normalization negotiations resulted only in temporary shelving of the issue. The passage of the TRA further aroused Chinese suspicion of U.S. intentions to resolve the problem. Second, presidential factors confirmed and increased Chinese fear and anxiety over U.S. arms sales to Taiwan. Presidential ideology, campaign promises, and the Taiwan backgrounds of Reagan's political advisers contributed to the rise of the arms sales issue. Third, conservative domestic inputs into the decisionmaking process also influenced Reagan's arms sales policies (see Figure 4.1). Fourth, various Chinese considerations might be dynamic factors in promoting the arms sales issue into a crisis.[83]

Figure 4.1   The FX Decisionmaking Process

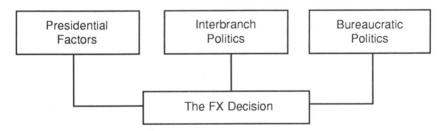

It became clear that maintaining a good relationship with China was an important goal of the Reagan administration's China policy. This foreign policy goal remained unchanged and in a way dictated U.S. government approach to the arms sales issue. The administration was not willing to sell arms to Taiwan to the extent that it would risk a possible retrogression in Sino-U.S. relations as long as Taiwan was not in danger. Given the choices, it turned out that the United States maximized its interests by managing the arms sales crisis in a way consistent with the China policy goals: it resolved the issue in a manner accepted by China and also maintained the U.S. credibility by not abandoning Taiwan.

The whole process of managing the arms sales issue took place in the executive arena. Although many were involved in the arms sales management process, only a handful of key players, apart from the president and the vice president, were charged with managing the crisis, namely, Secretary of State Haig and State Department bureaucrats. Both the final outcome and the policy process confirmed the rational actor explanation that the United States would not sell arms to Taiwan at the expense of its strategic relations with China. The case of the arms sales crisis provided further evidence to confirm that the rational actor model can provide good explanations for international crisis management both in terms of policy goals and crisis management processes.

In managing the arms sale crisis, both bureaucratic preferences and processes played an important role. Secretary Haig and State Department bureaucrats responsible for East Asian affairs preferred maintaining good relations with China over selling arms to Taiwan. They were able to translate their preference into the policy process by means of leaking information, developing policy options, and recommending to the president policies they preferred. Because the State Department was directly responsible for negotiations and policy recommendations, it was in an exclusive position to advance its interests and preference. While the president and his advisers were supervising the policy process, it was Haig and the State Department bureaucrats that made the workable recommendations and drafted the August Communiqué.

The interbranch politics approach is less helpful in understanding the outcome of U.S. arms sales policy. Interbranch politics explained the U.S. decision to sell military spare parts to Taiwan, but it did not explain the terms of the arms sales agreement. There was no formal congressional action involved in the management of the arms sales crisis. The congressional role was limited to publicly expressing concerns and privately exerting pressure on the president. In a crisis such as arms sales to Taiwan, the decisionmaking process was a closed one, with the executive developing policy options and conducting negotiations. There was not much interbranch consultation regarding the arms sales issue, despite the fact that Congress tried to play a more assertive role in the arms sales decisionmaking process.[84] In order to settle the issue by the desired date, the executive finessed congressional approval processes by agreeing on an arms sales communiqué with China.[85]

By reaching agreement on the August Communiqué, the executive in several ways eroded the TRA passed by Congress. First, it promised that future arms sales to Taiwan would not surpass, either in quality or in quantity, the level of previous arms sales. The TRA contained no provision in this regard. Second, it pledged to reduce and finally end U.S. arms sales to Taiwan as long as China maintained its fundamental peaceful approach with respect to Taiwan. The TRA did not pledge that the United States would reduce and finally terminate arms sales in light of Beijing's fundamental peaceful policy toward Taiwan. Third, although the TRA called for executive consultation with Congress regarding Taiwan, the executive precluded congressional participation in the formal policy process and reached an understanding with China on future arms sales to Taiwan.

In sum, the rational actor model and the bureaucratic politics model are the most useful in explaining the management of the crisis and the outcome of the U.S. arms sales policy. The interbranch politics model is helpful in providing a political context in which the Congress chose to let the conservative president take the leadership in making arms sales decisions and in managing the arms sales crisis (see Figure 4.2).

Figure 4.2   The Crisis Management Process and Outcome

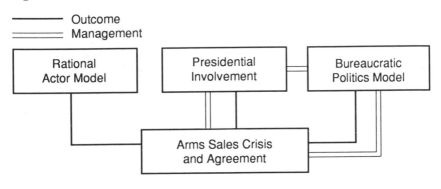

Notes

1. The text of the United States–China Joint Communiqué of August 17, 1982, can be found in Congress, House, Committee on Foreign Affairs, *China-Taiwan: United States Policy: Hearing Before the Committee on Foreign Affairs, House of Representatives*, 97th Cong., 2nd sess., 1982, pp. 31–32.

2. See Chapter 2.

3. Nayan Chanda and Robert Delfs, "China Ups the Ante," *Far Eastern Economic Review* (November 20, 1981), pp. 8–9.

4. *People's Daily* commentary, June 14, 1980, in Foreign Broadcast Information Service, *Daily Report: People's Republic of China*, December 18, 1978, pp. B4–B5 (hereafter cited as *FBIS* [China]).

5. U.S. Department of State, *U.S. Policy Towards China, July 15, 1971–January 15, 1979*, p. 48.

6. Instead of objecting to the U.S. statement, China only reaffirmed its position: "As for the way of bringing Taiwan back into the embrace of the motherland, it is entirely China's internal affair." Given Beijing's overtures for peaceful reunification, the Chinese position was understood to mean that any advance commitment not to use force would reduce a major long-term incentive for the Taiwan authority to accept peaceful reunification. See "Quarterly Chronicle and Documentation," *China Quarterly* 77 (March 1979), p. 209.

7. In fact, in the president's announcement and the U.S. statement on normalization, there was mention of U.S. expectation for a peaceful settlement of the Taiwan issue and no mention of U.S. arms sales. That confirmed the Chinese

belief that China's sincerity in adopting a peaceful approach to Taiwan reduced the need for arms.

8. China specialist A. Doak Barnett also pointed out that there was a certain degree of PRC tolerance in Carter's Taiwan policy. See Barnett, *U.S. Arms Sales: The China-Taiwan Tangle* (Washington, D.C.: Brookings Institution), 1982, p. 27.

9. The plan was an extension of an existing agreement with Taiwan, which was to expire in 1980, involving coproduction of Northrop's F-5E fighter in Taiwan. See Sutter, *The China Quandary*, pp. 145–146.

10. Ibid.

11. Congress, House, Subcommittee on Asian and Pacific Affairs of the Committee on Foreign Affairs, *Implementation of the Taiwan Relations Act: Hearings Before the Subcommittee on Asian and Pacific Affairs of the Committee on Foreign Affairs, House of Representatives*, 96th Cong., 2nd. sess., 1980, p. 28.

12. Taiwan had requested purchasing sophisticated U.S. aircraft such as the FX and certain types of missiles since 1972. But there had been U.S. deferral of answers to the requests up to the Carter administration. See Congress, House, *Implementation of the Taiwan Relations Act*, pp. 4–5.

13. Ibid., pp. 28–29.

14. It was unclear whether or not two U.S. companies, Northrop and GE, played any role in pressing members of Congress to send the letter to the president. The two companies had submitted the applications to the administration for sales of FX fighters to Taiwan. See Congress, House, *Implementation of the Taiwan Relations Act*.

15. Sutter, *The China Quandary*, p. 146.

16. See Kathy Sawyer, "Reagan Sticks to Stand on Taiwan Ties," *Washington Post*, August 23, 1980, p. 1; Philip Geyelin, "Reagan's 'Official' Position," *Washington Post*, September 1, 1980, p. 17.

17. "The Clock Must Not Be Turned Back," *FBIS* (China), June 16, 1980, pp. B4–B5.

18. Jay Mathews, "Bush Said to Reassure China on Policy," *Washington Post*, August 22, 1980, p. 2.

19. Haig, *Caveat*, p. 199.

20. Ibid., p. 126.

21. "Sino-Dutch Relations," *Beijing Review*, April 6, 1981, p. 8.

22. Haig, *Caveat*, p. 203.

23. Quoted by Martin L. Lasater in his *The Taiwan Issue in Sino-American Strategic Relations* (Boulder: Westview Press, 1984), p. 182.

24. Ibid.

25. President Ford had proposed to Beijing that the United States supply new arms to Taiwan and would also permit arms sales to China. China rejected such deals and made it clear that it would not compromise its sovereignty over Taiwan on U.S. transfer of sensitive technologies to China. See Michael Parks, "Ford Hopeful Taiwan Arms Sales Issue Can Be Solved," *Los Angeles Times*, March 28, 1981; "China Still Opposed to U.S. Arms Sales to Taiwan," April 3, 1981; "Sales of U.S. Military Gear to China Fail to Materialize," April 17, 1981.

26. Haig, *Caveat*, p. 207.

27. Karen Elliott House, "U.S. Foreign Policy Remains Muddled as Haig Ends 12-Day Far East Tour," *Wall Street Journal*, June 25, 1981, sec. 2, p. 30.

28. On August 25, the United States informed China that it was ready to discuss a considerable list of arms with Liu Huaqing, deputy chief of the People's Liberation Army, during his scheduled visit to the United States in September.

However, China postponed the trip indefinitely, dismissing the U.S. offer. See Haig, *Caveat*, p. 208.

29. Haig, *Caveat*, pp. 208–209.

30. According to the plan, Taiwan would be a special administrative region with complete autonomy; Taiwan would keep its political, economic, and social systems unchanged; Taiwan would maintain its own troops. The central government in Beijing would not interfere in local Taiwanese affairs and in their economic, cultural, and commercial relations with other nations. Later, Beijing broadened the plan and called for three "communications" (trade, postage, and shipping).

31. According to Haig, the conversation between Reagan and Zhao was running out of time, and Zhao had to cut off "one or two other things he wanted to discuss with Reagan." It turned out it was China's new proposal on the arms sales issue. See Haig, *Caveat*, pp. 209–210.

32. Ibid.

33. Ibid., p. 212.

34. It was reported that on December 11, 1981, the administration had informed Congress of its plan to sell arms to Taiwan. See Xinhua, "U.S. Decides to Sell Arms Spare Parts to Taiwan," *FBIS* (China), December 29, 1981, p. B1.

35. Ibid.

36. "China Resolutely Opposes Foreign Arms Sales to Taiwan," *FBIS* (China), December 31, 1981, p. B1.

37. The commentary said: "The Chinese Government has stated many times that we will endeavor to solve the Taiwan issue by peaceful means, and has also repeatedly announced that we are ready to apply a variety of methods to discuss with the Taiwan authorities the great matter of reunifying the motherland. On 1 January 1979 the Standing Committee of China's National People's Congress published a message to compatriots in Taiwan, and announced the general principles for achieving peaceful reunification. In the course of his visit to the United States, Vice Premier Deng Xiaoping further stated that as long as Taiwan returns to the motherland, we shall respect its status quo and existing systems. On 30 September this year, Chairman Ye Jianying clearly elaborated on the nine-point principles and policies concerning the return of Taiwan to the motherland for the realization of China's peaceful reunification. This fully expresses the Chinese Government's sincerity in endeavoring to solve the Taiwan issue by peaceful means. . . . This has also objectively created the most favorable conditions for the United States to halt its arms sales to Taiwan, to refrain from interfering again in China's internal affairs, and to eliminate the obstacle that threatens relations between the two countries" (*FBIS*, December 31, 1981, p. B1).

38. Ibid.

39. Department of State, "No Sale of Advanced Aircraft to Taiwan," *Department of State Bulletin* 82, no. 2059 (February 1982), p. 39.

40. China Protests U.S. Decision on Arms Sales to Taiwan, *"Beijing Review* (January 18, 1982), p. 8.

41. Haig, *Caveat*, p. 212.

42. The text of the letters can be found in Congress, House, *China-Taiwan: United States Policy*, pp. 38–39.

43. John W. Garver, "Arms Sales, the Taiwan Question, and Sino-U.S. Relations," *Orbis* 26, no.4 (Winter 1983), footnote 38, p. 1010.

44. "Critical Point in Sino-U.S. Relations," *Beijing Review* (May 15, 1982), p. 10.

45. Haig, *Caveat*, p. 213.

46. *New York Times*, March 28, 1982, p. 19.

47. Quoted from President Reagan's letter to Vice Chairman Deng Xiaoping, April 5, 1982. Both letters can be found in Congress, House, *China-Taiwan: United States Policy*, pp. 35–37.

48. "Protesting U.S. Sale of Military-Related Spare Parts to Taiwan," *Beijing Review* (April 26, 1982), p. 7.

49. Haig, *Caveat*, p. 211.

50. For instance, some officials revealed a recent U.S. proposal calling for a pledge by the United States not to provide Taiwan with military equipment beyond the quantity and quality of the current level. This proposal also indicated that there would be no need for additional sales if Taiwan and Beijing reconciled their differences. See Bernard Gwertzman, "Haig Meets with Peking Official to Discuss Arms Sales to Taiwan," *New York Times*, April 6, 1982, p. 1.

51. Haig, *Caveat*, p. 212.

52. Xinhua, *FBIS* (China), May 10, 1982, pp. B2–B3.

53. Haig, *Caveat*, p. 214.

54. Ibid., pp. 214–215.

55. John W. Garver wrote: "The Chinese had apparently been led to believe during the normalization negotiations that their emphasis on the peaceful reunification of China would be reciprocated by reductions in U.S. arms deliveries to Taiwan. According to key U.S. participants in the 1978 negotiations, the U.S. side used 'calculated ambiguity' to persuade the Chinese that such a linkage was understood. This 'ambiguity' included: (1) emphasizing the link between withdrawal of U.S. troops from Taiwan and the reduction of tension in the East Asian area that the 1972 communiqué had established; (2) optimistic statements that the Taiwan issue would solve itself without the use of force; and (3) President Carter's assurances that after normalization the United States would sell only carefully selected defensive weapons to Taiwan." See Garver's "Arms Sales, the Taiwan Question, and Sino-U.S. Relations," p. 1006.

56. See Congress, House, *Implementation of the Taiwan Relations Act*.

57. The official *Beijing Review* made critical comments on the TRA on several accounts. First, the TRA embarked on unacceptable interference in China's internal affairs by providing for arms sales to Taiwan. Second, it asserted a U.S. security guarantee to Taiwan, thereby substituting what the United States promised to abolish when it agreed to abrogate the 1954 mutual security treaty. Third, it violated the principle of the normalization communiqué that the Taiwan question was to be settled by the Chinese themselves by calling for appropriate U.S. action in response to "any threat to the security or to the social or economic system of the people of Taiwan." Fourth, it treated Taiwan as a "country" and the Taiwan authorities as "government," thereby violating the agreement that there would be only "unofficial, nongovernmental, people-to-people relations between the United States and Taiwan." See "U.S.-Taiwan Relations Act," *Beijing Review* (January 12, 1981), pp. 9–11.

58. Senate majority leader Howard H. Baker reported after his visit to Beijing that the Chinese leaders asked him about the possibility of amending the TRA. See Congress, Senate, *The United States and China: A Report to the United States Senate by the Senate Majority Leader* (Washington, D.C.: Government Printing Office, 1982).

59. Sawyer, "Reagan Sticks to Stand on Taiwan Ties," p. 4.

60. Howell Raines, "Reagan Backs Evangelicals in Their Political Activities," *New York Times*, August 23, 1980, p. 8.

61. Howell Raines, "Reagan, Conceding Misstatements, Abandons Plan on Taiwan," *New York Times*, August 26, 1980, p. 1.

62. For obvious reasons, China preferred Carter over Reagan to be elected. In fact, many political observers in the Chinese embassy in Washington and in Beijing had predicted a possible Carter victory in the election. Interview by author, Beijing, Spring 1984.

63. Robert S. Hirschfield, "The Reagan Administration and U.S. Relations with Taiwan and China," in Koenig, Hsiung, and Chang, *Congress, the Presidency, and the Taiwan Relations Act*, p. 117.

64. President Reagan was particularly known for his lack of interests in the details of policymaking, and for delegating much responsibility to his principal subordinates. See also Hirschfield, "The Reagan Administration and U.S. Relations with Taiwan and China," p. 114.

65. Hirschfield, "The Reagan Administration and U.S. Relations with Taiwan and China," p. 114.

66. Lasater, *The Taiwan Issue in Sino-American Strategic Relations*, p. 184.

67. Republican Senator Strom Thurmond and twenty-five other senators signed a letter asking Reagan to go ahead with arms sales to Taiwan. See Haig, *Caveat*, p. 213.

68. Ibid.

69. Department of State, Bureau of Public Affairs, "U.S. Relations with China," *Current Policy*, no. 297 (July 16, 1981), p. 1.

70. Congress, Senate, Committee on Foreign Relations, *U.S. Policy Toward China and Taiwan: Hearing Before the Committee On Foreign Relations*, 97th Cong., 2nd sess., 1982, p. 15.

71. Secretary Holdridge, in reply to Congressman Lagomarsino's question on the reactions of Asian countries to the arms sales communiqué, said that the fact the United States had managed to stabilize its relations with Beijing was going to "be perceived with a certain amount of relief, and this will be regarded as maintaining the peaceful environment which generally prevails in East Asia as of this moment." He pointed out that countries such as Japan, Australia, and South Korea were particularly worried about a setback in U.S.-China relations. See Congress, House, *China-Taiwan: United States Policy*, p. 22.

72. Congress, House, *China-Taiwan: United States Policy*, p. 17.

73. Senator Goldwater and some members of Congress were angry at Haig's alleged decision to prepare two different versions of the communiqué and pressed the president for Haig's resignation, which Reagan accepted. According to the July 2, 1982, *Washington Times*, the first version renounced "any long-term agreement" for arms sales to Taiwan. The second version pledged the United States "to reduce gradually such sales and to eventually terminate them." Quoted in Lasater, *The Taiwan Issue in Sino-American Strategic Relations*, p. 202.

74. See Haig's *Caveat*, Chapter 10.

75. Oksenberg, "A Decade of Sino-American Relations," p. 192.

76. Lasater, *The Taiwan Issue in Sino-American Strategic Relations*, p. 184.

77. It was reported that State Department bureaucrats responsible for Chinese and East Asian affairs had secretly prepared different drafts with Haig's knowledge. Goldwater condemned the trespass, saying that "it was clear to me and to the White House that President Reagan, Vice President Bush, and national security advisor William Clark had been lied to by the State Department about what they were planning." Quoted in Lasater, *The Taiwan Issue in Sino-American Strategic Relations*, p. 202.

78. Christopher S. Wren, "Bush Leaves China with New Ideas for Resolving Taiwan Arms Dispute," *New York Times*, May 10, 1982, p. 3.

79. Congress, House, *China-Taiwan: The United States Policy*, p. 35.

80. Haig assessed the political impact of mishandling the arms sales issue, pointing out, "If the President faltered in his relations with China, the Democratic opposition would leap on this question and turn it into a major issue in the 1984 elections. The refusal to search for a compromise on the issue of Taiwan could result in the most significant diplomatic disaster since the 'loss of China' in 1949, and the party judged responsible for this failure would, and should, pay heavy political consequences." Haig, *Caveat*, p. 214.

81. Don Oberdorfer, "Shultz Stresses U.S. Need to Deal with Palestinians," *Washington Post*, July 14, 1982, p. 15.

82. Quoted in Lasater, *The Taiwan Issue in Sino-American Strategic Relations*, pp. 203–204.

83. There were mainly two schools of thought offered by scholars in the field as to why China took a firm stance on the arms sales issue. One school explored the thinking of Chinese leaders. There were several possible explanations. One explanation was that the Chinese leader lost confidence in U.S. motives and intentions toward Taiwan as a result of Reagan's campaign promises, and thus decided to confront the issue at an early point in order to prevent closer U.S.-Taiwan ties. A second explanation relates to internal developments in Taiwan. As the old generation of mainlander leaders in Taiwan pass from the scene, chances of moving toward unification could diminish in the next decade. Thus, it was important to urge the U.S. government to encourage rather than discourage Beijing's unification initiatives. Selling arms to Taiwan at this moment would certainly have been viewed as a sign of a two-Chinas policy. A third explanation probed into PRC domestic politics. As economic and political reforms in China underwent difficulties, the Taiwan problem once again became a major issue. Some leaders felt that Deng had compromised too much on U.S. arms sales to Taiwan at the time of normalization and demanded a tougher position on U.S. Taiwan policy. This school of thought is represented by most U.S. China specialists, notably A. Doak Barnett and Robert A. Scalopino. (See A. Doak Barnett, *U.S. Arms Sales: The China-Taiwan Tangle* [Washington, D.C.: Brookings Institution, 1982], pp. 37–38; Robert A. Scalapino, "Uncertainties in Future Sino-U.S. Relations," *Orbis*. 26, no.3 [Fall 1982], pp. 681–696.) The other school seeks explanations from strategic orientation underlying the PRC's position on the arms sales issue. In his article "Arms Sales, the Taiwan Question, and Sino-U.S. Relations," Garver cited three rational actor explanations. One explanation offered by Martin Lasater claims that Beijing wanted to make an issue of arms sales to Taiwan in order to disengage itself from Sino-U.S. strategic cooperation, since Beijing saw a diminished Soviet threat and wanted to return to a more Third World–oriented position. The second explanation, advanced by Banning Garrett and Bonnie Glaser, maintains that China wanted to pressure the Reagan administration into a settlement of the arms sales issue in order to engage in broader strategic cooperation with the United States. This argument was based on the administration's view that China was so weak and in need of U.S. support that it had no option but to accept U.S. arms sales to Taiwan. It was to refute this view that China made an issue of U.S. arms sales. The third explanation, suggested by Thomas Robinson, holds that China was launching a long-term political-psychological war with the United States to force it to give up Taiwan in order to assure continued Chinese participation in the Sino-U.S. strategic partnership. (See Martin L. Lasater, "Why Peking May Want to Downgrade Relations with Washington," *Christian Science Monitor*, July 26, 1982, p. 23; Banning Garrett and Bonnie S. Glaser, "Peking: Balancing Soviets and U.S.," *New York Times*, July 19, 1982, p. 15; Thomas W. Robinson, "Choice and Consequences in Sino-American Relations," *Orbis* [Spring 1981], pp. 29–51.)

84. For example, Congress passed legislation in 1974 that established its right to review and veto, by a concurrent resolution, major arms sales. This legislative veto was subsequently incorporated into section 36(b) of the Arms Export Control Act, created through the enactment of the International Security Assistance and Arms Export Control Act of 1976. Subsequent congressional amendments to the act require the president to send to Congress various reports, including arms sales proposals and notification. For detailed information, see Congress, *Executive-Legislative Consultation on U.S. Arms Sales*, Congress and Foreign Policy Series, 7 (Washington, D.C.: Government Printing Office, 1982), pp. 5–8.

85. Congress, Senate, *U.S. Policy Toward China and Taiwan*, p. 24.

5

U.S. Nuclear Technology
Transfer to China

Technology transfer to China was another controversial issue in U.S. China policymaking. The agreement on nuclear cooperation between the United States and the People's Republic of China (hereafter, the nuclear agreement or the agreement) represented an important step taken by U.S. decisionmakers to advance relations with China in the field of high-technology cooperation.[1] The nuclear agreement provided a legal framework for U.S. nuclear companies to export to China nuclear material, equipment, and services. The agreement, however, survived a long process of diplomatic negotiations, political considerations, and policy process deliberations. The nuclear cooperation agreement was first considered by the two countries in 1982. It was initialed during President Reagan's visit to China in April 1984 but was not officially signed until July 1985 and was approved conditionally by Congress in December 1985.[2] The nuclear agreement was an important case for U.S. policy on the transfer of technology to China. It was the first high-technology transfer case since the Reagan administration relaxed its export control policies toward China.

Nuclear technology transfer was one important part of U.S. technology transfer policy toward China. Technology transfer was closely regulated by the U.S. government through export control laws. Liberalizing U.S. China export control policies, as part of U.S. efforts to strengthen ties with China, presented a challenge for U.S. policymakers. On the one hand, increasing U.S. technology transfer would help strengthen U.S.-PRC relations, promote U.S. business, improve the U.S. competitive position in the world technology market, and encourage China to purchase technology from the United States instead of from Japan and Western Europe. Some policymakers saw that technology transfer would have a positive effect of reinforcing those in the Chinese leadership who supported the open-door policy. Some policymakers, on the other hand, were concerned that the transfer of

Portions of this chapter are reprinted from *Asian Survey*, vol. 29, no. 9, pp. 870–882, by permission of the Regents of the University of California. Copyright ©1989 by the Regents of the University of California.

technology capable of dual applications might be used to enhance China's military capability in ways harmful to U.S. security interests or the security interests of its friends and allies. They were also concerned about the possibility that China might be willing to transfer acquired technology to third countries that would not be eligible in their own right for technological trade with the United States.

The nuclear agreement set up the basis for cooperation in a variety of peaceful applications of nuclear energy. It provided the legal framework for the export of nuclear reactors, fuel, and components and the exchange of technology, including cooperation in health, safety, and the environmental implications of peaceful uses of nuclear energy. Once the agreement was put into force, the U.S. nuclear industry would be able to export nuclear technology under licenses issued by the Nuclear Regulatory Commission, in accordance with existing law and export control policies.

This chapter examines the role and policy orientation of decisionmakers in the agreement process, as well as institutional interactions, especially between the executive and the Congress. What factors explain U.S. technology transfer policy toward China? How does the process work? What roles do Congress, the executive, and the bureaucracy play with regard to technology transfer?

Export Control Policies Toward China

The U.S. system of export control was, in general, designed to balance two sometimes conflicting goals: protecting national security by restricting the export of items that could bolster the military capabilities of unfriendly countries; and ensuring the ability of U.S. companies to export. The system was set up to identify and restrict U.S. exports that have military implications to certain countries, while making sure that such export control would not restrain trade in other items and to other parts of the world.[3]

Since normalization, U.S. technology transfer policies had generally reflected the belief that the benefits of increased technology sales to China outweighed the risks. Export controls on high-technology products to China had been gradually relaxed through the Export Administration Act amendments of 1977, which eased the equally restrictive trade policy toward all communist countries and delegated the power to the president to regulate the conduct of trade with different communist countries.[4] The Carter administration used the provision to facilitate a decision in April 1980 to move China from the more restrictive trade classification of Country Group Y (the classification for most East European countries and the Soviet Union) to a new classification created specifically for China, namely, Country Group P. Accordingly, in September 1980, the Department of Commerce made new, less restrictive guidelines that would govern the sale by the Carter administration of high-technology civilian goods with potential military applications.

Continuing the previous administration's policy of relaxing U.S. export controls, the Reagan administration further increased technology transfers to China. In June 1981, President Reagan issued a directive allowing for approval of technology and equipment to China at technology levels generally twice those approved for the Soviet Union. This "two times" policy, however, received criticism from involved government agencies, members of Congress, U.S. business leaders, and the Chinese government for its imprecise and unpredictable nature.[5] Partly in response to the criticism, the administration took further action to relax technology transfer, moving China from Country Group P to Country Group V—the same trade classification as that given to Japan and Western Europe.[6] Furthermore, the administration permitted exports to China of military items on the U.S. Munitions Control List on a case-by-case basis.

To accompany this change, the administration took the unusual step of establishing a "zone" system to deal with China exports. In May 1983, President Reagan directed that an interagency steering group on China technology transfer be created under the direction of the National Security Council, and this group was asked to define new technical guidelines that could be used to make licensing decisions. The goal was to restrict certain kinds of exports in the interest of national security while expediting the review of applications for nonsensitive exports by providing clear guidelines to license review officers.[7]

In September 1983, the interagency steering group established three technical guidelines: the green zone—routine licensing approval; the intermediate or yellow zone—case-by-case license review; and the red zone—most advanced technologies sensitive to national security.[8] According to the guidelines, cases falling in the green zone were reviewed by the Commerce Department. Cases falling in the yellow zone were reviewed case by case by both the Department of Defense and the Commerce Department. Items in the red zone were considered so sensitive as to pose a substantial threat to U.S. national security if exported.

Because of the time and technical efforts required to formulate the zones, the Commerce Department targeted seven commodity areas for special attention in license reviews.[9] These seven areas, which consisted of three-quarters of U.S. export license applications for China, were computers, computerized instruments, microcircuits, electronic instruments, recording equipment, semiconductor production equipment, and oscilloscopes.[10]

In theory, the most advanced technologies that have direct military applications fall in the red zone. Although no list of red zone items had been published, according to the State Department, included in the red zone were nuclear weapons and delivery systems, technologies and equipment used in intelligence gathering, electronic warfare, antisubmarine warfare, power projection, and air superiority.[11]

In practice, all non–green zone applications were reviewed and approved on a case-by-case basis. They required reviews by the Defense Department and other appropriate agencies. Approval procedures were somewhat complicated because they involved different agencies that might disagree over what kind of exports might or might not pose a threat to U.S. national security. Other factors could also affect approvals of export applications, such as the type of end user in China and the control that the U.S. firm would retain over the technology. In some situations, reviewing agencies placed certain conditions on exports—for instance, that the equipment must be operated by the U.S. firm or that it be leased but not sold to China.

The new guidelines clarified the ambiguity of the "two times" standard and accelerated the pace of bureaucratic reviews. The results of U.S. technology transfer liberalization could be seen in the licensing statistics. In 1982, the administration approved for export to China about 2,000 cases valued at about $500 million. In 1983, it approved over 3,000 cases, valued at over $1 billion. In 1984, it estimated 5,000 case approvals, with a total value of about $2 billion.[12]

There was, however, double-standard treatment with regard to technology transfers to China. Despite the fact that China was placed in the V category, which included Japan and Western Europe, the United States still treated China differently in that most dual-use technology transfers had to be reviewed on a case-by-case basis and "restrictions on certain products and technologies" would be necessarily applied.[13]

Prospects for Nuclear Cooperation with China

China's ambitious plans for its nuclear industry in the 1980s gave rise to new prospects for foreign nuclear technology to be exported to China's nuclear market. Developing nuclear technology had been given top priority in China's sixth and seventh five-year plans for the years 1981-1985 and 1986-1990. The Chinese leadership viewed nuclear power plants as an important aspect of the peaceful utilization of nuclear energy and an important step in meeting increasing demands for energy. China had announced plans to build at least ten nuclear power plants with a total generating capacity of 10,000 megawatts (MW) of nuclear power by the year 2000.[14] Chinese officials had expressed interest in importing foreign nuclear technology equipment and engineering services for most of these projects. Three nuclear power plants had been projected in the 1980s as a first step in laying down foundations for further nuclear power expansion by the end of this century.

The first nuclear power plant was a 300MW plant near Shanghai (Qinshan).[15] Despite the emphasis on self-reliance by the Chinese government, the Ministry of Nuclear Industry in 1982 was soliciting company bids for foreign components, for which the State Council had allocated $100 million.[16]

The second nuclear power plant to be built was the Daya Bay plant in Guangdong Province, using two 900MW reactors. This large project would be largely financed by foreign investors and built with foreign nuclear technology.[17] The third one would be an 1800MW facility to be built in Jiangsu (Sunan).

The three nuclear power plant projects provided foreign companies with alluring prospects. Since it was perhaps the last and the largest potential nuclear power market, China had attracted foreign competitors. Several countries wanted to sell complete reactor systems: the United States, France, West Germany, Japan, and the Soviet Union all could export pressurized water reactors (PWRs). Japan and West Germany had first taken steps to bid in the Qinshan project and secured supplies of two major reactor components—the pressure vessel and cooling pumps.[18]

The Daya Bay project involved the import of all important components. It thus attracted British, French, and German companies to bid for contracts. It was expected that France would supply the nuclear island, including reactor, primary pumps, and steam generators, and Great Britain would provide the generating components.[19] France and West Germany were also expected to compete for contracts in the Sunan project. Earlier in 1985, requests for quotations for construction of the project were issued to France and West Germany.[20]

These nuclear projects and the potential market presented a good prospect for U.S. companies. The United States had a certain advantage in its nuclear technology exports. It was the first country that had transferred the complete technology, as distinct from selling the equipment. The French, German, and Japanese designs were actually developed from U.S. PWR technology, and royalties had been paid to U.S. companies. The Chinese preferred to deal with U.S. companies directly. Westinghouse, for instance, would have been a strong competitor in the Daya Bay project.[21] In fact, the Chinese delegation visiting the United States expressed their favorable view of U.S. nuclear power technology.[22]

In the absence of an agreement for nuclear cooperation with China, the United States could not participate in the Chinese nuclear projects and thus lost some opportunities to its competitors. The Chinese had ordered major equipment items for the Qinshan project from West German and Japanese companies. For the two 900MW units, U.S. companies had tried hard to persuade the Chinese to defer their decisions in giving contracts to French and British companies until they were in a position to compete. But since there was no prospect for a Sino-U.S. nuclear agreement in early 1985, the Chinese could not wait any longer and granted contracts to U.S. competitors.[23]

U.S. Goals of Nuclear Cooperation with China

U.S. legal requirements to ensure U.S. participation in China's nuclear energy development created a need for an agreement on peaceful nuclear cooperation. The Reagan administration saw that such an agreement could advance U.S. political as well as economic interests. There were initially two goals sought by the administration in proposing a nuclear agreement with China: securing a share in China's nuclear market and further improving U.S.-China relations.

Economic considerations were the primary motive of the proposed nuclear agreement. According to the U.S. nuclear industry's estimates in 1984, for the first ten nuclear plants, U.S. industry could enjoy $10 billion in exports over five to ten years on the power plants alone, not including the opportunities this would open for the United States in related fields such as transmission and distribution systems, lighting, and factory installations.[24] Such nuclear trade could also represent as many as 200,000 person-years of direct employment and roughly double that amount if indirect employment was considered.[25] Even officially adopted figures in some conservative studies showed that in the Chinese nuclear market, as it was planned by the government, the United States could anticipate trade benefits from $3 billion to $7 billion, and about 160,000 person-years of employment.[26]

Because China represented one of the few remaining markets for significant near-term sales of nuclear equipment and technology, there was strong foreign competition for a share in the market. Assistant Secretary for East Asian and Pacific Affairs Paul Wolfowitz spelled out the challenge and opportunity before the House Foreign Affairs Committee:

> There will be opportunities for American companies to compete for nuclear power business in China. The market is there, and European and Japanese competitors are already active in it. China will look to the outside primarily for assistance in building up its indigenous nuclear power plant manufacturing industry. Over the long run, more than anything, China will want to import technology, modern management methods, and old-fashioned engineering know-how. In these areas—which are vitally important for the safety and efficiency of reactor operation—U.S. companies have a wealth of experience and flexibility, which put them in a strong competitive position.[27]

To secure U.S. competitiveness in China, however, a nuclear agreement was badly needed. Without it, U.S. companies would be barred by domestic law from exporting nuclear materials, equipment, and services. Ambassador-at-Large and Special Adviser to the Secretary of State on Non-Proliferation Policy and Nuclear Energy Affairs Richard T. Kennedy pointed out that such an agreement would establish the basis for cooperation in a variety of the peaceful applications of nuclear energy. It would set up the basis for the export of nuclear reactors, fuel, and components, and for the exchange of technology, including cooperation in health, safety, and the environmental implications of the peaceful uses of nuclear energy.[28]

In the absence of an agreement, U.S. companies had already lost several opportunities to bid in the three nuclear projects, which, according to the National Council for U.S.-China Trade, meant a possible loss of sales of $1.8 billion worth of reactors in 1984.[29] An official agreement could also engage the Export-Import Bank in supporting U.S. efforts to sell nuclear equipment and services to China. Japan had provided a $2 billion loan to finance its nuclear sales to China. The French and Germans were also offering financing at very attractive rates for China's nuclear program.[30]

In light of China's plan to build ten new power plants by the year 2000, both the administration and the nuclear industry saw an opportunity to sell billions of dollars worth of nuclear materials, equipment, and services to China. The State Department, with the technical assistance and concurrence of the Department of Energy and in consultation with the Arms Control and Disarmament Agency (ACDA), initiated and negotiated the agreement.

Negotiating the Agreement: Issues and Delays

The first talks about the possibility of an agreement for peaceful nuclear cooperation were held in September 1981, when Assistant Secretary of State for Oceans and Environment James Malone visited China. Former Deputy Secretary of State Walter Stoessel revealed U.S. discussions with the Chinese in a speech to the National Council on United States–China Trade in June 1982.[31] However, talks did not go far because the government agencies were unable to present a position paper to the president. Two major issues confronted U.S. negotiators.

First, China was still critical of the Nuclear Nonproliferation Treaty of 1970 and refused to sign it. It was not ready to join the International Atomic Energy Agency (IAEA), which required safeguard procedures on any nuclear exports. The possibility of Chinese involvement in international nuclear commerce in the 1980s worried U.S. policymakers. They viewed China's practice of exporting nuclear materials as undermining U.S. nonproliferation policy since China did not require safeguards against possible diversion for military use. Some agencies were especially concerned about intelligence leaks, suggesting that China was helping Pakistan's uranium enrichment efforts for use in weapons.[32]

On January 28, 1983, U.S. intelligence sources further leaked that China had provided Pakistan with sensitive information about the design of nuclear weapons. The sources said that by confirming for Pakistan that a particular bomb design could work, the Chinese may have made it possible for Pakistan to proceed with its efforts to build atomic bombs without staging an early nuclear test. This would bring a cutoff of a $3.2 billion security assistance program.[33]

The second issue was related to the requirements of the 1978 Nuclear Nonproliferation Act. Under the act, the United States was barred from selling nuclear materials to any countries that failed to accept requirements for inspection. It also called for U.S. controls over separation of weapons-usable plutonium from spent nuclear fuel. China was not yet ready to open its nuclear facilities to international on-site inspection.[34]

Those two issues aroused the concerns of U.S. negotiators, even though the issue of aiding Pakistan's nuclear project was based on "intelligence sources" that might be questionable.[35] Nevertheless, U.S. concerns about nonproliferation and on-site inspection were responsible for the impasse on the agreement. In February 1983, during Secretary George Shultz's visit to Beijing, the United States formally attached progress toward a bilateral agreement of nuclear cooperation to Beijing's assurances of its nonproliferation policy.[36]

Initialing and Signing of the Agreement

After more than a year of negotiations, the U.S.-China nuclear agreement on peaceful cooperation was officially initialed when President Reagan visited China in April 1984. The progress on the agreement reflected the desire of the U.S. nuclear industry to enter into China's nuclear market and the administration's effort to pursue its goal of developing cooperation with China in preventing international nuclear proliferation. The administration noticed that China had expressed its intention to join the IAEA and to observe and comply with IAEA safeguards since mid-1983. Furthermore, the administration was encouraged by the change in Chinese declaratory policy toward nuclear proliferation. Those developments led to an interagency's recommendation to move forward with the initiation.[37]

The nuclear agreement, however, was signed on July 23, 1985, by Chinese Vice Premier Li Peng and Secretary of Energy John S. Herrington. The signed agreement was identical to the earlier one initialed in Beijing after a fifteen-month delay.[38] The delay was caused by congressional opposition and bureaucratic concerns about the language of the agreement.

One factor that contributed to the delay was that congressional concerns about China's nonproliferation policies postponed the executive signing of the agreement. In 1984, some members of Congress took up intelligence allegations about China's nuclear aid program in Pakistan. Senator Cranston charged in a June 21, 1984, Senate floor speech that China was helping Pakistan construct a nuclear bomb.[39] On December 21, 1984, several senators signed a letter to Secretary Shultz, expressing their concerns about China's nuclear cooperation with other nations such as Pakistan and Brazil. The possibility of undermining U.S. nonproliferation efforts, they wrote, "is most troubling in the absence of clarification of PRC pledges made at the initialing of the proposed United States/PRC cooperative agreement not to help other nations develop nuclear weapons."[40]

Another reason for the delay was that what had seemed a successful diplomatic maneuver for the 1984 reelection campaign instantly became a liability as concerns about the agreement's language mounted. To avoid the possible political consequences of such a controversial agreement, the president's political strategists decided to shelve the agreement until after the election.[41] Officials from the executive branch and Congress had expressed their doubts on some of the key provisions in the agreement. They considered the language misleading for future nuclear business. In his letter to Senator William Proxmire (D-Wis), Nuclear Regulatory Commission Chairman Nunzio J. Palladino said that the commission "would have preferred that the agreement contain a clear statement of U.S. consent rights for the subsequent reprocessing or enrichment of U.S.-supplied nuclear reactor fuel or fuel used in U.S.-supplied reactors."[42]

To assure Congress of the Chinese position on the nonproliferation policy, the administration conducted a series of talks with China. Ambassador-at-Large Richard T. Kennedy prepared a classified memorandum containing various assurances and presented it to responsible Chinese officials during his trip to Beijing in June 1985.[43] Kennedy reportedly obtained their oral consent on the assurances, although they declined to sign the memorandum.[44] With the classified assurances, the administration was able to reach an interagency consensus in time to sign the agreement during the Chinese president's July visit.[45]

On July 24, 1985, President Reagan submitted the nuclear cooperation agreement to Congress for approval, together with his determination that the agreement had met all the requirements of U.S. law.[46] The U.S.-China nuclear cooperation agreement, after this delay, then became the subject of congressional deliberations in a long congressional approval process.

Legislative Intent and the Congressional Role

As concerns U.S. nuclear cooperation with foreign countries, Congress has passed several laws regulating U.S. nuclear commerce. Under the Atomic Energy Act of 1954 (AEA), Congress established the framework for U.S. nuclear exports. This act imposed few specific conditions on nuclear exports.[47] After India exploded a nuclear device from material supplied by the United States, Congress passed the Nuclear Nonproliferation Act (NNPA) in 1978, which tightened and standardized the export rules.[48]

The NNPA, which revised and amended the AEA, established the requirements for the end use of nuclear exports. One of the major revisions of the act, section 103, required that safeguards be set forth in the agreement for cooperation to guarantee that all transferred nuclear materials and equipment would be used for peaceful purposes only.[49] It stipulated that the United States must grant consent before the export recipient can reprocess the U.S.-supplied fuel or other fuel used in U.S.-supplied reactors. It required similar consent for use of plutonium obtained by reprocessing spent fuel. It also required U.S. permission before any U.S.-made items or materials and their by-products could be transferred to a third country.

Another statute set up legislative procedures and processes for Congress to review executive branch decisions. Under the Proxmire Amendment to the Export Administration Amendments Act, passed in June 1985, the president sent to Congress a nuclear cooperation agreement either with or without a "waiver" of the requirements of the NNPA.

If the president submitted an agreement with a waiver, either initially or in response to a committee request, it would not become effective unless both houses of Congress passed a resolution of approval within sixty working days. If the president determined that an agreement conformed to the NNPA requirements, he would submit it without a waiver to Congress for approval. The House Foreign Affairs Committee or the Senate Foreign Relations Committee would then have a thirty-day consultation period to determine whether the agreement did indeed conform to the act. If either committee determined otherwise, the president would be expected to either renegotiate the agreement or resubmit it with a waiver of the violated legal requirement. If the agreement were not challenged by Congress, it would automatically take effect unless both Houses passed a resolution of disapproval within ninety working days. This particular legislative process made it difficult for Congress to disapprove since the president would almost certainly veto any resolution of disapproval, and Congress would have to obtain a two-thirds majority to override the veto.

Congressional Concerns and Preferences

When President Reagan transmitted the agreement and accompanying papers to Congress for ratification, he sent a clear message that the agreement had met all the requirements of U.S. law.[50] Despite the executive's insistence on the legality of the agreement, Congress had a distinctly different orientation toward the agreement. While making sure that the agreement met the requirements of law, the executive was more interested in developing commercial nuclear relations with China. Congress, however, saw its responsibility primarily as making the executive adhere to a strict interpretation of the NNPA in the approval process, thus vigorously exercising its oversight function of the executive's nuclear agreement. Some key members of Congress, Senator John Glenn, Senator Allan Cranston, and Representative Edward J. Markey (D-Mass.), who were interested in and responsible for nuclear matters, took the lead in defining issues and congressional preferences in four areas.

China's nonproliferation policies. Some members of Congress asserted that the agreement did not provide satisfactory evidence of China's nonproliferation policies. They rejected the executive's claim that China's assurances had been contained in the classified "summary of discussions," or memorandum, on the ground that the memorandum had not been officially recognized by the Chinese government. These members felt it important to have the PRC's account of its policies to ensure a full understanding of PRC nonproliferation policies, including its commitment not to assist Pakistan and other nations in developing nuclear weapons capabilities. Therefore, members of Congress demanded that the president certify that China would provide a public, written, detailed description of its nonproliferation policies, and that those policies would correspond in all essential elements and details to the description of such policies contained in the Department of State's summary of discussions.[51]

Verification of exported items. In the State Department's legal memorandum, the executive took the position that IAEA safeguard procedures regarding the verification of peaceful uses on exported material and equipment were not required by the NNPA, since China was already a nuclear weapon state.[52] Some members of Congress took a harder position on the verification question, arguing that less strict application of the NNPA would undermine the objectives of U.S. nonproliferation policies and therefore the protection of U.S. national security.[53] Those members viewed the language on verification as inadequate, although the agreement provided that the two countries would "establish mutually acceptable arrangements for exchanges of information and visits" through diplomatic channels. The bill introduced by Senator Glenn called for the inclusion of the verification of peaceful uses on U.S. exported items, as required by the IAEA safeguards provisions.[54]

U.S. consent rights. Another congressional concern was over U.S. consent rights to various activities, including the further enrichment of U.S.-supplied fuel, the reprocessing of spent fuel of U.S. origin, and the reprocessing of spent fuel that had passed through a U.S. reactor. The agreement stated that "in the event that a party would like at some future time to undertake such activities, the parties will promptly hold consultations to agree on a mutually acceptable arrangement. . . . The parties agree that the consultations referred to above will be carried out in a manner to avoid hampering, delay, or undue interference in their respective nuclear program." The State Department claimed that the language adequately guarantees U.S. rights of prior approval to these future activities. Senator Glenn, however, regarded the language as "unorthodox" and subject to different interpretations. Some members were concerned that the language was so biased toward acceding to Chinese requests that, in essence, the United States had given up its consent rights. They demanded Chinese recognition that the language neither favorably nor unfavorably disposed the United States to exercise its consent rights in any particular direction.[55]

Future U.S. export laws and regulation. Finally, members of Congress were concerned with one part of the agreement that might restrict the ability of Congress to apply future nuclear export laws and regulations to China. This part, which was added to Article 2 at the request of the Chinese, reads: "The parties recognize, with respect to the observance of this agreement, the principle of international law that provides that a party may not invoke the provisions of its internal law as justification for its failure to perform a treaty."[56] The "unorthodox" language, as members of Congress put it, may be interpreted to suggest that the application of any new U.S. export legislation to nuclear trade with China could be a violation of the agreement. They argued that, since the agreement for cooperation was not a treaty that would require ratification by a two-thirds majority vote of the Senate, it was meant to be a framework for engaging in nuclear trade; it did not obligate the United States to transfer nuclear technologies, nor was it a substitute for binding contracts.[57]

Congressional Deliberations and Processes

The House Foreign Affairs and Senate Foreign Relations committees held two public hearings on the agreement, as did the Special Subcommittee on U.S.-Pacific Rim Trade of the House Energy and Commerce Committee. The public debates by members of Congress, administration officials, and other witnesses were centered on the four issues mentioned above.[58]

Congressional opponents of the agreement sought first to alter the review process provided by the Proxmire amendment, but to no avail.[59] Then came another congressional move. On October 9, Senators Glenn and Roth introduced a bill (S. 1754) spelling out four conditions on nuclear exports to China: peaceful-use verification equivalent to IAEA safeguards; U.S. prior consent rights regarding reprocessing U.S.-origin spent fuel; a written statement of China's nonproliferation policies; and Chinese acknowledgment of future U.S. legislation governing U.S. nuclear exports to China.[60] An identical bill (H.R. 3537) was introduced in the House by members of Congress Edward Feighan and Howard Wolpe on the same day.

The Glenn bill was strongly opposed by the White House and State Department officials on the grounds that China would not accept such conditions. The Foreign Relations Committee, through the joint efforts of Senator Cranston and administration officials, worked out a compromise incorporating some aspects of the Glenn bill into a joint resolution of approval (S.J. Res. 238). The compromise resolution, as Cranston contended, provided effective safeguards without requiring any renegotiation of the agreement with China.[61]

The resolution dropped Glenn's requirement for a written Chinese nonproliferation statement, instead requiring that the president certify to Congress that China had provided "additional information on its nuclear nonproliferation policies." It also gave up Glenn's condition on verification in compliance with IAEA safeguard requirements. It only called on the president to certify that "reciprocal arrangements are effective in ensuring peaceful uses" of nuclear technology licensed and resold by China. The committee resolution kept Glenn's two other conditions, requiring the president to certify that the agreement did not impose restrictions on future U.S. nuclear legislation and that it did not predispose the United States in approving Chinese reprocessing requests.[62]

The Senate committee approved S.J. Res. 238 on November 13 by a 12-3 vote.[63] On the revised conditions, Deputy Assistant Secretary of State James B. Devine commented that the administration examined the resolution and concluded that "it will not undercut the implementation of the agreement."[64]

The Senate approved S.J. Res. 238 by voice vote on November 21 without debate. There was no accompanying report by the Foreign Relations Committee. However, an amendment to the agreement was unexpectedly introduced by Senator Glenn during a Senate debate on the fiscal 1986 continuing appropriations. The Glenn amendment was approved by the Senate to be attached to the Senate's omnibus spending bill after the Senate rejected an effort to kill it.[65] The amendment went beyond S.J. Res. 238, which required that, before any nuclear technology was exported to China, the president must certify to Congress that China had clarified its nonproliferation policies and had accepted standards equivalent to those enforced by the IAEA.[66]

The Glenn amendment became the center of intense maneuvering within a House-Senate conference committee on the spending omnibus bill. Chinese officials had already stated that "any unilaterally imposed additional provisions beyond the agreement are completely unacceptable."[67] The administration had also pointed out that the amendment would kill the U.S.-China agreement. The State Department sent conferees a letter stating that the amendment "would do serious damage to U.S.-China relations."[68] The administration finally persuaded the conferees, and the conference voted 15-7 on December 16 to drop the amendment. President Reagan then signed the resolution.

The congressional resolution went beyond the mere approval of the U.S.-China nuclear agreement as the administration demanded. It set conditions on the implementation of the agreement that no transfer to China of nuclear materials, facilities, or components could take place until thirty days of continuous congressional session after the president had certified to Congress

1. that the United States and China had made arrangements that were "designed to be effective" in ensuring that U.S. nuclear exports would be used solely for "intended peaceful purposes" (the resolution did not specifically require arrangements equivalent to IAEA requirements, as the Glenn resolution had demanded);

2. that the Chinese government had provided "additional information" about its nonproliferation policies and that, based on this and all other information available to the U.S. government, China was not in violation of provisions of the NNPA (the resolution did not require a "public, written statement" from the Chinese government); and

3. that a clause in the agreement obligating the United States to "consider favorably" a Chinese request for permission to enrich or reprocess fuels of U.S. origin would not prejudice the U.S. decision on whether to approve or deny such a request.

The resolution further placed a condition on the administration barring nuclear licenses or transfers to China until the president sent Congress a report detailing the history and current developments of China's nuclear nonproliferation policies.

It should be noted that the resolution, in spite of the conditions, did not require any renegotiation of the terms that both the administration and China opposed. It merely asked the executive to provide more information on China's nonproliferation policies, and it restated congressional interpretation of some provisions of the agreement.

A Long-Delayed Agreement: An Analysis

The U.S.-China nuclear agreement endured a four-year process by which it was negotiated, signed, and approved. The final approval of the agreement was conditioned by the congressional resolution. There were two essential questions that deserve explanation. First, what are the factors that can account for the U.S.-China nuclear agreement? Second, what are the factors that can best explain the delay and the conditions of the agreement?

With regard to the first question, the new export control policy, the executive's goals of improving Sino-U.S. relations and expanding economic ties set priorities for interested agencies to pursue. As to the second question, bureaucratic factors and congressional intervention played a large role in delaying the process, and the coalition of liberal and conservative members of Congress pressured congressional leaders and the executive to come up with compromises on conditions to be attached to the agreement.

Executive Rationale and Business Interests

The rationale of the Reagan administration for its China policy was basically that of the previous administration: Developing a good and friendly relationship is in the interests of the United States. This rationale became the driving force of further relaxing technology transfer. The rationale behind U.S. technology exports policy toward China was summarized by President Reagan in a 1983 directive on technology transfer, which stated that supporting "a secure, friendly and modernized China" was in the interests of the United States.[69] Holding this basic view of U.S.-China policy, the United States had worked to strengthen and broaden political and economic ties with China for the past several years. It had also sought to regularize its relations with China in several areas. The United States had established a structure of arrangements and agreements in areas such as trade, investment, finance, civil aviation, and scientific, technological, and industrial cooperation.

In proposing nuclear cooperation with China, the administration responded primarily to the interests of the U.S. nuclear industry in China's nuclear market. The U.S. nuclear industry had closely followed developments in China's nuclear industry and saw its interests at stake in China's new and competitive nuclear market. In order to engage in nuclear trade with China, U.S. companies, by law, needed a Sino-U.S. nuclear agreement. It appeared that the lobby efforts by the U.S. nuclear industry corresponded with the administration's interests of expanding U.S.-China economic relations and with the goal of recent relaxed export control policies to further bilateral relations. It was these combined factors that helped initiate the agreement.[70]

As estimated by the U.S. nuclear industry, the potential value of U.S. exports for China's nuclear power program could be between $10 to 20 billion before the end of this century. And China has repeatedly expressed interest in foreign nuclear technology. This prospect for the U.S. nuclear industry, however, was hindered by the fact that bilateral nuclear trade was barred by U.S. law because the United States did not have a nuclear cooperation agreement with China. The U.S. nuclear industry was also badly in need of government help in competing with other countries for China's market. It already faced stiff competition from Canada, the United Kingdom, France, West Germany, Sweden, and Japan. Companies from some of these countries were fiercely competing to obtain contracts for building Chinese nuclear power plants. Some were competing with important aid and assistance from their governments, especially in marketing and financing nuclear reactors. Given this situation, a nuclear agreement and the necessary

U.S. government export financing support, as demanded by the U.S. nuclear industry,[71] would certainly be desirable.

To enter into nuclear trade with China was consistent with the U.S. objective of expanding the scope of Sino-U.S. economic relations. This economic objective was set by the Carter administration when it entered MFN relations with China. It was carried out by the Reagan administration. The United States saw China succeeding beyond the expectation of many analysts in its economic development programs. In 1983, China achieved a 10 percent growth rate in its industrial sector and had foreign exchange reserves in excess of $17 billion in 1984.[72] U.S.-China trade had expanded greatly since both countries signed a trade agreement in 1979, estimated at $5.5 to $6 billion in 1985, according to the testimony by the Council for United States-China Trade.[73] China was also shifting its imports from traditional agricultural products to technology-related trade. In 1983, China had a 14 percent increase in nonagricultural trade, and in the first six months of 1984, there was a 24 percent increase in Chinese imports of goods that required licensing from the United States.[74] The shift made it possible for the U.S. nuclear industry to sell $1.8 billion worth of reactors in 1984, if the nuclear cooperation agreement could be concluded in that year.[75]

U.S. economic objectives were further supported by the U.S.-China export control policy that the Reagan administration had made as a gesture to improve U.S.-China relations after the arms sales crisis. The nuclear cooperation agreement was the first agreement that embodied relaxed U.S. technology transfer policy toward China since 1983. Such an agreement provided U.S. companies with the necessary legal means to take advantage of the new export control policy as they applied for export licenses.

To advance U.S. nonproliferation objectives was another U.S. goal of peaceful nuclear cooperation with China. This goal was promoted only after the initial negotiation in 1981 by the State Department and interested bureaucratic agencies. The Reagan administration hoped that through nuclear cooperation with China it could influence China's nonproliferation policy.[76]

The promotion of the nonproliferation goal to the top of the U.S. objectives in the negotiation indeed had some impact on the process and on the clarification of China's nonproliferation policies. Since the introduction of its domestic reforms and its open-door policy, China had undergone a change in its orientation toward the international system.[77] China had moved toward more active participation on disarmament issues in general and on nonproliferation in particular.[78] In the 1980s, China had taken a series of nonproliferation steps, moving to accept basic nonproliferation practices and norms. On January 1, 1984, China joined the International Atomic Energy Agency (IAEA). As a member of the IAEA, China would require IAEA safeguards on its nuclear exports to non–nuclear weapon states. This policy was formally implemented in late 1984 when the China-Brazil civil nuclear cooperation agreement encompassed a reciprocal IAEA safeguards requirement for items transferred under the agreement.[79]

During his January 1984 visit to the United States, Premier Zhao stated that China does not "engage in nuclear proliferation ourselves, nor do we help other countries to develop nuclear weapons."[80] On May 15, 1984, in an address to the sixth National People's Congress, Zhao restated China's nonproliferation policy, which the Congress subsequently endorsed. He pointed out that China was critical of the discriminatory Nuclear Nonproliferation Treaty and declined to accede to the treaty, but he emphasized that China in no way favored nuclear proliferation, nor would China engage in such proliferation by helping other countries to develop nuclear weapons."[81]

Ironing Out Bureaucratic Differences

Liberalization of technology transfers to China initially did not go as far as the rationale allowed. There had been a gap between China policy objectives and the actual formulation of liberal technology transfer policies. One of the main reasons had been bureaucratic resistance to actualizing such a rationale.[82] It was not until 1983, when President Reagan directed that China be treated as a "friendly, non-allied country," that technology transfer policies toward China were formulated.[83] Under the new policy, China was placed in the Country Group V category in terms of export controls, and a "zone" system was set up specifically for China to guide bureaucratic controls of technology transfers.

Bureaucratic positions and preferences with regard to the nuclear agreement played a large role in redefining the goal of U.S. nuclear technology policies and delaying the initiation and approval of the agreement. Different agencies viewed the agreement from their own bureaucratic perspectives, advancing their preferences or priorities in initiating the agreement.

The Energy Department, which signed the agreement with its Chinese counterpart, was responsible for policies affecting the U.S. nuclear industry. Since the industry was facing a sluggish domestic nuclear market, it exerted pressure on the Energy Department to help it find foreign markets. In light of China's ambitious nuclear energy plan, the Energy Department saw that a multibillion-dollar business opportunity was at stake and that if the United States did not act, other nations would. Secretary Herrington made a point in his testimony that the United States needed to be a player in the Chinese market for the "survival" of the U.S. nuclear industry. He stressed that if the United States "is not allowed to compete in this [market] by signing this agreement, we are damaging the long-term security and viability of the nuclear industry in this country."[84] It was clear that the Energy Department's position was to help U.S. industry in obtaining a share of China's nuclear market. Thus, it not only favored an agreement, but it took the lead in sponsoring it.[85]

However, since the Energy Department had limited power in diplomacy, the State Department assumed the principal responsibility of negotiating the agreement. It was interested in improving overall Sino-U.S. relations and such an agreement served its interests. But unlike the Energy Department, whose sole interest was in the market, State had other interests as well, namely, the nonproliferation issue. That was why the negotiations broke off in 1982 after the two countries had explored the possibility in 1981. State shifted its focus in the negotiations to China's stance on the nonproliferation issue, after the press and members of Congress expressed their concerns. Subsequently, State promoted China's nonproliferation policy to the top of the three objectives in negotiating the agreement.[86] Thus, while State took a supportive position on the agreement, it preferred a cautious and deliberate approach in the negotiation process. Even after the initiation of the agreement in April 1984, State was still holding back the agreement for the signing. Ambassador-at-Large Kennedy went to Beijing to renegotiate the understanding of China's nonproliferation policy. One State Department official explained the delay, saying U.S. negotiators were not "sure that we have a complete understanding" about the Chinese position on the issue, but "we are getting there slowly but surely."[87]

Two other regulatory agencies, the Arms Control and Disarmament Agency (ACDA) and the Nuclear Regulatory Commission (NRC), also influenced the process of negotiations and the signing of the agreement. The NRC went even further in influencing the congressional approval process. As the regulatory agency on nuclear matters, its primary concerns were nonproliferation safeguards issues. The ACDA's main goal in the agreement was to bolster "vital nonproliferation norms and standards." The ACDA succeeded in putting its goal at the top of the three objectives shared by the State Department.[88] To achieve this goal, it insisted on clarifying matters related to the implementation of China's nuclear policies if it would delay the process. Kenneth L. Adelman, director of the ACDA, stated clearly that "we did not want to proceed until we were completely satisfied. We were willing to wait as long as need be."[89] The NRC had serious reservations over the agreement, even though it was recommended by the State Department for presidential approval. The NRC's position provided some members of Congress with the ammunition needed to attack the agreement in the approval process.[90]

Congressional Orientation and Processes

Unlike the executive, Congress stressed the legal aspect of the agreement. It was predisposed to take a different approach from that of the executive by adhering to the strict interpretation of the AEA, as amended. This approach helped some active members set congressional priorities in the process. While the majority of members were inclined to support the agreement, they found themselves following the cause of some leading opponents to revise the agreement. The Glenn resolution and the Feighan resolution raised four priorities that they wanted Congress to stress in considering the agreement.

There was an unusual congressional coalition formed by liberals and conservatives who aimed to block the executive agreement in the process. Though for different reasons, this coalition was formed to prevent U.S. nuclear technology transfers to China.[91] It affected the executive's effectiveness in persuading the Congress not to put any conditions on the agreement. It enhanced the congressional perception that some measures should be taken to balance the executive approach to developing nuclear cooperation with China. The coalition eventually produced the final resolution, which was a compromise to the Glenn resolution.

Leaders of both Senate and House committees and executive lobbying in the final process played an important role in reshaping congressional orientation and in producing the final outcome. The chairs of two House Foreign Affairs subcommittees (on Asian and Pacific Affairs and on International Economic Policy and Trade), Stephen J. Solarz (D-N.Y.) and Don Bonker (D-Wash.), influenced the majority opinion when they concluded that they could uncover no evidence to support Senators Cranston and Glenn's claims that China was currently helping other countries develop nuclear weapons.[92]

Both full committee leaders were responsible for ensuring the passage of the agreement without serious amendment in the congressional process. In the initial process, both committees' leaders set aside the demand of resubmitting the agreement to Congress with a waiver, which would have made the approval more difficult. Then they saw to reconciling the hard-line resolutions into a more acceptable joint resolution. They took the lead in working closely with the executive and key members of the committees to come up with a carefully drafted resolution. Furthermore, they chose the best strategy to set up the rule to ensure the passage of the resolution without any floor amendment. In the Senate, the majority leader brought the resolution up for a vote during a break in the debates, when some leading critics were not present.[93] (It should be noted that the Senate leaders had already received the majority votes; it was doubtful that this strategy would have worked if the vote had been close.) In the House, the leaders of the Foreign Affairs Committee asked the Committee on Rules for a closed rule to bar any amendment before the floor action.[94]

The strenuous lobbying efforts by the executive in the final process encouraged a balance of the objectives of the two institutions. The administration committed its resources to convincing the House-Senate conference to give up the Glenn amendment. These resources included Vice President Bush's last minute lobbying,[95] a State Department warning letter to the House committee,[96] and special phone calls from Beijing by U.S. Ambassador to China Winston Lord.[97] The executive was even prepared to use the last resort of the presidential veto to make sure the amendment was dropped.[98] This interbranch interaction helped reconcile institutional differences into a compromise policy that both the executive and the Congress could accept.

Conclusion

The nuclear agreement was the outcome of a long, deliberate process in which the executive, Congress, and bureaucratic agencies played a role in influencing the negotiations and approval of the agreement. There were different political orientations and considerations associated with the agreement, which determined the roles that concerned officials played in the process. The approval process opened up an arena for individual decisionmakers to exert their influences in the making of the agreement. It also provided an opportunity for the executive and Congress to interact in seeking a mutual ground on which the agreement could be approved.

The driving force of the agreement was U.S. economic interest in China's newly opened nuclear market. Largely in response to China's interest in foreign nuclear technology and to the U.S. nuclear industry's demands in entering the market, the United States initiated an agreement with China. The initiation was also explained by the Reagan administration's interest in improving Sino-U.S. relations, which was demonstrated in its earlier decision to relax its export control policy toward China.

The rational actor model assumes that the United States would provide China with nuclear technology to advance its political and economic interests without risking its security interests. This assumption was only partially confirmed by the outcome. The nuclear agreement did establish the framework for nuclear technology transfers to China as predicted.

But the rational actor model does not and cannot predict that there will be a delay in the process. It cannot forecast the conditions attached to the agreement, since it assumes that there is only one process in which the rational actor establishes the goal and selects the means to maximize the goal. The model did not take into account other policy processes in which various actors had played a role. For example, the ACDA and the State Department helped define the nonproliferation objective, the most important objective of the agreement.

Bureaucratic politics were largely responsible for the agreement, not only in terms of negotiations, but also in terms of the content of the agreement. The nature of the agreement was intricate, technical, and detail oriented. The administration from the beginning left most of the responsibility for developing the agreement to bureaucratic agencies. Even Secretary Shultz, who was in charge of the negotiations, left the whole matter to his aides.[99] Despite the Energy Department's and U.S. nuclear industry's interest in an early agreement, the State Department and the ACDA controlled the pace and the content of the negotiations. Since the two agencies were charged with negotiating power, they were favorably positioned to translate their preferences and objectives, through the process, into the content of the agreement.

Bureaucratic interests were also responsible for delaying the signing of the agreement. The Defense Department opposed the agreement, and its officials sought to form an alliance with members of Congress who did not support the agreement.[100] The NRC had serious reservations on U.S. consent rights and preferred a stricter approach to the agreement. Because of different views among bureaucratic agencies on China's nonproliferation policies, the State Department had to go back to Beijing to seek additional assurances even one year after the agreement was initiated. In Senator Cranston's words, "It is American bureaucrats reassuring each other."[101]

The State Department played a special role throughout the process. It coordinated bureaucratic action in the negotiations and was the chief negotiator. It recommended to the president appropriate options to adopt. Its role did not end after the signing of the agreement; it was charged with the responsibility to see to the passage of the agreement through the Congress. Not only did it play a coordinating role among bureaucratic agencies, it also functioned as a liaison between the executive and the Congress and the main lobbying force for the agreement.

The interbranch politics assumption that there would be joint efforts by the executive and Congress in determining U.S. technology transfer policies was confirmed both by the outcome and the process. Congress had a different orientation toward balancing executive interests in nuclear technology transfers to China and played an assertive oversight role in stressing U.S. nonproliferation interests in the process. The congressional approval procedures and processes, as provided for in the NNPA, opened up an arena for members of Congress and the executive to act and interact. This open process enabled those leading members of Congress who were interested in and concerned about U.S. technology transfers to China to shape the congressional orientation toward a more restrictive adoption of the NNPA. Those members of Congress had preferred more specific and more orthodox language in the agreement and had employed the rules and the process to try to skew the policy toward what they preferred.

These open processes and procedures, however, provided a mechanism to balance policy outcomes. The rules and norms governing the interaction between the executive and the Congress throughout the approval process embodied such a mechanism. The rules provided for differences of opinion to be expressed in the open process and set up the limits on congressional behavior. These norms, defined as both branches sharing the power of foreign policymaking, required the two branches to compromise their differences, thus enabling the policy to be negotiated and bargained in the closed, behind-the-door process. The strength of the bargaining position depended on the latitude of law, congressional cohesiveness, and resources committed by the executive.

Two congressional factors also contributed to the balance in policy outcomes. The Republican majority in the Senate appeared unwilling to embarrass the president by opposing or amending the delicately crafted agreement. Senate leaders made sure that the rules and procedures were applied in such a way as to fend off any potential action that would have killed the agreement. In the House, some key leaders, whose committees or subcommittees had jurisdiction over the agreement, were instrumental in shaping the majority orientation in the process. Endorsement by the influential chairman of the Committee on Energy and Commerce, Representative John Dingell (D-Mich.), and by members of Congress Solarz and Bonker, was apparently significant in gaining the support of a large majority of the members.[102]

In short, the rational actor model provided a rationale for the development of nuclear cooperation with China. But the bureaucratic politics model and the interbranch politics model are more useful in accounting for the making of U.S. China policy as regards nuclear technology transfer (see Figure 5.1).

Figure 5.1   Decisionmaking on Nuclear Technology Transfer

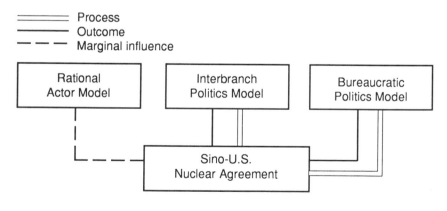

Notes

1. For the text of the nuclear agreement, see U.S. Congress, House, *Agreement Between the United States and the People's Republic of China Concerning Peaceful Uses of Nuclear Energy: Message from the President of the United States, Transmitting an Agreement for Cooperation Between the Government of the United States and the Government of the People's Republic of*

China Concerning Peaceful Uses of Nuclear Energy, House Document 99–86, 99th Cong., 1st sess., 1985.

2. Congress passed a joint resolution (S.J. Res. 238), with conditions attached, approving the agreement. See *Public Law 99–183*, December 16, 1985.

3. Congress, Office of Technology Assessment (hereafter, OTA), *Energy Technology Transfer to China: A Technical Memorandum* (Washington, D.C.: Government Printing Office, 1985), p. 48.

4. Congress, House, Committee on Foreign Affairs, *The Export Administration Act Amendments of 1978*, 96th Cong., 1st sess., 1979.

5. See the statement by Secretary of Commerce Malcolm Baldrige, "U.S. Policy on Exports of Advanced Technology to China," in Department of State, *American Foreign Policy: Current Documents, 1983* (Washington, D.C.: Government Printing Office), p. 1005.

6. In announcing the change, the administration noted that there would be continuance on an expedited basis of national security reviews of all license applications. See Department of Commerce, *Export Administration Annual Report 1983* (Washington, D.C.: Government Printing Office, 1984), p. 9.

7. Congress, OTA, *Energy Technology Transfer to China: A Technical Memorandum*, p. 48.

8. For a statement of the guidelines for U.S. technology transfer to China, see testimony of Secretary of Commerce Malcolm Baldrige before the Special Subcommittee on U.S. Trade with China of the Committee on Energy and Commerce in Congress, House, Special Subcommittee on U.S. Trade with China of the Committee on Energy and Commerce, *Exports to China: A Review on the 200th Anniversary of U.S.-China Trade*, 98th Cong., 2nd sess., 1984, pp. 5–8.

9. By 1985, there were eight major categories. Two of the seven had been merged, and two more had been added (microwave, numerically controlled machine tools). See Congress, OTA, *Energy Technology Transfer to China*, footnote 6, p. 48.

10. Congress, House, *Exports to China*, p. 4.

11. See Department of State, "U.S. Exports Controls and China," *GIST*, Bureau of Public Affairs, March 1985.

12. Congress, House, *Exports to China*, p. 4.

13. See Department of Commerce, *Export Administration Annual Report 1983*, p. 9.

14. For details, see Minister of Nuclear Industry Jiang Xinxiong, "China's Nuclear Industry in the Last 30 Years and Its Future," *Industrial Equipment and Materials* 6, no. 4, Hong Kong.

15. This project was said to be growing out of China's naval propulsion program. It was originally named the 728 project, standing for 1970 (7), February (2), and eight (8), which symbolized the commencement of Chinese domestic R & D authorized by Premier Zhou. The project endured several ups and downs due to political turbulence and economic readjustment, and construction finally began in 1985. See Martin Weil, "The First Nuclear Power Project," *China Business Review* 19, no. 5 (September-October 1982), pp. 40–44.

16. Weil, "The First Nuclear Power Project," p. 41.

17. Congress, OTA, *Energy Technology Transfer to China*, p. 32.

18. Congress, House, Committee on Foreign Affairs, *Proposed Nuclear Cooperation Agreement with the People's Republic of China: Hearing and Markup Before the Committee on Foreign Affairs, House of Representatives*, 99th Cong., 1st sess., 1985, p. 165.

19. Alan T. Crane and Richard P. Suttmeier, "Nuclear Trade with China," *Columbia Journal of World Business* 21 (Spring 1986), p. 37.

20. Congress, House, *Proposed Nuclear Cooperation Agreement with the People's Republic of China*, p. 165.

21. Weil, "The First Nuclear Power Project," p. 43.

22. Congress, Senate, Committee on Foreign Relations, *United States–People's Republic of China Nuclear Agreement: Hearing Before the Committee on Foreign Relations, United States Senate*, 99th Cong., 1st sess., 1985, p. 123.

23. Congress, House, Special Subcommittee on U.S. Trade with China of the Committee on Energy and Commerce, *Nuclear Energy Cooperation with China: Hearing Before the Special Subcommittee on U.S. Trade with China of the Committee on Energy and Commerce, House of Representatives*, 98th Cong., 2nd sess., 1984, p. 4.

24. Ibid., p. 56.

25. Ibid., p. 6.

26. See the prepared statement by Secretary of Energy John S. Herrington in Congress, Senate, *United States–People's Republic of China Nuclear Agreement*, pp. 118–128.

27. Department of State, Bureau of Public Affairs, *U.S.-China Nuclear Cooperation Agreement*, Current Policy no. 729, 1985, p. 4.

28. Ibid., pp. 2–3.

29. See the prepared statement by Roger W. Sullivan, vice executive president, National Council for U.S.-China Trade, in Congress, House, Committee on Foreign Affairs, House of Representatives and its Subcommittees on Asian and Pacific Affairs and on International Economic Policy and Trade, *United States–China Relations: Hearings Before the Committee on Foreign Affairs, House of Representatives and Its Subcommittees on Asian and Pacific Affairs and on International Economic Policy and Trade*, 98th Cong., 2nd sess., 1984, pp. 111–114.

30. Congress, House, *Nuclear Energy Cooperation with China*, p. 5.

31. Martin Weil, "The Elusive U.S.-China Agreement," *China Business Review* 9, no. 5 (September–October 1982), p. 45.

32. Suspicions about Chinese aid to Pakistan were disclosed in August 1982 by James I. Malone, assistant secretary of state for oceans and international environmental and scientific affairs. It was reported that Pakistan had been trying to develop its own ability to produce highly enriched uranium as a fuel for research reactors that could also be converted for developing nuclear weapons. See Judith Miller, "U.S. Is Holding Up Peking Atom Talks: China's Reluctance to Accept Checks on Nuclear Exports Viewed as an Obstacle," *New York Times*, September 19, 1982, p. 11.

33. Miller, "U.S. Is Holding Up Peking Atom Talks."

34. Weil, "The Elusive U.S.-China Agreement," p. 45.

35. According to the author of "The Elusive U.S.-China Agreement," there had been rumors for years that China had been assisting Pakistan in its weapons development, but none had yet been proven. Some of the rumors originated with the Soviet Union. Another piece of information came from a friendly government (the British). The British, however, did not attach nearly as much significance to the information as the United States did. Thus, Weil questioned the reliability of U.S. intelligence analysis. The leaks of such sources, the author pointed out, resulted from the factional dispute within the U.S. government over nuclear cooperation with China. See Weil, "The Elusive U.S.-China Agreement," p. 46.

36. Bernard Gwertzman, "Shultz Snaps at U.S. Businessmen in Peking," *New York Times*, February 4, 1983, p. 9.

37. Interview with State Department officials, Washington, D.C., August 1987.

38. *Congressional Quarterly Weekly Report,* July 27, 1985, p. 1479.

39. Ibid.

40. The copies of the letter were also sent to Secretary Caspar W. Weinberger and Secretary of Energy Donald P. Hodel. The letter was obtained by the author from Senator Glenn's office.

41. Christopher E. Paine, "Fuzzy Safeguards for U.S.-China Deal," *Bulletin of the Atomic Scientists* 41 (October 1985), pp. 6–7.

42. Ibid.

43. According to Representative Edward J. Markey, this memorandum was a "non-paper" since the Chinese neither agreed to it nor signed it. See his testimony before the House Foreign Affairs Committee on July 31, 1985, in Congress, House, *Proposed Nuclear Cooperation Agreement with the People's Republic of China.*

44. Paine, "Fuzzy Safeguards," p. 6.

45. The executive branch prepared a legal memorandum responding to members of Congress on issues of safeguards and reprocessing and other fuel cycle activities. According to the memorandum, the president was recommended by the unanimous advice of the secretaries of state and energy and the director of the Arms Control and Disarmament Agency that the requirements of law relating to the issues had been met. For the details of the memorandum, see Congress, House, *Proposed Nuclear Cooperation Agreement with the People's Republic of China,* pp. 202–226.

46. Under the Proxmire amendment to the Export Administration Amendments Act, passed in June 1985, the president must submit a nuclear cooperation agreement to Congress for ratification.

47. *Authorization of Appropriations for Fiscal Years 1980–1985, Public Law 98–553, United States Statutes at Large,* vol. 98, part 3, October 30, 1984, p. 2825.

48. *Nuclear Nonproliferation Act of 1978,* Public Law 95–242, *United States Statutes at Large,* vol. 92, part 1, March 10, 1978, p. 120.

49. Under section 127(1) of the NNPA, nuclear cooperation with non–nuclear weapons states required, as a condition, the IAEA safeguards that call for on-site inspections and audits of nuclear facilities. Since China is a nuclear state, IAEA safeguards were not provided for in the agreement. It, however, provided for arrangements for exchanges of information and visits by U.S. government officials to materials, facilities, and components subject to the agreement.

50. For his message and accompanying papers, see *House Document 99–86,* 96th Cong., 1st sess., 1985.

51. See Glenn, "Sino-American Nuclear Verification Act of 1985," S. 1754, a Senate bill introduced by Senator Glenn, in *Congressional Record,* October 9, 1985, p. S13012.

52. Congress, House, *Proposed Nuclear Cooperation Agreement with the People's Republic of China,* p. 264.

53. See Representative Markey's letter to House Foreign Affairs Chairman Dante B. Fascell (D-Fla.), ibid., p. 36.

54. Glenn, "Sino-American Nuclear Verification Act of 1985."

55. Ibid.

56. See Daniel Horner and Paul Leventhal, "The U.S.-China Nuclear Agreement: A Failure of Executive Policy Making and Congressional Oversight," *The Fletcher Forum* 11, no.1 (Winter 1987), footnote 18, p. 113.

57. Glenn, "Sino-American Nuclear Verification Act of 1985."

58. At the insistence of Senator Cranston, the Foreign Relations Committee demanded that knowledgeable intelligence agency officials testify on these

reports of Chinese activities. Subsequently, both committees held two closed hearings on U.S. intelligence information indicating a 1983 Chinese test of a nuclear device built by Pakistan and designed by China and on reports of unsafeguarded Chinese nuclear exports. Although these briefings were classified, it could be inferred from the subsequent congressional actions that the reports were either inconclusive or inaccurate.

59. Under the Proxmire amendment, it would be relatively easy for opponents to block the agreement submitted with a waiver of statutory requirements, while an agreement submitted without a waiver would be difficult to block since Congress needed a two-thirds majority to override a presidential veto on a disapproval resolution. On September 20, 1985, Congressman Markey introduced a resolution (H. Res. 269) with thirty-six cosponsors, calling for resubmitting the agreement with certain waivers to the AEA, as amended. The resolution asked for waivers on the AEA requirements on safeguards for U.S.-origin nuclear equipment and material, as well as U.S. consent rights for the reprocessing of U.S.-origin fuel (H. Res. 269, in *Congressional Record*, 99th Cong., 1st sess., 1985, p. H11765) The Markey resolution, which was referred to the House Foreign Affairs Committee, however, was not supported by the committee and died without a hearing. A similar proposal was drafted in the Foreign Relations Committee, but no further action was taken by the committee.

60. See *Congressional Record*, October 9, 1985, p. S13012.

61. Joanne Omang, "Nuclear Pact with China Wins Senate Approval," *Washington Post*, November 22, 1985, p. 3.

62. The Senate resolution took special note when it said that it did favor the agreement "notwithstanding the requirements of Section 103 of the Atomic Energy Act." It added, "Nothing in this Agreement or this resolution may be construed as providing a precedent or other basis for the negotiation or renegotiation of any other agreement for nuclear cooperation." By so doing, Congress waived the statutory requirements on nuclear safeguards and consent rights, something the president was required to do by the NNPA. For the text of S.J. Res. 238, see *Congressional Record*, December 11, 1985, p. H11761.

63. In the House committee, a similar action was taken to replace the Feighan bill with a mild resolution (H.J. Res. 404) sponsored by members of Congress Don Bonker and Stephen Solarz. The original resolution approved the agreement with various "whereas" clauses but no legally binding language. The Senate committee's passage of S.J. Res. 238 put supporters of a more restrictive agreement on the House committee in a fix. The agreement would go into effect automatically after ninety days of continuous session without congressional approval, which could mean that differing versions of the two Houses would put the agreement into force without any conditions. Thus, on November 13, the House committee chose to amend H.J. Res. 404 to add some conditions identical to the ones reported by the Senate committee and approved it by voice vote. See *House Report 99–382*, 99th Cong., 1st sess., 1985.

64. Patrick E. Tyler, "Hill Panels Add Conditions to U.S.-China Nuclear Pact," *Washington Post*, November 14, 1985, p. 1.

65. See Amendment 1347 to H.J. Res. 456, December 9, 1985, *Congressional Record*, 99th Cong., 1st sess., p. S17141.

66. In the House, the sponsors of the House resolution were blocked in their first attempt to bring the resolution to the floor on December 5. House leaders withdrew their attempt to bring the measure up for a vote when Representative Dan Burton objected to a motion allowing action by unanimous consent. The measure did not reach the floor until December 11. In a procedural vote, 158 members voted against the rule under which the resolution was brought to the

floor and the rule prohibiting amendments on the floor. H. Res. 333 set up the rule with regard to the floor action, which prevented possible amendment by those who were encouraged by the Senate's action on the Glenn amendment. According to H. Res. 333, there was a three-hour debate on the measure, and it was a closed rule, so it could not be amended. Once the rule was set, opponents in the House could express their opposition in the debate but could not amend the agreement. The House finally approved S.J. Res. 238 by a vote of 307–112. See *Congressional Record*, December 11, 1985, p. H11785.

67. Joanne Omang, "China Assails Changes in Nuclear Pact," *Washington Post*, December 12, 1985, p. 35.

68. *Congressional Quarterly Weekly Report*, December 14, 1985, p. 2654.

69. Department of State, Bureau of Public Affairs, *The U.S.-China Relationship*, Current Policy no. 594, May 31, 1984, p. 2.

70. Horner and Leventhal argued that the agreement was initiated and approved mainly due to industry lobbying. This argument, however, did not take into account the executive's economic objectives and export control policy regarding China. See Horner and Leventhal, "The U.S.-China Nuclear Agreement: A Failure of Executive Policymaking and Congressional Oversight," pp. 113–114.

71. Congress, House, *Nuclear Energy Cooperation with China*, p. 5.

72. Prepared statement by Roger W. Sullivan, executive vice president, National Council for United States–China Trade, in Congress, House, *United States–China Relations*, p. 108.

73. Ibid.

74. Ibid.

75. Ibid., p. 110.

76. That is to acknowledge and accept international nonproliferation practices and norms and to "implement their general nonproliferation policies in a manner consistent with the basic nonproliferation practices" that the United States and other nuclear suppliers would follow and advocate. Congress, House, *Nuclear Energy Cooperation with China*, p. 60.

77. For details of China's foreign policy in the 1980s, see Harry Harding, ed., *China's Foreign Relations in the 1980s* (New Haven: Yale University Press, 1984), particularly Chapter 6.

78. China in the past had opposed the monopoly of nuclear weapons by the two superpowers. Like France, it especially criticized the Nuclear Nonproliferation Treaty as discriminatory. But, at the same time, China's actions were more restrained than its declaratory policy.

79. Congress, House, *Proposed Nuclear Cooperation Agreement with the People's Republic of China*, p. 167.

80. Congress, House, *Nuclear Energy Cooperation with China*, p. 17.

81. Congress, Senate, Committee on Foreign Relations, *United States–China Relations: Today's Realities and Prospects for the Future; Hearing Before the Committee on Foreign Relations, United States Senate*, 98th. Cong., 2nd. sess., 1984, p. 4.

82. Hobart Rowen, "Reagan Permits China to Buy Computers, Other Disputed Items," *Washington Post*, June 21, 1983, p. A8.

83. For more details of the president's directive, see Department of State, Current Policy, no. 594.

84. Congress, House, *Proposed Nuclear Cooperation Agreement with the People's Republic of China*, p. 99.

85. The fact that the energy secretary signed the agreement showed that such an agreement was on Energy Department turf.

86. According to Wolfowitz, the other two objectives were giving U.S. firms the opportunity to enter into China's market and reinforcing the overall framework of U.S.-China relations. See State Department, "U.S-China Nuclear Cooperation Agreement," p. 5.

87. Charlotte Saikowski, "Reagan Under Pressure to OK Reactor Pact with China: U.S. Industry Concerned Congress May Not Ratify Nuclear Partnership," *Christian Science Monitor*, March 4, 1985, p. 5.

88. Since the ACDA was the main regulatory body regarding nuclear matters, it had the expertise and power needed by the State Department in the negotiations. In fact, the ACDA fully participated in all stages of the negotiations.

89. U.S. State Department, "U.S.-China Nuclear Cooperation Agreement," p. 2.

90. In his letter to Senator William Proxmire, the NRC chairman, Nunzio J. Palladino, expressed his concerns about the assurances of China's nuclear policies, U.S. consent rights, and U.S. future law regarding nuclear trade with China. See Joanne Omang, "NRC Cites Concerns on China Treaty: Uncertainties Seen About Arms Spread," *Washington Post*, October 5, 1985, p. 3.

91. Liberal members of Congress were mainly concerned with the proliferation issue and opposed the agreement on the grounds that the agreement did not fully comply with U.S. law. Conservative members, on the other hand, objected to the agreement purely on the ideological grounds that any technology transfer to communist countries would be strategically detrimental to U.S. interests.

92. Solarz disclosed that intelligence agency representatives had told his subcommittee that China either had stopped giving nuclear weapons assistance or had developed ties that posed no real danger of nuclear proliferation. See *Congressional Quarterly Weekly Report*, December 14, 1985, p. 2654.

93. Omang, "Nuclear Pact with China Wins Senate Approval."

94. *Congressional Record*, December 11, 1985, p. 11758.

95. Patrick E. Tyler, "Nuclear Pact with China Nears Last Test on Hill," *Washington Post*, December 16, 1985, p. 23.

96. The State Department sent Congressman Broomfield a letter before the House floor action, strongly opposing any amendment to S.J. Res. 238, warning that it would set back all the progress the United States had made with China in the nonproliferation area. For the letter, see *Congressional Record*, December 11, 1985, p. H11762.

97. Ambassador Lord telephoned several key members in the conference, stressing the possible damage to U.S.-China relations caused by the Glenn amendment. See *Congressional Quarterly Weekly Report*, December 14, 1985, p. 2654.

98. According to Senators Glenn and William S. Cohen, President Reagan would veto the entire stopgap spending bill if the China nuclear agreement was encumbered by further restrictions. See Tyler, "Nuclear Pact with China Nears Last Test on Hill."

99. According to my interview with an official (name unattributable) from Ambassador Richard T. Kennedy's office in the summer of 1987, Kennedy's office was responsible for coordinating different agencies and was instrumental in the negotiations.

100. Bernard Gwertzman, "Cranston Assails U.S.-China Accord," *New York Times*, October 22, 1985, p. 6.

101. *Congressional Quarterly Weekly Report*, July 27, 1985, p. 1479.

102. "U.S.-China Nuclear Pact: Congressional Approval Appears Likely," *Nuclear News*, November 1985, p. 128.

6

Conclusion:
China Policy and Its Making

At the beginning of this study, a question was posed as to whether U.S. China policy since normalization has been a function of strategy or governmental processes. The question may represent a false dichotomy. This study found that there is a necessary linkage between strategic interests and governmental processes in which strategic and other political interests are transformed into foreign policies. U.S. strategic considerations have been an important motive in developing U.S.-China relations since normalization. Although perceptions of the importance of Sino-U.S. strategic relations may vary across administrations and over time, U.S. strategic goals have remained more or less the same in U.S. policy toward China. However, U.S. China policy is not automatically the function of strategic concerns. Due to the rapid expansion of Sino-U.S. relations since normalization, it is also a function of U.S. governmental processes. U.S. strategic interests are frequently subject to the interpretation of policymakers and are balanced and weighted by concerned governmental institutions and agencies in the process. Governmental processes involve different institutions and agencies with differences of opinion and interests in U.S. China policy. Governmental processes are responsible for transforming the China policy interests and preferences of different governmental institutions and agencies into policies.

The relationship between the United States and the People's Republic of China developed at unprecedented speed in the early postnormalization period. U.S.-China relations extended from diplomatic arenas to exchanges involving trade, tourism, business, culture, education, health, environment, science, and technology. Although U.S.-China official relations cooled in the initial Reagan administration, the relationship continued to expand in other areas, especially in trade, business, tourism, and people-to-people exchange. Further progress was achieved in the area of U.S.-China technological cooperation as a result of the relaxation of U.S. export control policy toward China.

The rapid expansion of Sino-U.S. relations has had a profound impact on governmental processes regarding U.S. China policymaking. First and foremost, U.S. China policy objectives diversified as a result of such expansion. The diversification of China policy goals is signified by plural and decentralized U.S. China policymaking. Before normalization, the United

States was largely motivated by strategic considerations in its dealings with China. During three successive administrations, U.S. China policymakers were preoccupied with this strategic concern in relation to normalization. The presidents and their principal advisers and officials were able to define normalization as a China policy goal in a global strategic context. With this goal in mind, U.S. policymakers were able to present their China policy to the public and slowly build a bipartisan consensus on the means to achieve it. Once U.S.-China relations were normalized, however, rapid expansion into other aspects of bilateral relations called for an ordering of China policy priorities. Apart from strategic interests, U.S. policymakers had to deal with bilateral issues, U.S.-Taiwan relations in the context of U.S. China policy, and U.S.-China cooperation in areas of other international concerns. Further erosion of U.S.-China strategic relations as a result of the Reagan administration's reevaluation of China's global position and the change of the international scene rendered the initial China policy goal insufficient in guiding the making of China policy. Thus, the postnormalization period saw different China policy goals advanced, debated, and defined by interested government agencies with less direct involvement by the president and his top officials.

Second, U.S.-China relations were institutionalized as the United States and China moved to develop commercial, trade, educational, scientific, technological, and other cooperative ties. Institutionalization rendered bureaucratic agencies more powerful in handling day-to-day bilateral matters on a regular and direct basis. In effect, U.S.-China relations were bureaucratized in the areas of diplomacy, commerce, trade, and technology transfers. With the signing of a series of bilateral agreements, different government agencies were charged with the responsibility of implementing those agreements. In doing so, bureaucratic agencies developed institutional interests in dealing with China affairs. And such interests motivated bureaucratic agencies to maintain and expand their "turfs," thus contributing to decentralizing U.S. China policymaking.

Third, rapid expansion of U.S.-China ties led to an increasing role for Congress in providing a legal framework for China policy and sharing China policymaking power with the executive. Congress, through regulating commerce and export control, often linked bilateral economic issues with Chinese political and social issues. This linkage of issues characterized Congress as an institution with its China policy predisposition distinctly different from that of the executive. Consequently, linked issues are often different from executive China policy goals, which aimed more at strategic and bilateral relations than at Chinese domestic issues, and thus complicated U.S. China policymaking. The executive found itself unable to enjoy the discreet China policymaking that so marked the normalization process. It had to engage Congress in the new decisionmaking process that highlighted conflicts of China policy goals, bargains in approaches, and compromises on decisions. Through this interactive governmental process, Congress was able to address its concerns over such areas as trade, arms sales, technological transfers, and human rights.

How do these changes affect U.S. China policy and the policymaking process? First, because U.S. China policy goals are diversified, it is more difficult for U.S. policymakers to agree on a goal in the process and formulate a consensual China policy. What is important depends on who sees it and who is able to define the goal. The conventional wisdom has been that the president sets the direction of China policy. U.S. China policy has often been associated with Nixon's dramatic Beijing visit, Carter's decision on normalization, and Reagan's rhetoric on Taiwan. The fact is that postnormalization expansion of Sino-U.S. relations covered such a wide range of areas that China policymaking went from the small circle of decisionmakers to larger and larger circles. This new pattern of decisionmaking suggests that the existing understanding of how the president makes U.S. China policy is no longer adequate. China policymaking needs to incorporate different policy goals, to reconcile priorities, to compromise in approaches, and to encompass governmental processes.

Second, institutionalization of U.S.-China relations formally defined the jurisdiction of governmental agencies in managing China policy. Each department and federal agency set up corresponding China domains, which are in turn responsible for competing for its China interests in the bureaucratic process. China policy and its making has been decentralized, and bureaucratic players have exerted great influence in China policymaking.

Lastly, and importantly, the U.S. Congress, which played an important role in China policy in the past, has been drawn into China policymaking arenas by new issues as U.S.-China ties have expanded. As a governmental institution, Congress has inevitably asserted its role in making several important U.S. China policies. The congressional assertiveness renders the interbranch process more important in transforming U.S. China policy goals, including the strategic goal, into final policies. This is done by way of consultations, resolutions, amendments, and, above all, compromises. In this regard, the interbranch policy process is the key to explaining and understanding U.S. China policy since normalization. (This point will be expanded in the theoretical discussion.)

U.S. China Policy: What Is It? For What Purpose?

U.S. China policy after normalization aimed to improve and expand Sino-U.S. relations for several policy objectives. First, maintaining strategic cooperation with China in the context of U.S.-Soviet relations was considered an important U.S. China policy objective, which also included U.S. interest in Taiwan's future political stability and economic prosperity.

Second, U.S. interests in Asia could be served by improved Sino-U.S. relations that could help stabilize Asian affairs, especially the situation on the Korean peninsula. Third, expanding economic ties with China could promote U.S. political and economic interests in China. The fourth objective involved Sino-U.S. cooperation in such international matters as arms sales, environmental protection, crime control, and drug enforcement. These U.S. China objectives were largely shared by the Carter and Reagan administrations and members of Congress in formulating U.S. China policy.

U.S. China policy encompassed a wide range of issues, from political disputes over U.S.-Taiwan relations to economic and technological cooperation. It has undergone a profound transformation from addressing single-minded, long-term strategic cooperation to embracing multidimensional, short-term, or day-to-day bilateral affairs. The foregoing cases represented some major China policies in dealing with postnormalization Sino-U.S. relations. Those policies were made to resolve different bilateral issues, but together they constituted overall U.S. China policy governing postnormalization U.S.-China relations.

U.S. Taiwan Policy in the Context of Sino-U.S. Relations

The first major issue in postnormalization U.S.-China relations was future U.S. relations with Taiwan. The obvious differences between the executive and Congress over the future U.S. Taiwan policy posed a serious question for the Chinese government: Can the United States abide by the normalization principles regarding the Taiwan question? The passage of the Taiwan Relations Act (TRA) in 1979 presented another question: Who actually makes China policy?

To answer the second question first, the unique thing about this case is the assertive orientation of Congress in formulating the TRA. But Congress did more than just assert its role in U.S. Taiwan policy. Congress was determined to play an active role in U.S. China policymaking. In doing so, Congress made a point that U.S. China policymaking was not simply the president's domain. Congress, if it chooses to, can be just as important as the executive in making U.S. China policy.

The TRA was a compromise among U.S. policymakers. The making of the TRA in the context of a new U.S.-China relationship showed that there was no consensus among U.S. policymakers as to whether the United States should conduct U.S.-Taiwan relations within the framework of U.S. China policy. Some policymakers wanted U.S. Taiwan policy to be favored independent of the Sino-U.S. normalization agreement, linking U.S. security interests with Taiwan's security. The Carter administration's initial Taiwan legislation meant to provide a legal framework for a continuation of commercial, cultural, and other relations between the American people and the people on Taiwan on an unofficial basis. The TRA was not merely a piece of legislation governing unofficial U.S.-Taiwan relations. It was a policy that reflected some U.S. policymakers' perceptions of future U.S.-China relations. It is in the interests of the United States to improve Sino-U.S. relations, but improving bilateral relations should not affect U.S. interests in Taiwan's security and prosperity.

Apart from the substantive provisions governing the conduct of U.S.-Taiwan unofficial relations, the TRA contained some hypothetical assumptions about the potential Chinese threat to Taiwan's security. The purpose of these assumptions was to justify U.S. concerns over Taiwan's security, hence, the U.S. China policy statement in the TRA. However, no hypothetical assumptions were made in the TRA as to what the United States would do if relations between Taiwan and Mainland China improved. The lack of peaceful assumption could have a perceptual and psychological impact upon some policymakers in the United States, China, and Taiwan in future U.S.-China-Taiwan relations. China has already felt frustrated by Taiwan and the United States for not responding adequately to its Taiwan peace initiatives.[1]

Going beyond the perceptual and psychological impact, the TRA has also posed a policy question to U.S. policymakers: Will the United States have to sell arms to Taiwan when such sales affect U.S.-China relations? The TRA contained a provision allowing sales of arms to Taiwan, which the Carter administration initially did not want to include. Since the power of executing the TRA was vested in the executive, different administrations might treat it differently. Therefore, the execution of the TRA can be a potential destabilizing source for Sino-U.S. relations. In fact, Chinese leaders viewed the treatment of the TRA by President Reagan as a test case of his new China policy.

In sum, the TRA case signified congressional assertiveness and a new pattern of executive-congressional relations in U.S. China policymaking in the postnormalization era. The TRA implied potential U.S.-China disputes over the treatment of future U.S.-Taiwan relations. It also attested to the importance of emerging interbranch politics in making U.S. China and Taiwan policy.

U.S. Economic Policy Toward China

While the passage of the TRA caused some political tensions in the immediate postnormalization U.S.-China relations, Sino-U.S. economic cooperation took place in a larger strategic and political setting. Significantly, the bilateral economic issues were dealt with on an economic basis, but in relation to the international situation and bilateral political relations.

The U.S-China trade agreement represented an important U.S. economic policy toward China. For the first time, the United States granted China

MFN treatment, thus separating its China economic policy from its generally restrictive East-West economic policy. The trade agreement was a crucial step toward further expanding U.S.-China economic relations by ending discriminatory tariff treatment; facilitating business activities; providing for reciprocal and equivalent protection of patents, trademarks, and copyrights; and safeguarding against disruption of each other's domestic market.

The trade agreement was a first attempt to institutionalize an important part of U.S.-China economic relations. It served as an example for regularizing other bilateral economic activities. In initiating the trade agreement, the Carter administration attached great importance to developing U.S.-China relations. A significant political implication of the trade agreement was that the Carter administration for the first time disowned Carter's evenhanded foreign economic policy toward the Soviet Union and China. By waiving the Jackson-Vanik amendment requirement, thus granting the MFN treatment to China, the administration sent out a clear political message: U.S. China policy would not depend on an absolute mathematical calculation for an evenhanded foreign policy, but rather on U.S. strategic, political, and economic interests in the new international situation.

The Arms Sales Crisis and Crisis Management

The implication of the TRA came to the surface when the arms sales to Taiwan evolved into a crisis in U.S.-China relations. Precisely because of the lack of assumptions about possible improvement of relations between Taiwan and mainland China, U.S. policymakers were put into a dilemma when China protested U.S. arms sales to Taiwan. It seemed ironic that the United States should sell arms to Taiwan when there was such a reduction of tensions between the two parts of China. The arms sales crisis started with the question of whether the United States should sell FX fighter planes to Taiwan as requested. Due to China's protest over such a sale, the United States decided not to sell the FX; instead, it would sell some military spare parts.

There were sharply different perceptions of arms sales by leaders of the two governments. President Reagan saw arms sales as a commitment to the execution of the TRA as well as to the security of his own allies, whereas Chinese leaders viewed arms sales as U.S. encroachment upon its sovereignty and interference in China's internal affairs. As a result, U.S.-China relations deteriorated rapidly, to a point where something had to be done to halt the possible retrogression of diplomatic relations. It took concerted efforts by both sides to reevaluate the differences over the arms sales issue, and a solution was reached on the common ground that stabilizing a bilateral relationship and creating a peaceful environment around the Taiwan Strait could promote U.S. and Chinese foreign policy objectives.

The arms sales case presented a unique case study of crisis management. It was the first crisis in U.S.-China relations since normalization. The ability to manage this crisis became a full test of the survival of a newly established relationship. There was no doubt that the goal of maintaining good, strategic relations with China outweighed the risk of selling arms to Taiwan, and this goal was responsible for Reagan's decision not to sell the FX and his determination to reach an agreement settling the issue. But a successful management of the crisis on both sides not only helped resolve the immediate arms sale problem, but, more important, it also enhanced the understanding that the long-term resolution of the Taiwan issue would rest not on arms but on peaceful means and constructive U.S.-China relations.[2] The communication and mutual trust that gradually developed during the crisis led to further expansion of U.S.-China relations, especially in the fields of economic cooperation and technology transfer.

U.S. Technology Transfer to China

With the successful management of the arms sales crisis, both governments were able to focus on further expanding Sino-U.S. relations. President Reagan further decided in 1983 to relax U.S. export control policy toward China, moving China from a more restrictive trade classification to the one given to Japan and Western Europe. Despite the relaxation, however, fewer high technologies were transferred than actually expected. China complained that it was not treated fully as a friendly country in terms of technology transfers. Many high-technology transfers were strictly scrutinized on a case-by-case basis.

The U.S.-China nuclear cooperation agreement was the first major agreement reflecting U.S. intent to address the issue to extend technological cooperation with China. Apart from its economic applications, the agreement contained a message further liberalizing U.S. policies concerning technology transfer to China. The nuclear agreement established the basis for Sino-U.S. cooperation in various peaceful applications of nuclear energy. It set up the legal framework for the export of nuclear reactors, fuel, and components, and for the exchange of technology, including cooperation in health, safety, and the environmental implications of the peaceful uses of nuclear energy. The agreement put the United States into a competitive position in terms of exporting U.S. nuclear technology to the new China nuclear market, since the United States was leading in nuclear technology.

U.S. initiation of the agreement was largely in response to China's interest in acquiring foreign nuclear technology and to the U.S. nuclear industry's desire to enter into China's nuclear market. This nuclear cooperation policy was consistent with the U.S. objective of expanding the scope of Sino-U.S. economic relations. Furthermore, the nuclear agreement helped the United States clarify China's nuclear nonproliferation policies, which served U.S. interests in curbing international nuclear proliferation.

The implication of the agreement, however, went beyond the potential economic gains. It had several political implications. First, the initiation of the agreement represented U.S. sincerity in improving the bilateral relations that had been affected by the arms sales issue. Second, the agreement was the first one that the United States signed with a major communist country. It represented an expansion of bilateral relations into a new, sensitive field. Successful nuclear cooperation would further tie the United States to China's modernization drive. Third, the United States successfully linked the agreement with China's nonproliferation policy.

* * *

In conclusion, U.S. China policy since normalization has been built upon a widely shared belief that maintaining a good relationship with China serves U.S. foreign policy interests. U.S.-China policy has been directed toward improving and strengthening bilateral relations. Despite ups and downs in developing the new relationship, U.S. China policy during this period has been consistent with U.S. foreign policy goals shared by the majority of U.S. policymakers.

U.S. China policy, however, has also been a function of governmental processes. There are factors in the governmental process affecting bilateral issues: U.S. policy differences over Taiwan, U.S. security concerns, and ideology. Some issues, such as U.S. arms sales to Taiwan, arose because of the U.S. policy disagreements over Taiwan. Other issues, like technology transfer, were caused by security concerns about whether Chinese access to U.S. technology would provide them with unintended military advantages or interfere with other U.S. foreign policy objectives. While fundamental differences in ideology could cause variations in U.S. China policy, they often interplay with other differences in traditional values and cultural ethnics. A good example for the argument was the case of the termination of U.S. funds to a United Nations agency that supported China's family planning program.[3]

U.S. China Policymaking: Are Models Useful?

Efforts to explain U.S. China policy in the past have concentrated largely on a realist perspective. Many theories derived from this perspective sought to explain U.S. China policy in terms of strategic need or balance of power. Those theories all assume that U.S. China policy was made by the rational actor—the United States—who can define U.S. national interests in strategic terms, set China policy goals, develop policy options, and select appropriate means to maximize the goals. Since U.S. China policy was developed out of a bipartisan consensus and there were some shared national interests in dealing with China in the strategic context, the rational actor approach had some validity in terms of identifying China policy goals.

The rapid expansion of U.S.-China relations resulted in some bilateral issues that affected U.S. China policymaking in two ways. First, issues, especially those concerning bilateral trade, government economic assistance, and technological transfer, broadened the scope of U.S. decisionmaking, requiring governmental processes to be involved in establishing additional legal framework, making new rules and regulations. Second, the resolution of those issues often relied on the reconciliation of China policy goals, policy preferences, and approaches because different governmental institutions and agencies were brought into the decisionmaking process. China policymaking, therefore, cannot escape an open, democratic policymaking process in which governmental officials and bureaucratic players compromise on policy goals, bargain on policy interests, and build a coalition for certain policies. In this respect, the rational actor explanations seem inadequate in explaining postnormalization U.S.-China relations. It is necessary to look into the "black box" or domestic political institutions and policy processes for extra accounts of U.S. China policy.

The Rational Actor Model

The rational actor model seeks an explanation of U.S. China policy from a political calculation of international affairs and domestic situation. Based on this calculation, the state actor defines what national interests are at stake and what the goal of U.S. China policy should be. This approach explained U.S. decisions to normalize Sino-U.S. relations.

The rational actor model, to a certain extent, explained those policies that reflected the continuous U.S. efforts to expand and develop U.S.-China ties since normalization. This is because U.S. policymakers have shared some China policy goals. The model was able to predict China policy outcomes according to the identified China policy goals. The power of the model depends on whether there are agreed-upon goals in foreign policymaking. If national foreign policy goals are shared and supported by a wide range of political groups, the state can act as a unitary actor to make foreign policy decisions without being constrained by domestic political forces. In the United States, shared foreign policy goals enable the president to pursue foreign policy in a relatively free way. In the trade agreement case, the United States granted MFN status to China because there existed a widely shared consensus on further U.S.-China economic relations, which gave the president a free hand to make a decision as he deemed appropriate. A shared foreign policy goal can be defined by three factors: bipartisan consensus, supportive public opinion, and lack of public opinion. On some issues, there existed bipartisan agreements on U.S. China policy objectives and approaches. In resolving the arms sales issue, President Reagan had the majority support from both parties. On other issues, public opinion emerged as a cue for defining U.S. China policy goals.[4] This is increasingly evident with regard to U.S. responses to China's human rights practices. Still, on other issues, there was no distinct public opinion, and, therefore, U.S. policymakers defined China policy goals according to their perceptions, institutional interests, and political skills. For example, in engaging China in cooperation on some international issues of common concern, the executive often took liberties in defining and pursuing China policy goals.

In dealing with international crises, the state can sometimes act as a rational actor because of the urgency of time and the need for unity. And such a crisis management process necessarily preempts the normal policy process and policy players. Usually, the shorter the crisis is, the fewer the players involved, and vice versa. In the arms sales crisis, the United States managed to resolve the issue in such a fashion that the president and his advisers defined the goal (retaining U.S-China ties and preserving Taiwan security), provided policy alternatives (different version of the agreement), and selected the best means to achieve the goal (sending the vice president to Beijing and letting the secretary of state be in charge of the negotiations).

However, the rational actor model does not sufficiently explain U.S. China policy after normalization, for two reasons. First, the model loses its explanatory power when the state actor cannot define policy goals or there is no national consensus on foreign policy goals. The model fails to explain fully some major postnormalization U.S. China policies because U.S. China policy interests and goals became diversified, and, as a result, more and more players are involved in the policymaking process. In the nuclear agreement case, the bureaucratic process revealed how different bureaucratic agencies were able to advance their interests and policy goals. The executive, apart from its own divisions over China policies, has to share with Congress the power of making China policy.

Second, the rational actor model does not take into account the policymaking process. According to the model, the process does not matter. Outcomes reflect goals. By discounting the process, the model severs the linkage between the goal and the outcome. It excludes factors that may influence policy initiation and formulation in the process. Yet, the process does matter when there are diverse goals. In the nuclear case, decisionmakers have to engage in a bargaining process in order to reconcile different policy emphases and preferences between the executive and the Congress. The model was also proven less useful in that the outcomes do not necessarily reflect U.S. foreign policy goals at the same time. In the TRA case, the model does not predict the policy outcomes that reflected U.S. Taiwan interests. Congress, as an important player, used the process to address its concerns over Taiwan, which had been neglected by the executive.

It may be too easy for critics to dismiss the rational actor model as useless just because it assumes that the state is a unitary actor. To say that the state always acts as a unitary actor is just as fallacious as to say that the state never acts as a unitary actor. It depends on foreign policy goals shared by the public and various political sectors, and the nature of international events with which the state tries to deal.

The Bureaucratic Politics Model

Though the rational actor model has been widely used to explain U.S.-China strategic cooperation, the bureaucratic politics model has proven to be important in understanding the initial stage of China policymaking and U.S. bargaining positions in the negotiations with China. Given the intricate and technical nature of foreign economic and technological issues, bureaucratic expertise and policy preferences have much influence on recommending and initiating specific U.S. China policies concerning economics and technology transfer. In the trade and nuclear cases, bureaucratic politics was largely responsible not only for negotiating the agreements, but also for the technical terms and contents of the agreements.

The State Department is a very important bureaucratic player, whose policy preferences often win over other bureaucratic preferences in the bureaucratic process because it has both interests and resources in China policymaking. As a governmental agency for foreign relations, the State Department has an interest and a stake in maintaining good relations with China. Due to its role in diplomacy, it often serves as a coordinator for concerned bureaucratic interests in formulating U.S. China policy in the areas of economics and technological transfer. In the nuclear case, State was effective in promoting the U.S. nonproliferation goal despite the preference of the Energy Department to reach an early agreement. Moreover, in negotiating the agreements, State is often in an advantageous position as the chief negotiator in recommending to the president appropriate options to adopt. In the arms sales agreement, the State Department's preferences regarding the terms of the agreement may not have pleased the Defense Department, but State managed to persuade the president to accept them. Lastly, State serves another important function as a liaison between the executive and Congress in China policy matters concerning both branches of the government. State, by building a coalition with members of Congress, can affect the policy process. In the trade case, State worked with some members of Congress to modify Brzezinski's pro-China policy by delaying the approval of China's MFN status.

The bureaucratic politics model has several major limits. First, it cannot offer an understanding of the whole China policymaking process. Bureaucratic players may be policy initiators, but not final policymakers. Once a policy deliberation moves out of the bureaucratic process for further approval, bureaucratic politics loses its influence over the final outcome. Very often, bureaucratic policy initiation and formulation were either subject to presidential approval or at the mercy of an interbranch political process. In the arms sales case, the final version of the communiqué had to be approved by the president. In the trade and the nuclear cases, the two negotiated agreements could not take effect without congressional action.

Second, bureaucratic politics did not cause inconsistencies in U.S.-China policies. Its fissures on certain issues might have slowed down policy deliberations, which could have provided members of Congress with different information to advance their interests, but bureaucratic fissures were not responsible for issues affecting U.S.-China relations, such as the arms sales issue and the TRA. Bureaucratic fissures can be explored by policymakers from two directions. For example, in the arms sale case, the leaking of the CIA and the Defense Department evaluation, which stated that Taiwan did not need the FX planes, was obviously exploited by those who did not want arms sales to affect Sino-U.S. relations adversely. On the other hand, the leaking of information stating that China aided Pakistan in the nuclear case resulted in a long process of negotiation and congressional approval. Third, the presence and intensity of presidential attention can be an important intervening variable that may strengthen or weaken bureaucratic effectiveness in China policymaking. Effectiveness in making China economic policies was also a function of presidential control of other foreign policy goals, such as security concerns.

In short, the bureaucratic politics model provides a useful tool for looking into the bureaucratic policy process in an attempt to understand China policy intention, initiations, negotiations, and formulation. But the influence of bureaucratic politics in decisionmaking is also subject to presidential interests and attention.

The Interbranch Politics Model

The interbranch politics model is so far the best of the three models for describing, explaining, and understanding U.S. China policies since normalization.[5] Unlike the other two models, it stresses the importance of an interactive policy process in which the executive and Congress approach issues with different institutional preferences and predispositions. Each branch of government acts as a coherent, unitary institution in the process, trying to influence each other on U.S. China policy. The model is particularly helpful in understanding why Congress gets involved in China policymaking and how Congress affects the executive in the policy process. It is interesting to note that Congress, according to conventional wisdom, engages in short-term, parochial, and narrow-focused policymaking. But this study finds, to the contrary, that Congress is more concerned with rather broader and long-term aspects of U.S. China policy.[6] It also helps to understand the extent to which the executive balances congressional preferences and demands in formulating China policies.

By emphasizing the policy process by which the two branches of government interact to make foreign policy, the interbranch politics model contributed to a better understanding of U.S. China policymaking. It not only offered good explanations as to how and why U.S. China policy was made, but it also provided insights into the fissures of the two government branches concerning respective institutional interests and roles in foreign policymaking. Interbranch fissures were often the cause of disagreements over China policy goals and approaches. And the process of the two branches pulling and hauling each other over their differences became critical in understanding the contents of the final China policies.

The utility of the interbranch politics model lies in its inclusion of Congress as a foreign policymaking institution in the policy process. It takes into account the assertive role that Congress played in reaction to the executive's China policy orientation after normalization. Congress, as an equal player in the model, did more than oversee and approve the executive's China policies. It asserted itself, as it did in the TRA, by initiating China policies, playing what is normally considered the executive role.[7] The rational actor and the bureaucratic politics models are obviously defective in excluding the congressional process. Therefore, they cannot explain why many U.S. policies bear congressional imprints. As U.S.-China relations expanded, the interbranch politics model became more effective in explaining U.S. Taiwan policy and economic and technology transfer policies toward China.

This model also helps explain in what direction Congress pulls the executive in the China policymaking process. The conventional wisdom on congressional behavior is that Congress engages in parochial, short-term policymaking. But in the TRA case, Congress was trying to balance the executive's Taiwan policy by amendments addressing Taiwan's security and arms sales. These amendments have long-term implications in U.S. dealings with Taiwan and China. In the nuclear case, it was the executive that was interested in the economic benefit of nuclear cooperation with China. Congress, on the contrary, was pulling the executive toward stressing the rather broader goal of nuclear nonproliferation policy by attaching a condition requiring the president to certify China's nonproliferation policies.[8]

The power of the model lies in its ability to identify the critical factors that would mold different institutional interests and preferences into a single policy. One of the crucial factors, as identified by Pastor, is "the degree of trust and responsiveness which flowed in both directions between the branches."[9] Congressional consultations and executive responses to congressional concerns often form the base for a bipartisan China policy. Through consultations and responses, Congress raises an issue, the executive considers it, an interbranch policy process weighs benefits and costs, and finally a policy is made. In the TRA case, the Congress addressed its concerns over Taiwan security, the executive responded, and a compromise was finally reached on the issue. The nuclear cooperation agreement reflected less trust and responsiveness between the Congress and the executive over the nonproliferation issue. As a result, Congress imposed conditions, despite the executive objection, that barred nuclear licenses or transfers to China until the president sent Congress a report on China's nuclear nonproliferation policies.

Whether institutional preferences converged into a policy was a function of two factors: consultation and responsiveness between the branches and the degree of institutional cohesiveness. How strong Congress held its preferences and what resources the executive had committed to dealing with Congress for a given issue can affect the bargaining process and thus the outcome. In the TRA case, the majority of the members of Congress were deeply committed to having a certain degree of security guarantee written in the TRA. Although the executive would have preferred not to have the arms sales provision written into the TRA, it had to give up its preference in order to produce a TRA that it could accept. The outcomes enabled the United States to continue its unofficial relations with Taiwan, but also stressed U.S. concerns over Taiwan's security. In the case of the nuclear agreement, due to the loose congressional opposition and the heavy executive lobbying, the executive was able to persuade the Congress to adopt a more balanced approach to China's nonproliferation policy. The outcome dropped the demand on China's additional clarification of its nonproliferation policies and its acceptance of standards equivalent to those enforced by the IAEA, which avoided the risk of jeopardizing the long-negotiated agreement.

In sum, this study found that it is most useful to combine the strategic approach with an approach stressing governmental processes in studying U.S. China policy from 1979 to 1985. The strategic approach provides a global context in identifying U.S. China policy goals. The governmental process leads us to see how foreign policy goals and other political interests are translated into final policies. In this regard, the interbranch politics model is the most helpful in explaining and understanding many China policy decisions.

The three models provide three different analytical tools in studying U.S. China policy. They focus on different aspects of decisionmaking, such as national interests, China policy goals, institutional preferences and priorities, the roles of individual decisionmakers, and policy processes. However, these models are not mutually exclusive; rather, they complement each other in explaining U.S. decisions during this period. First, national interests may not be differently defined by each model. In other words, there are some shared views as to what U.S. national interests are involved in China policymaking. The three models do not necessarily reject the notion that U.S. national interests were served by developing U.S.-China relations.

Second, while emphasizing different political preferences and priorities in making China policy, the three models do not exclude the possibility of U.S. decisionmakers sharing some basic China policy goals. They differ in sensitivity to Chinese attitudes toward U.S. China policy moves, in priorities of ranking China policy goals, and in approaches to achieve these goals. Third, excluding the rational actor model, the other two models embrace policy processes in which bureaucratic agencies and Congress may influence each other on particular issues. In the bureaucratic politics process, bureaucratic players may ally with members of Congress to affect a particular outcome. This was the case in reaching the nuclear agreement.

In examining the processes of U.S. China policymaking, other ad hoc factors were found to be important in explaining China policy, apart from the three models. A single important international event can have an effect on China policymaking in terms of being capable of changing policymakers' perceptions and positions in the decisionmaking process. The Soviet invasion of Afghanistan, in effect, changed some U.S. policymakers' perceptions of an "evenhanded" policy toward the Soviet Union and China. It influenced the positions of those members of Congress who had initially objected to granting the MFN status to China. Such international events may alter policymakers' perceptions of the balance of power and U.S. strategic interests, if not their basic belief systems. Reagan's perceptions of a Soviet threat, to a certain extent, suppressed the residual effect of presidential ideology in dealing with the arms sales crisis.

Furthermore, U.S. policymakers' perceptions of China factors are also important in making China policies.[10] Policymakers' perceptions of China's reactions to certain U.S. policies affect their policy positions, especially in the bargaining process between the executive and Congress. The executive usually is more sensitive in perceiving China's reaction to certain U.S. policy moves, therefore making it more likely for the executive to effectively engage Congress in bargaining out differences in the interbranch politics process.[11] In the TRA case, the executive strongly opposed the proposed security provision because it perceived that China would certainly regard this provision as violating the normalization principles and would therefore reject it. In the case of the nuclear agreement, the executive tried hard to water down the Glenn amendment, because it thought that the amendment would be unacceptable to the Chinese, which would thus effectively break the agreement.

Last, the nature of different issues can have an independent effect on China policymaking processes. It helps define who should be major policymakers, what type of policy should be made, and how it should be made. Different issues may require different players in the game and may pose direct questions that need to be answered. Different issues may also spell out different decisionmaking processes and thus place a limit to the access other policymakers may have in decisionmaking (see Figure 6.1). The arms sales issue involved the executive decision to sell arms to Taiwan and was primarily handled by the executive decisionmakers. Congress did not involve itself in the process, because there was no requirement for congressional actions. In most crisis management situations, the nature of the issue requires prompt responses, thus limiting the possibility of involving many other players and processes. On the other hand, the TRA, the trade and the nuclear policies, by the rule of the game, all required congressional action.

Figure 6.1 Explaining Foreign Policy Issues

Rational Actor Model	Interbranch Politics Model	Bureaucratic Politics Model
Security, arms sales, regional conflict, nuclear nonproliferation, international environment, drug and crime control	Human rights, trade, most-favored-nation status, Taiwan-related issues, technology transfer, funding, and aid legislation	Diplomacy, negotiation, trade and economic policies, export control, human rights, educational and cultural exchange

While the issue variable may not have a direct effect on the outcome of China policy, it can identify U.S. decisionmaking institutions and processes for future U.S. China policymaking. Congress will be a constant decisionmaker of China policy, and the continuous, interactive interbranch policy process will be a major policy process through which U.S. China policies will be made. One can expect that the U.S. Congress will interact with the executive on a more frequent basis in making China policies concerning the Taiwan issue, Sino-U.S. economic relations, U.S. technology transfer to China, trade, indirect U.S. aid,[12] and other domestic issues that may affect Sino-U.S. relations. In other areas, especially human rights and Tibet, Congress will probably act independently of the executive branch in shaping public opinion, pushing its policy agenda, and initiating China policies.

* * *

Two points perhaps can be drawn from this exercise of U.S. China policymaking. First, specific issues and their causes may pose potential threats to future Sino-U.S. relations. The successful management of different foreign policy interests and objectives is at least as important as the emphasis on identical interests and objectives in the development of widely diverse interests that in turn affect bilateral relations in many other areas. Successful management of differences is a means of limiting the issue should it arise and of preventing a consequential spillover. To be able to do so requires a deep understanding of each other's domestic political structures and policy processes. Second, U.S. China policy reflects the importance of U.S. political institutions, public opinion, political and cultural values, and strategic interests. It is inadequate to assume that U.S. China policymaking is always guided by strategic considerations and that Congress and the bureaucracy have no important impact on the policy outcome. Any attempt to reduce the complexity of U.S.-China relations to the mere assertion of balance of power would only result in miscalculation of policy intention and misunderstanding of policy outcomes.

Notes

1. The Chinese government has made several public statements that the United States could and should play a constructive role in helping resolve the Taiwan issue and bring the two separate parts together.
2. Oksenberg pointed out that "the August 17 Communiqué accepts the premise that the well-being of the people of Taiwan is best obtained not through exclusive reliance on arms but through constructive and binding Sino-U.S. ties." See his "A Decade of Sino-American Relations," p. 195.
3. This is an example of how different political forces in U.S. Congress can make a joint effort in influencing U.S.-China policy. In 1985, Congress passed a law prohibiting U.S. aid to the United Nations for population activities if the executive determined annually that the Chinese family planning program included coerced abortion. The legislation was proposed and supported by members of Congress for different reasons; conservative members voted for anticommunist ideology, liberal members for human rights, and other members for antiabortion.
4. Nathan and Oliver argued that there were three types of public moods that offered cues for U.S. foreign policy in the late 1970s: a liberal internationalism making up 25 percent of the population, a conservative or "military" internationalism consisting of a third of the population, and a noninternationalism, which can usually be associated with conservative internationalism when stimulated by world affairs. The Soviet global offensive in the late 1970s made the latter two groups a dominant public voice to which Carter and the Reagan administrations responded by adopting a hard-line foreign policy. James A. Nathan and James K. Oliver, *Foreign Policy Making and the American Political System*, 2d ed. (Boston: Little, Brown, 1987), Chapter 6.
5. This statement does not imply that the model can explain all decisions and policies. Its utility rather depends on how China policy is defined, or on the nature of issues. For a discussion of when and how the interbranch politics model is useful in explaining U.S. foreign policy, see Robert A. Pastor, "Interbranch Politics and U.S. Foreign Policy," an unpublished manuscript, September 14, 1990.
6. This finding is rather inconclusive since the study focuses only on the interactive aspect of the congressional-executive relations in China policymaking. Congress, in other cases, is found to be more issue-specific, for example, in its stance on China's family planning policies.
7. Contrary to what some congressional literature has concluded—that congressional involvement tends to be sporadic and episodic—the effects of congressional involvement in China policy are long term and lasting. See also

Oksenberg, "Congress, Executive-Legislative Relations, and China Policy," pp. 207–230.

8. The evidence in these two cases, suggesting that Congress, as an institutional decisionmaker, engage itself in long-term China policy goals, was rather inconclusive. Congress may just want to fill up whatever policy openings that are left unattended by the executive.

9. Pastor, *Congress and the Politics of U.S. Foreign Economic Policies*, p. 345.

10. This conclusion in a way confirms the cognitive model of decisionmaking, which stresses that the behavior of a policymaker is a function of that person's perception of the decisionmaking environment. For a nation, foreign policy results from its perception of other nations' reactions to its own actions. See Ole R. Holsti, "Foreign Policy Formation Viewed Cognitively," in Robert Axelrod, ed., *Structure of Decision: The Cognitive Maps of Political Elites* (Princeton: Princeton University Press, 1976), pp. 18–54; John D. Steinbruner, *The Cybernetic Theory of Decision* (Princeton: Princeton University Press, 1974); and Michael J. Shapiro, "Cognitive Process and Foreign Policy Decision-Making," *International Studies Quarterly* 17, no. 2 (June 1973), pp. 147–174.

11. Snyder and Diesing would argue that bargaining involves a process of manipulating policy preferences and perception of them. See Snyder and Diesing, *Conflict Among Nations*, p. 183.

12. Refers to U.S. contributions to international agencies that support China's domestic programs—for instance, U.S. aid to the United Nations Fund for Population Activities.

Bibliography

Books

Allison, G. T. *Essence of Decisions: Explaining the Cuban Missile Crisis.* Boston: Little, Brown, 1971.

Barnds, William J. *China and America: The Search for a New Relationship.* A Council on Foreign Relations book. New York: New York University Press, 1977.

Barnett, A. Doak. *China Policy: Old Problems and New Challenges.* Washington, D.C.: Brookings Institution, 1977.

————. *China's Economy in Global Perspective.* Washington, D.C.: Brookings Institution, 1981.

————. *The FX Decision: "Another Crucial Movement" in U.S.-China-Taiwan Relations.* Washington, D.C.: Brookings Institution, 1981.

————. *U.S. Arms Sales: The China-Taiwan Tangle.* Washington, D.C.: Brookings Institution, 1982.

Brzezinski, Zbigniew K. *Power and Principle: Memoirs of the National Security Adviser, 1977–1981.* New York: Farrar, Straus, Giroux, 1983.

Chang, Jaw-ling Joanne. *United States–China Normalization: An Evaluation of Foreign Policy Decision Making.* Denver: Graduate School of International Studies, University of Denver, 1986.

Chen, Frederick T., ed. *China Policy and National Security.* New York: Transnational, 1984.

Cohen, Benjamin J., ed. *American Foreign Economic Policy: Essays and Comments.* New York: Harper and Row, 1968.

Congressional Quarterly Almanac. *Trade: U.S. Policy Since 1945.* Washington, D.C.: Congressional Quarterly, 1984.

Corwin, Edward S. *The President: Office and Powers.* 4th ed. New York: New York University Press, 1957.

Crabb, Cecil V., Jr., and Patt M. Holt. *Invitation to Struggle: Congress, the President, and Foreign Policy.* Washington, D.C.: Congressional Quarterly, 1980.

Dahl, Robert. *Congress and Foreign Policy.* New York: Norton, 1950.

————. *Pluralist Democracy in the United States: Conflict and Consent.* Chicago: Rand McNally, 1967.

Destler, I. M. *Presidents, Bureaucracies, and Foreign Policy.* Princeton: Princeton University Press, 1972.

Downen, Robert. *The Taiwan Pawn in the China Game: Congress to the Rescue.* Washington, D.C.: The Center for Strategic and International Studies, Georgetown University, 1979.

Edwards, Randle R., Louis Henkin, and Andrew J. Nathan. *Human Rights in Contemporary China.* New York: Columbia University Press, 1986.

Fenno, Richard F. *Congressmen in Committees.* Boston: Little, Brown, 1973.

Franck, Thomas M., and Edward Weisband. *Foreign Policy by Congress.* New York: Oxford University Press, 1979.

Frost, Michael. "Taiwan's Security and United States Policy: Executive and Congressional Strategies in 1978–1979." *Occasional Papers in Contemporary Asian Studies,* No. 4, School of Law, University of Maryland, 1982.

Haig, Alexander. *Caveat: Realism, Reagan, and Foreign Policy.* New York: Macmillan, 1984.

Halperin, Morton H. *Bureaucratic Politics and Foreign Policy.* Washington, D.C.: Brookings Institution, 1974.

Harding, Harry, ed. *China's Foreign Relations in the 1980s.* New Haven: Yale University Press, 1984.

Henkin, Louis. *Foreign Affairs and the Constitution.* New York: Norton, 1976.

Holsti, Ole, R. Siverson, and A. George, eds. *Change in the International System.* Boulder: Westview Press, 1980.

Hsiao, Gene T., and Michael Witunski, eds. *Sino-American Normalization and Its Policy Implications.* New York: Praeger, 1983.

Hsiung, James C., and Winberg Chai, eds. *Asia and U.S. Foreign Policy.* New York: Praeger, 1981.

Jacobson, Gary. *The Politics of Congressional Elections.* Boston: Little, Brown, 1987.

Katzenstein, Peter J., ed. *Between Power and Plenty: Foreign Economic Policies of Advanced Industrial States.* Madison: University of Wisconsin Press, 1978.

Keohane, Robert, and Joseph Nye. *Power and Interdependence: World Politics in Transition.* Boston: Little, Brown, 1977.

Kingdom, John. *Congressmen's Voting Decisions.* New York: Harper and Row, 1973.

Kissinger, Henry. *White House Years.* Boston: Little, Brown, 1979.

Knorr, Klaus, and Sidney Verba, eds. *The International System: Theoretical Essays.* Princeton: Princeton University Press, 1961.

Krasner, Stephen. *Defending the National Interest: Raw Materials, Investment, and United States Foreign Policy.* Princeton: Princeton University Press, 1978.

Kusnitz, Leonard A. *Public Opinion and Foreign Policy: America's China Policy, 1949–1979.* Westport, Conn.: Greenwood Press, 1984.

Lasater, Martin L. *The Taiwan Issue in Sino-American Strategic Relations.* Boulder: Westview Press, 1984.

Lauren, Paul G., ed. *Diplomacy: New Approaches in History, Theory, and Policy.* New York: The Free Press, 1979.

Lehman, John F. *The Executive, Congress, and Foreign Policy: Studies of the Nixon Administration.* New York: Praeger, 1976.

Maass, Arthur. *Congress and the Common Good.* New York: Basic Books, 1983.

Mayhew, David. *Congress: The Electoral Connection.* New Haven: Yale University Press, 1974.

Miliband, Ralph. *The State in Capitalist Society.* New York: Basic Books, 1969.

Moens, Alexander. *Foreign Policy Under Carter: Testing Multiple Advocacy Decision Making.* Boulder: Westview Press, 1990.

Nathan, Andrew J. *China's Crisis: Dilemmas of Reform and Prospects for Democracy.* New York: Columbia University Press, 1990.

Nathan, James A., and James K. Oliver. *Foreign Policy Making and the American Political System*. 2d ed. Boston: Little, Brown, 1987.

Neustadt, Richard E. *Presidential Power: The Politics of Leadership from FDR to Carter*. New York: John Wiley and Sons, 1980.

Oksenberg, Michel, and Robert B. Oxnam. *Dragon and Eagle: United States–China Relations: Past and Future*. New York: Basic Books, 1978.

———. *Explorations in Sino-American Relations*. Boulder: Westview Press, 1989.

Oye, Kenneth A., Robert J. Lieber, and Donald Rothchild, eds. *Eagle Defiant: United States Foreign Policy in the 1980s*. Boston: Little, Brown, 1983.

Pastor, Robert A. *Congress and the Politics of U.S. Foreign Economic Policy 1929–1976*. Berkeley: University of California Press, 1980.

Pious, Richard M. *The American Presidency*. New York: Basic Books, 1979.

Pollack, Jonathan D. *The Lessons of Coalition Politics: Sino-American Security Relations*. A Project Air Force Report. Santa Monica, Calif.: Rand Corporation, 1984.

Robinson, James A., *Congress and Foreign Policy Making: A Study in Legislative Influence and Initiative*. Rev. ed. Homewood, Ill: Dorsey Press, 1967.

Rowe, David Nelson. *Informal "Diplomatic Relations": The Case of Japan and the Republic of China, 1972–1974*. Hamden, Conn.: Shoestring Press, 1975.

Snyder, Glen H., and Paul Diesing. *Conflict Among Nations: Bargaining, Decision-making, and System Structure in International Crises*. Princeton: Princeton University Press, 1977.

Solomon, Richard H., ed. *The China Factor: Sino-American Relations and the Global Scene*. Englewood Cliffs, N.J.: Prentice-Hall, 1981.

Spanier, John, and Eric Uslaner. *American Foreign Policy Making and the Domestic Dilemmas*. 4th ed. New York: Holt, Rinehart and Winston, 1985.

Sullivan, Michael P. *International Relations: Theories and Evidence*. Englewood Cliffs, N.J.: Prentice-Hall, 1976.

Sutter, Robert G. *The China Quandary: Domestic Determinants of U.S. China Policy, 1972–82*. Boulder: Westview Press, 1983.

———. *China Watch: Toward Sino-American Reconciliation*. Baltimore: Johns Hopkins University Press, 1978.

Thompson, Kenneth W. *The President, the Congress, and Foreign Policy*. Lanham, Md.: University Press of America, 1986.

Truman, David B., ed. *The Congress and America's Future*. 2d ed. Englewood Cliffs, N.J.: Prentice-Hall, 1973.

Tung, Rosalie L. *U.S.-China Trade Negotiations*. New York: Pergamon Press, 1982.

Vance, Cyrus R. *Hard Choices: Critical Years in America's Foreign Policy*. New York: Simon and Schuster, 1983.

Waltz, Kenneth N. *Theory of International Politics*. Reading, Mass.: Addison-Wesley, 1979.

Westerfield, Bradford H. *Foreign Policy and Party Politics: Pearl Harbor to Korea*. New Haven: Yale University Press, 1955.

Articles in Journals, Magazines, and Books

Allison, G. T. "Conceptual Model and the Cuban Missile Crisis." *American Political Science Review* 63 (September 1969): 689–718.

Art, Robert J. "Bureaucratic Politics and American Foreign Policy: A Critique." *Policy Science* 4, no. 4 (December 1973):467–490.

Baldrige, Malcolm. "U.S. Policy on Exports of Advanced Technology to China." *American Foreign Policy: Current Documents, 1983*. Department of State, Bureau of Public Affairs.

Bax, Frans R. "The Legislative-Executive Relationship in Foreign Policy: New Partnership or New Competition?" *Orbis* 20 (Winter 1977): 881–904.

"Beijing and Moscow: No Progress." *Newsweek* (November 2, 1981): 29.

Chanda, Nayan, and Robert Delfs. "China Ups the Ante." *Far Eastern Economic Review* (November 20, 1981): 8–9.

"China Protests U.S. Decision on Arms Sales to Taiwan." *Beijing Review* (January 18, 1982): 8.

"Claims-Assets Settlement." *China Business Review* 6, no. 1 (January-February 1979): 50–51.

Clarke, William. "Commercial Implications of Normalization." *The International Trade Law Journal* 5, no. 1 (Fall-Winter 1979): 95.

Crabb, Cecil V., Jr. "An Assertive Congress and the TRA: Policy Influence and Implications." In Koenig, Louis W., James C. Hsiung, and Kin-yuh Chang, eds. *Congress, the Presidency and the Taiwan Relations Act*. New York: Praeger, 1985, pp. 85–110.

Crane, Alan T., and Richard P. Suttmeier. "Nuclear Trade with China." *Columbia Journal of World Business* 21 (Spring 1986): 35–40.

"Critical Point in Sino-U.S. Relations." *Beijing Review* (May 15, 1982): 10.

Freeman, Charles. "The Japanese Model: Could U.S. Relations with Taiwan Also Be Conducted Through 'Private' Incorporated Associations?" An unpublished paper, East Asian Legal Studies, Harvard Law School, March 17, 1975.

————. "Legal/Economic Consequences of Derecognition for American Economic Relations with Taiwan." An unpublished paper, East Asian Legal Studies, Harvard Law School, March 3, 1975.

Garson, John R. "The American Trade Embargo Against China." In Eckstein, Alexander, ed., *China Trade Prospects and U.S. Policy*. New York: Praeger (for the National Committee on United States–China Relations), 1971.

Garver, John W. "Arms Sales, the Taiwan Question, and Sino-U.S. Relations." *Orbis* 26, no. 4 (Winter 1983): 999–1035.

George, Alexander L., and Timothy J. McKeown. "Case Studies and Theories of Organizational Decision-making." *Advances in Information Processing in Organizations* 2 (1985): 21-58.

Gregor, James. "The United States, the Republic of China, and the Taiwan Relations Act." *Orbis* 24 (Fall 1980): 611–612.

Hirschfield, Robert S. "The Reagan Administration and U.S. Relations with Taiwan and China." In Koenig, L. W., J. C. Hsiung, and K. Chang, eds., *Congress, the Presidency, and the Taiwan Relations Act*. New York: Praeger, 1985, pp. 111–139.

Holsti, Ole. "Foreign Policy Formation Viewed Cognitively." In Axelrod, Robert M., ed., *Structure of Decision: The Cognitive Maps of Political Elites*. Princeton: Princeton University Press, 1976, pp. 18–54.

Holzman, F. D., and R. Legvold. "The Economics and Politics of East-West Relations." In Bergsten, C. F., and L. B. Krause, eds., *World Politics and International Economics*. Washington, D.C.: Brookings Institution, 1975, pp. 275–322.

Horner, Daniel, and Paul Leventhal. "The U.S.-China Nuclear Agreement: A Failure of Executive Policymaking and Congressional Oversight." *The Fletcher Forum* 11, no.1 (Winter 1987): 105–122.

Hsiao, Gene T. "The Sino-Japanese Rapprochement: A Relationship of Ambivalence." In Hsiao, ed., *Sino-American Detente and Its Policy Implication*. New York: Praeger, 1974, 160–188.

Ikenberry, John, David A. Lake, and Michael Mastanduno. "Introduction: Approaches to Explaining American Foreign Economic Policy." *International Organization* 42 (Winter 1988): 1–14.

Javits, Jacob K. "Congress and Foreign Relations: The Taiwan Relations Act." *Foreign Affairs* 60, no. 1 (Fall 1981): 54–62.

Jiang, Xinxiong. "China's Nuclear Industry in the Last 30 Years and Its Future." *Industrial Equipment and Materials* 6, no. 4, Hong Kong, citing Crane, Alan T., and Richard P. Suttmeier, "Nuclear Trade with China," *Columbia Journal of World Business* 21 (Spring 1986): 36.

Krasner, Stephen D. "Are Bureaucracies Important? (Or Allison Wonderland)." *Foreign Policy*, no.7 (Summer 1972): 159–179.

Oksenberg, Michel. "China Policy for the 1980s." *Foreign Affairs* 61, no. 2 (Winter 1980/81): 304–322.

————."Congress, Executive-Legislative Relations, and American China Policy." In Thompson, Kenneth W., *The President, the Congress, and Foreign Policy*. Lanham, Md.: University Press of America, 1986.

————. "A Decade of Sino-American Relations." *Foreign Affairs* 61, no. 1 (Fall 1982): 175–195.

————."The Dynamics of the Sino-American Relationship." In Solomon, R.H., ed., *The China Factor*. Englewood Cliffs, N.J.: Prentice-Hall, 1981.

Paine, Christopher E. "Fuzzy Safeguards for U.S.-China Deal." *Bulletin of the Atomic Scientists* 41 (October 1985): 6–7.

Perlmutter, Amos. "The Presidential Political Center and Foreign Policy: A Critique." *World Politics* 27, no. 1 (October 1974): 87–106.

Pillsbury, Michael. "U.S.-China Military Ties?" *Foreign Policy*, no. 20 (Fall 1975): 50–64.

"Protesting U.S. Sale of Military-Related Spare Parts to Taiwan." *Beijing Review* (April 26, 1982): 7.

"Quarterly Chronicle and Documentation." *China Quarterly* 77 (March 1979): 209.

Robinson, Thomas W. "Choice and Consequences in Sino-American Relations." *Orbis* 20, no. 1 (Spring 1981): 29–51.

Rosati, Jerel A. "Developing a Systemic Decision-making Framework: Bureaucratic Politics in Perspective." *World Politics* 33, no. 2 (January 1981): 234–252.

Scalapino, Robert A. "Uncertainties in Future Sino-U.S. Relations." *Orbis* 26, no. 3 (Fall 1982): 681–696.

"Sino-Dutch Relations." *Beijing Review* (April 6, 1981): 8.

Teske, Gary R., Hedija H. Kravalis, and Allen J. Lenz. "U.S. Trade with China: Prospects Through 1985." *Business America* (February 12, 1979): 3–7.

Thomson, James C., Jr. "On the Making of U.S. China Policy, 1961–69: A Study in Bureaucratic Politics." *China Quarterly* 50 (April-June 1972): 220–243.

"U.S.-China Nuclear Pact: Congressional Approval Appears Likely." *Nuclear News* 28 (November 1985): 124–128.

"U.S.-Taiwan Relations Act." *Beijing Review* (January 12, 1981): 9–11.

Weil, Martin. "The Elusive U.S.-China Agreement." *China Business Review* 9, no. 5 (September-October, 1982): 45–47.

————. "The First Nuclear Power Project." *China Business Review* 19, no. 5 (September-October 1982): 40–44.

Articles in Newspapers

Bacon, Kenneth H. "U.S. China Initial Accord to Widen Trade But Benefits Are Not Expected for a While." *Wall Street Journal*, May 15, 1979, p. 8.

"Chinese Trade Pact Is Sent to Congress." *New York Times*, October 24, 1979, p. 1.

"The Clock Must Not Be Turned Back." *FBIS* (China), June 16, 1980, pp. B4–B5.

Garrett, Banning, and Bonnie S. Glaser. "Peking: Balancing Soviets and U.S." *New York Times*, July 19, 1982, p. 15.

Geyelin, Philip. "Reagan's 'Official' Position." *Washington Post*, September 1, 1980, p. 17.

Goshko, John M. "Carter Will Seek Favored Status for China Trade." *Washington Post*, July 4, 1979, p. 22.

———. "Glenn Says China Pledge on Taiwan Is Essential." *Washington Post*, January 25, 1979, p. 21.

———. "President Warns Hill On Taiwan." *Washington Post*, January 27, 1979, p. 1.

———. "Two Senators Urge Giving a Security Pledge to Taiwan." *Washington Post*, January 23, 1979, p. 11.

Gwertzman, Bernard. "Cranston Assails U.S.-China Accord." *New York Times*, October 22, 1985, p. 6.

———. "Haig Meets with Peking Official to Discuss Arms Sales to Taiwan." *New York Times*, April 6, 1982, p. 1.

———. "Shultz Snaps at U.S. Businessmen in Peking." *New York Times*, February 4, 1983, p. 9.

———. "U.S. Seeking Pledge Soviet Union Won't Curb Rate of Emigration." *New York Times*, May 18, 1979, p. 1.

House, Karen E. "U.S. Foreign Policy Remains Muddled as Haig Ends 12-Day Far East Tour." *Wall Street Journal*, June 25, 1981, sec. 2, p. 30.

Kaiser, Robert G. "House and Senate Adopt Taiwan Bills." *Washington Post*, March 14, 1979, p. 10.

———. "Senators Insist U.S. Give Strong Support to Taiwan." *Washington Post*, February 6, 1979, p. 15.

———. "Trade Benefits for Russia, China Eyed." *Washington Post*, January 5, 1979, p. 8.

Lasater, Martin L. "Why Peking May Want to Downgrade Relations with Washington." *Christian Science Monitor*, July 26, 1982, p. 23.

Marder, Murrey. "State Department and Kennedy Discussed China Speech." *Washington Post*, August 17, 1977, p. 17.

Mathews, Jay. "Bush Said to Reassure China on Policy." *Washington Post*, August 22, 1980, p. 2.

———. "China and U.S. Initial Accord Aiding Trade." *Washington Post*, May 15, 1979, p. 20.

———. "Jackson Says Peking Dissatisfied About Trade Status." *Washington Post*, August 25, 1979, p. 18.

———. "Kreps Hopeful on Claims Accord, Doubtful on Sino-U.S. Trade Pact." *Washington Post*, May 10, 1979, p. 37.

McBee, Susanna. "Strauss: China Business Needed to Help U.S. Overcome $30 Billion Trade Deficit." *Washington Post*, January 8, 1979, p. 6.

Miller, Judith. "U.S. Is Holding Up Peking Atom Talks: China's Reluctance to Accept Checks on Nuclear Exports Viewed as an Obstacle." *New York Times*, September 19, 1982, p. 11.

New York Times, March 28, 1982, p. 19.

Oberdorfer, Don. "Shultz Stresses U.S. Need to Deal with Palestinians." *Washington Post*, July 14, 1982, p. 15.

———. "Trade Benefits for China Are Approved by Carter." *Washington Post*, October 24, 1979, p. 2.

———. "U.S. Moves to Grant Soviets Trade and Tariff Benefits." *Washington Post*, May 17, 1979, p. 1.

Omang, Joanne. "China Assails Changes in Nuclear Pact." *Washington Post*, December 12, 1985, p. 35.

———. "Nuclear Pact with China Wins Senate Approval." *Washington Post*, November 22, 1985, p. 3.

Parks, Michael. "China Still Opposed to U.S. Arms Sales to Taiwan." *Los Angeles Times*, April 3, 1981.

———. "Ford Hopeful Taiwan Arms Sales Issue Can Be Solved." *Los Angeles Times*, March 28, 1981.

———. "Sales of U.S. Military Gear to China Fail to Materialize." *Los Angeles Times*, April 17, 1981.

Parry, Robert. "China Pact Hits Snag on Emigration." *Washington Post*. November 2, 1979, p. D2.

People's Daily commentary, June 14, 1980, in Foreign Broadcast Information Service, *Daily Report: People's Republic of China* (hereafter cited as *FBIS* [China]), December 18, 1978, pp. B4–B5.

People's Daily (in Chinese), August 17, 1982.

Raines, Howell. "Reagan Backs Evangelicals in Their Political Activities." *New York Times*, August 23, 1980, p. 8.

———. "Reagan, Conceding Misstatements, Abandons Plan on Taiwan." *New York Times*, August 26, p. 1.

Rowen, Hobart. "Blumenthal, in China, Foresees Closer Trade Ties." *Washington Post*, February 25, p. 24.

———. "Reagan Permits China to Buy Computers, Other Disputed Items." *Washington Post*, June 21, 1983, p. A8.

———. "U.S. Closer to Trade Treaty with China." *Washington Post*, March 3, 1979, p. D8.

———. "U.S. Signs Pact to Grant China Favored Status." *Washington Post*, July 8, 1979, p. 1.

———. "U.S. to Hold China Treaty Until a Textile Pact Is Secured." *Washington Post*, May 16, 1979, p. 1.

Russell, Mary. "Bill On Taiwan Ties Survives Early Tests in Senate and House." *Washington Post*, March 9, 1979, p. 2.

Saikowski, Charlotte. "Reagan Under Pressure to OK Reactor Pact with China: U.S. Industry Concerned Congress May Not Ratify Nuclear Partnership." *Christian Science Monitor*, March 4, 1985, p. 5.

Sawyer, Kathy. "Reagan Sticks to Stand on Taiwan Ties." *Washington Post*, August 23, 1980, p. 1.

"Strauss Holds Little Hope for Chinese Textile Pact." *Washington Post*, May 29, 1979, p. D7.

Tyler, Patrick E. "Hill Panels Add Conditions to U.S.-China Nuclear Pact." *Washington Post*, November 14, 1985, p. 1.

———. "Nuclear Pact with China Nears Last Test on Hill." *Washington Post*, December 16, 1985, p. 23.

Walsh, Edward. "Resolution on Taiwan Stirs Struggle." *Washington Post*, February 2, 1979, p. 14.

Wren, Christopher S. "Bush Leaves China with New Ideas for Resolving Taiwan Arms Dispute." *New York Times*, May 10, 1982, p. 3.

Xinhua. *FBIS* (China), May 10, 1982, pp. B2–B3.
————. "China Resolutely Opposes Foreign Arms Sales to Taiwan." *FBIS* (China), December 31, 1981, p. B1.
————. "U.S. Decides to Sell Arms Spare Parts to Taiwan." *FBIS* (China), December 29, 1981, p. B1.

Government Documents

Amendment 1347 to H.J. Res. 456. 99th Cong., 1st sess. *Congressional Record* (December 9, 1985), p. S17141.
An Act to Extend the Authorities Under the Export Administration Act of 1979, and for Other Purposes. Public Law 98-207. Washington, D.C.: Government Printing Office, 1983.
Authorization of Appropriations for Fiscal Years 1980–1985. Public Law 98-553. *United States Statutes at Large*, vol. 98, part 3. October 30, 1984, p. 2825.
Nuclear Nonproliferation Act of 1978. Public Law 95-242. *United States Statutes at Large*, vol. 92, part 1. March 10, 1978, p. 120.
Taiwan Relations Act. Public Law 96-8. Washington, D.C.: Government Printing Office, 1979.
Trade Act of 1974. Public Law 93-618. *United States Statutes at Large*, vol. 88, part 2 (1976).
U.S. Congress. *Executive-Legislative Consultation on U.S. Arms Sales.* Congress and Foreign Policy Series 7. Washington, D.C.: Government Printing Office, 1982.
U.S. Congress. House. *Agreement Between the United States and the People's Republic of China Concerning Peaceful Uses of Nuclear Energy: Message from the President of the United States, Transmitting an Agreement for Cooperation Between the Government of the United States and the Government of the People's Republic of China Concerning Peaceful Uses of Nuclear Energy.* House Document 99-86. 99th Cong., 1st sess., 1985.
U.S. Congress. House. *Agreement on Trade Relations Between the United States and the People's Republic of China: Communication from the President of the United States Transmitting Proclamation Extending Non-discriminatory Trade Treatment to the Products of the People's Republic of China, Together with Related Reports, Pursuant to Section 407 of the Trade Act of 1974,* House Document 209. 96th Cong., 1st sess., 1979.
U.S. Congress. House. Committee on Foreign Affairs. *China-Taiwan: United States Policy: Hearing Before the Committee on Foreign Affairs, House of Representatives.* 97th Cong., 2nd sess., 1982.
U.S. Congress. House. Committee on Foreign Affairs. *Executive-Legislative Consultations on China Policy, 1978-79.* Washington, D.C.: Government Printing Office, 1980.
U.S. Congress. House. Committee on Foreign Affairs. *The Export Administration Act Amendments of 1978.* 96th Cong., 1st sess., 1979.
U.S. Congress. House. Committee on Foreign Affairs. H.J. Res. 404. *House Report 99-382.* 99th Cong., 1st sess., 1985.
U.S. Congress. House. Committee on Foreign Affairs. *Proposed Nuclear Cooperation Agreement with the People's Republic of China: Hearing and Markup Before the Committee on Foreign Affairs, House of Representatives.* 99th Cong., 1st sess., 1985.
U.S. Congress. House. Committee on Foreign Affairs. Subcommittee on Asian

and Pacific Affairs. *Normalization of Relations with the PRC: Practical Implications Hearings.* 95th Cong., 1st sess., September 20, 21, 28, 29; October 11, 13, 1977.

U.S. Congress. House. Committee on Foreign Affairs. Subcommittees on Asian and Pacific Affairs and on International Economic Policy and Trade. *United States-China Relations: Hearings Before the Committee on Foreign Affairs, House of Representatives and Its Subcommittees on Asian and Pacific Affairs and on International Economic Policy and Trade.* 98th Cong., 2nd sess., 1984.

U.S. Congress. House. Committee on Foreign Affairs. *Taiwan Legislation: Hearings Before the Committee on Foreign Affairs, United States House of Representatives.* 96th Cong., 1st. sess., 1979.

U.S. Congress. House. Committee on Ways and Means. *Approving the Extension of Nondiscriminatory Treatment to the Products of the People's Republic of China,* House Report 96-733, 96th Cong., 1st. sess., 1979.

U.S. Congress. House. *Relations with Taiwan: Message from the President of the United States.* House Document 96-45. Washington, D.C.: Government Printing Office, 1979.

U.S. Congress. House. A resolution introduced by Representative Edward Markey, asking for waivers on the AEA requirements on safeguards for U.S.-origin nuclear equipment and material, as well as U.S. consent rights for the reprocessing of U.S.-origin fuel. H. Res. 269. 99th Cong., 1st sess. *Congressional Record* (September 20, 1985), p. H11765.

U.S. Congress. House. Special Subcommittee on U.S. Trade with China of the Committee on Energy and Commerce. *Exports to China: A Review on the 200th Anniversary of U.S.-China Trade.* 98th Cong., 2nd sess., 1984.

U.S. Congress. House. Special Subcommittee on U.S. Trade with China of the Committee on Energy and Commerce. *Nuclear Energy Cooperation with China: Hearing Before the Special Subcommittee on U.S. Trade with China of the Committee on Energy and Commerce, House of Representatives.* 98th Cong., 2nd sess., 1984.

U.S. Congress. House. Subcommittee on Asian and Pacific Affairs of the Committee on Foreign Affairs. *Implementation of the Taiwan Relations Act: Hearings Before the Subcommittee on Asian and Pacific Affairs of the Committee on Foreign Affairs, House of Representatives.* 96th. Cong., 2nd sess., 1980.

U.S. Congress. House. Subcommittee on Asian and Pacific Affairs of Committee on Foreign Affairs. *Playing the China Card: Implications for United States-Soviet-Chinese Relations: Report Prepared for the Subcommittee on Asian and Pacific Affairs of Committee on Foreign Affairs, U.S. House of Representatives.* 96th Cong., 1st sess., 1979.

U.S. Congress. House. Subcommittee on International Trade and Commerce of Committee on International Relations. *Trading with the Enemy: Legislative and Executive Documents Concerning Regulation of International Transactions in Time of Declared National Emergency.* 94th Cong., 2nd sess., 1976.

U.S. Congress. House. Subcommittee on Trade of the Committee on Ways and Means. *United States–China Trade Agreement: Hearings Before the Subcommittee on Trade of the Committee on Ways and Means, House of Representatives.* 96th. Cong., 1st sess., 1979.

U.S. Congress. Joint Economic Committee. *China Under the Four Modernizations: Selected Papers Submitted to Joint Economic Committee.* 97th Cong., 2nd sess., 1982.

U.S. Congress. Office of Technology Assessment. *Energy Technology Transfer to China: A Technical Memorandum.* Washington, D.C.: Government Printing Office, 1985.

U.S. Congress. Senate. Amendment No. 3264. *Congressional Record* (July 25, 1978), p. S22571.

U.S. Congress. Senate. Committee on Foreign Relations. *The Taiwan Enabling Act: Report of the Committee on Foreign Relations, United States Senate, Together with Additional Views on S. 245,* 96th Cong., 1st sess., 1979.

U.S. Congress. Senate. Committee on Foreign Relations. *Taiwan: Hearings Before the Committee on Foreign Relations.* 96th Cong., 1st sess., 1979.

U.S. Congress. Senate. Committee on Foreign Relations. *United States–China Relations: Today's Realities and Prospects for the Future: Hearing Before the Committee on Foreign Relations, United States Senate.* 98th Cong., 2nd sess., 1984.

U.S. Congress. Senate. Committee on Foreign Relations. *United States–People's Republic of China Nuclear Agreement: Hearing Before the Committee on Foreign Relations, United States Senate.* 99th Cong., 1st sess., 1985.

U.S. Congress. Senate. Committee on Foreign Relations. *U.S. Policy Toward China and Taiwan: Hearing Before the Committee On Foreign Relations.* 97th Cong., 2nd sess., 1982.

U.S. Congress. Senate. *Sino-American Nuclear Verification Act of 1985.* S. 1754, a Senate bill introduced by Senator John Glenn, 96th Cong., 1st sess. *Congressional Record* (October 9, 1985), p. S13012.

U.S. Congress. Senate. Subcommittee on Foreign Agricultural Policy of the Committee on Agriculture, Nutrition, and Forestry. *Agricultural Trade with the People's Republic of China and Taiwan: Hearing Before the Subcommittee on Foreign Agricultural Policy of the Committee on Agriculture, Nutrition, and Forestry.* 96th Cong., 1st sess., March 13, 1979.

U.S. Congress. Senate. Subcommittee on International Trade of the Committee on Finance. *Agreement on Trade Relations Between the United States and People's Republic of China: Hearings Before the Subcommittee on International Trade of the Committee on Finance.* 96th Cong., 1st sess., November 1979.

U.S. Congress. Senate. *The United States and China: A Report to the United States Senate by the Senate Majority Leader.* Washington, D.C.: Government Printing Office, 1982.

U.S. Department of Commerce. *Export Administration Annual Report 1983.* Washington, D.C.: Government Printing Office, 1984.

U.S. Department of State. Bureau of Public Affairs. "Economic and Commercial Relations with Taiwan." *Department of State Bulletin* 79, no. 2023 (February 1979).

U.S. Department of State. Bureau of Public of Affairs. "No Sale of Advanced Aircraft to Taiwan." *Department of State Bulletin* 82, no. 2059 (February 1982): 39.

U.S. Department of State. Bureau of Public Affairs. *U.S.-China Nuclear Cooperation Agreement.* Current Policy no. 729, 1985.

U.S. Department of State. Bureau of Public Affairs. *The U.S.-China Relationship.* Current Policy no. 594, May 31, 1984.

U.S. Department of State. Bureau of Public Affairs. *U.S. Exports Controls and China. GIST,* March 1985.

U.S. Department of State. Bureau of Public Affairs. *U.S. Policy Toward China, July 15, 1971–January 15, 1979.* Selected Documents no. 9. Bureau of Public Affairs, Office of Public Communication, 1979.

U.S. Department of State. Bureau of Public Affairs. *U.S. Relations with China.* Current Policy no. 297, July 16, 1981.

U.S. Department of State. Bureau of Public Affairs. "Vice President: Visit to East Asia." *Department of State Bulletin* 79, no. 2031 (October 1979): 10–13.

U.S. President. Press Conference. Office of the Federal Register. *Weekly Compilation of Presidential Documents* 15, no.15 (April 10, 1979): 640.

Index

About the Book and Author

This unique book evaluates U.S. policy toward China since normalization, exploring the importance of government institutions (Congress, the executive, etc.), the interactions among those institutions, and the roles that specific individuals have played in policymaking.

Focusing on four case studies (the Taiwan Relations Act, U.S. arms sales to Taiwan, the U.S.-China trade agreement, and U.S. technology transfer to China), Tan emphasizes the necessary linkage between strategic interests and government processes in foreign policymaking. His examination of the variance in U.S. China policy explains why some policies reflected the convergence of strategic interests and intergovernmental politics, while others did not. His richly detailed analysis is the first to illuminate the impact of the U.S. *political* process on China policymaking.

Tan Qingshan is assistant professor of political science at Cleveland State University.